# CURES

## A GAY MAN'S ODYSSEY

# MARTIN DUBERMAN

A DUTTON BOOK

DUTTON
Published by the Penguin Group
Penguin Books USA Inc., 375 Hudson Street,
New York, New York 10014, U.S.A.
Penguin Books Ltd, 27 Wrights Lane,
London W8 5TZ, England
Penguin Books Australia Ltd, Ringwood,
Victoria, Australia
Penguin Books Canada Ltd, 2801 John Street,
Markham, Ontario, Canada L3R 1B4
Penguin Books (N.Z.) Ltd, 182–190 Wairau Road,
Auckland 10, New Zealand

Penguin Books Ltd, Registered Offices:
Harmondsworth, Middlesex, England

First published by Dutton, an imprint of New American Library, a
division of Penguin Books USA Inc.
Distributed in Canada by McClelland & Stewart Inc.

First Printing, April, 1991
10 9 8 7 6 5 4 3 2 1

 REGISTERED TRADEMARK—MARCA REGISTRADA

LIBRARY OF CONGRESS CATALOGING-IN-PUBLICATION DATA:
Duberman, Martin.
    Cures : a gay man's odyssey / by Martin Duberman.
    p.  cm.
    1. Duberman, Martin.   2. Gay men—United States—Biography.
3. Homosexuality—Psychological aspects.   I. Title.
HQ75.8.D82A3   1991
305.38'9664'092—dc20                                          90-46658
ISBN 0–525–24955–9                                           CIP

Printed in the United States of America
Set in New Baskerville
Designed by Leonard Telesca

for Eli Zal
who has done so much to improve this book—
and my life

## Other Books by Martin Duberman

*Hidden from History: Reclaiming the Gay and Lesbian Past* (1990) (with Martha Vicinus and George Chauncey, Jr.)

*Paul Robeson* (1989)

*About Time: Exploring the Gay Past* (1986)

*Visions of Kerouac* (1977)

*Male Armor: Selected Plays 1968–1974* (1976)

*Black Mountain: An Exploration in Community* (1972)

*The Memory Bank* (1970)

*The Uncompleted Past* (1969)

*James Russell Lowell* (1966)

*The Antislavery Vanguard*, ed. (1965)

*In White America* (1964)

*Charles Francis Adams, 1807–1886* (1963)

# CURES

## ACKNOWLEDGMENTS

I'm deeply grateful to those who have read this manuscript in whole or in part and whose comments have helped to improve it: my editor, Arnold Dolin; my agent, Frances Goldin; my sister, Lucile Duberman; my lover, Eli Zal; and my encouraging, supportive friends, Arnie Kantrowitz, Seymour Kleinberg, Kenneth Lewes, Lawrence D. Mass, Barbara Hart Weiss, and Jon Wiener.

## NOTE

Where the individual's public persona is essential to the narrative (for example, Elaine May, Agnes de Mille, or Richard Barr), I have kept actual names. In most other cases, I have used pseudonyms, as indicated by quotation marks on first presentation.

# CURES

# PROLOGUE

A RRIVING AT PRINCETON IN 1962 to teach in the history department, I felt like an outsider from the start. I was a bachelor in a community dominated by couples, a Jew on a faculty notably Christian, an outspoken supporter of the civil rights movement on a campus that had been historically anti-black. But I was also white, male, a prize-winning historian, Anglo-Saxon in appearance and manner, and therefore a comparatively acceptable representative of several deviant categories—especially since I was not yet known to be gay as well.

The other department members treated me with an unfailing politeness that at times seemed actually cordial, and I got the requisite number of invitations to faculty homes. Though I had already spent more than a decade in the starchy corridors of the Ivy League, what I found in Princeton drawing rooms surpassed in formality and complacency anything I had previously known. At one dinner party at a colleague's house, black tie was *de rigueur*, and following dinner the men literally retired to the library for cigars, liqueur, and the kind of serious political talk at which women were thought notoriously inept. That night the talk focused on the necessity of our engaging Communism in Southeast Asia.

Undergraduates can often be a leaven to faculty pretensions—

if only because youthful exuberance almost reflexively cuts through cant. Not so at Princeton. In the early sixties there were no women undergraduates, only two or three blacks, and a sizable contingent of unreconstructed Southern whites whose families had been sending their scions to the safety of Princeton since before the Civil War. Uniformly bright, the undergraduates seemed uniformly committed to playing parts from a fifties script, according to which paternal white men benignly ruled a prosperous country devoid of serious conflict.

Few Princeton students believed in the necessity of suffering (at least other people's) and, when forced to confront the evidence produced by the black struggle then mounting in intensity, shrugged it off. The remedy, they would argue in my classes, lay entirely within the reach of the sufferers themselves. Were blacks consigned to menial jobs? Let them work harder, study more, demonstrate their abilities, and then, as the night follows the day, opportunities would open for them.

I was myself no more than a liberal in these years. Unlike most of my students, I acknowledged and protested the country's serious inequities, but still believed that the "pragmatic, undogmatic approach" (as I wrote in my diary in the fall of 1962) "offers the best hope of flexible, realistic solutions. I am in full sympathy with this generation's lack of patience with ideology, with abstraction, with systems."

Yet even as a mere liberal on his way to becoming radicalized, I was appalled by the attitudes I heard in my classes. I can still recall the session where one of my students denounced the "immorality" of social security legislation and then argued—to the general nodding of heads in agreement—that putting blacks on welfare rolls would only serve to encourage their "laziness" and to destroy their "incentive and self-respect." "Incentive?" I asked—"to become janitors, factory hands, unskilled laborers?" The blame lay with blacks themselves, I was told. They had failed "to raise themselves up" so that they might better "deserve" equality.

Not every Princeton undergraduate held such views. By 1963, after James Meredith had been shot trying to integrate Ole Miss, Martin Luther King jailed in Birmingham, and Medgar Evers killed in Jackson, a small group of Princeton students finally got around to forming a council on human rights. Asked to speak to the group, I let loose some of my accumulated anger, couched in sarcasm: "I have always thought the tiger, sleepless, animated, alert, was a strangely inappropriate symbol for Princeton; some sluggish, dull bovine animal might be much more to the point—a nice dairy cow, perhaps Guernsey, which is not too large and usually white." In my diary, I added this: "Here they are, the members of the coming white elite, with little awareness of the social and power structure of our country, of the realities of life for the underprivileged, and most horrifying of all, with almost no simple compassion for the less fortunate. What a generation this is! Bound in their private worlds—and proud of it!"

*My* private world was not nearly so comfortable. I lived in faculty housing—a small pseudocolonial unit built to sit "picturesquely" next to an artificial pond—and my personal life was a neat match for the antiseptic surroundings. Except for one local pub where ambivalent glances were rumored to have been exchanged between men awaiting their turn at the dart board, and the town of New Hope, about an hour's drive from Princeton, where a gay bar was actually known to exist (though subject to police raids), the only other hope for contact was in the bushes and the men's room at the Princeton railroad station, dim prospects in every sense. Even if Princeton had offered more opportunities, I would have been ambivalent about taking advantage of them. In these pre-Stonewall liberation years, a few brave souls had publicly declared themselves and even banded together for limited political purposes, but the vast majority of gay people were locked away in painful isolation and fear, doing everything possible *not* to declare themselves. Many of us cursed our fate, longed to be straight. And some of us had actively been seeking "cure." In my case, for a long time.

# 1

---

# CALGARY

W|E ARRIVED AT THE Calgary Stampede—Canada's "legendary yearly event, the World's Greatest Rodeo"—in July 1948, just before my eighteenth birthday. I was on a Youth Hostel trip with a group of some twenty other teenagers, and we had already put in a month of grueling but happy cross-country biking and backpacking. Calgary was a rest stop. We had heard great tales of its spectacular fairgrounds and rodeo events and rushed to take it all in. We watched the opening-day parade of high school bands, covered wagons, cows and cowhands, dashed to the arena to see the chuck wagon races, thrilled to the feats of daredevil Dick Griffith as he jumped over a Buick car while straddling two horses.

Come evening, we headed out for the midway and amusement park, a vast stretch of dirt road that included (as I gushed in a letter home to my parents) "roller coasters, ice cream and soda stands, circus barkers, gyp joints, international exhibits such as the Ford Company, freak shows, girlie reviews, even Sally Rand herself doing the one and only fan dance!" What I didn't tell my parents was that as the evening grew late and the rest of our group went off to bed, I stayed on alone.

The midway was still feverish with activity, packed with carousers, most of them men, most of them (from my vantage point) middle-aged, clustered in groups of three or four, noisily drunk, vaguely frightening and exciting me with their self-confident swagger, their unpredictable shouts, the sudden way they halted at a duck-shoot booth to challenge each other's prowess or to grab a kiss from any woman within reach. The booth owners egged them on, yelling out encouragement even as they scurried to nail down a scuffed tent peg, run test spins on a roulette wheel, line up rows of oversized dolls to tempt the contestants.

Every fourth or fifth booth advertised a fortune teller. Why so many? I wondered. Didn't everybody know that fortune tellers were a pack of thieves and liars? Most of them weren't even real gypsies—just renegade Spaniards from Brooklyn. Plus they had every known disease, since they never bathed or washed their hair. Boy, people were gullible! You had to be a dope to hand over real dough to some filthy hag, just to watch her shuffle a deck of cards and spout prepackaged mumbo-jumbo at you. I guess it *could* be fun, if you took it in that spirit, maybe worth a laugh or two, something to write home to the folks about—that is, if it only cost a few bucks, and you kept one eye over your shoulder in case somebody tried to bop you over the head. Yeah, maybe as a joke, a kind of lark, it might be worth trying . . .

She was sitting on a small camp stool in front of a tent. She must have been watching me because when I glanced over I had the feeling she had already been staring at me. I didn't like that. It felt creepy, like she'd picked *me* out. If I was going to waste money on a parlor trick, *I'd* pick the parlor. She smiled at me. That made me feel really stupid, like I was some scared kid who had to be reassured. So I smiled back. I didn't want to be rude, after all; this was a carnival, where people were supposed to be friendly. Besides, she looked pretty decent; clean, too; and sort of young.

"How are you tonight?" she called over. "Are you having a good time?" I was surprised at her neutral, quiet voice, and that she spoke English. Didn't gypsies speak their own language, called something like "romanoff"? I told her I'd only been in Calgary a few hours, but it looked fine so far. She asked where I was from. I said New York and explained that I was with a group of other kids biking across the country for the summer.

Before I knew it, we were having a regular chat. She wanted to know about the group, what places we'd been, where we were headed next. She seemed so ordinary, I soon felt at ease. She told me her family were *real* gypsies, that they traveled from fair to fair making a living telling fortunes. She said real fortune tellers, like real gypsies, were rare, and gestured with disdain toward the other booths nearby: "Fakers, liars! Fortune-telling is an art"—her eyes blazed—"a *heritage* passed down from generation to generation."

The more we chatted on, the more pleased I felt with myself. I could hardly wait to write my parents about my gutsy encounter with the exotic Gemma (for that turned out to be her name). After we'd talked for some fifteen minutes, Gemma asked me if I "had any interest in learning about what the future held for me"—whether I was "brave enough" to live with such knowledge. I started to feel nervous again.

"Do you mean do I want to have my fortune told?"

"Yes." She stared hard at me.

I stammered something like, "Gosh, I don't know . . . I mean I've never thought about it."

"That is untrue. You must never say anything to me that is not true."

Now I felt really nervous—because she was right. I did want my fortune told, even though I thought it was a lot of hocus-pocus. How did she know I wanted to?

"That is why you came to the midway tonight. That is why you came to me." Her eyes stayed on me.

"Well, I guess the idea . . . did . . . well, kinda cross my mind."

"Why are you so afraid?" Her voice was warm again.

"I don't know . . . but I am." Then to my surprise, I blurted out, "I really don't believe in . . . in anyone being able to . . . in fortune-telling."

"Only a very few are able. I am one of the few. You showed excellent judgment in seeking me out."

"I did? I mean . . . did I?"

She smiled at me. "You answer that question."

"Well, I . . . I did come over to say . . . hello."

"There is no reason to be afraid." She was now very calm, dignified.

"But I am afraid."

"I can tell you why. If you will let me. It doesn't matter whether you believe in my powers. I can still help you. Particularly with the one problem that most troubles you."

"What problem?" I asked, already knowing what she meant, even if she didn't.

"One question above all others is on your mind. Constantly on your mind. It troubles you far, far more than any other question. Should I tell you what it is?"

"No—NO!" I could feel my panic rising. "Not *here*. Not here, for God's sakes—anybody could overhear us!"

Gemma rose and moved toward the flap opening into her tent.

"I agree," she said. "It is better said inside."

"You dumb schmuck!" I silently yelled at myself as I followed her inside. How can you fall for such an obvious sales pitch? You didn't even ask her how much it would cost!

"Ten dollars is my usual fee," she said as soon as we were inside the tent. "But I will only charge you five. Money is not important when weighed against pain. You are full of pain, deep pain. It moves and saddens me. A fine young man like you should not be carrying so heavy a load of pain. I can relieve it. Pay me only what you can afford."

I fought back tears as Gemma closed the tent flap behind us and secured it with a peg. I put down the five dollars, and she motioned for me to sit on one of the two chairs drawn up to a table in the middle of the room. Above the table was a dim light, and in the center of it sat a large, square-shaped piece of glass.

"What's *that*?" I said, the quaver in my voice compromising my attempt at mockery. "Don't tell me that's a *crystal ball*, for God's sake!"

"It is a piece of crystal. Why does it bother you?"

"It's so corny! I thought you were . . . the 'real thing.' " I was pleased at the bravado in my voice.

"The crystal can be a useful tool. But not a necessary one. I can remove it if it bothers you."

I felt foolish again. "Why should it bother me?" I managed to mumble.

"Good. Then we can begin. I want you to write down"— seemingly from nowhere she produced a pad and pencil—"the

one question that most preys on your mind. Do you understand?"

"I thought you already knew the question."

Gemma smiled enigmatically. "I feel I need to provide you
with proof."

"One question?"

"Keep it brief. As short as possible. After writing down the
question, fold the paper once and then place it under the piece
of glass. Be sure to fold the paper over, so that the writing is
not visible. After you have done that, I want you to sit back,
close your eyes, and concentrate as deeply as possible on the
question you have written down. I, too, shall close my eyes. I
will empty my mind to receive your message. But you must
concentrate very hard or you will not succeed in transmitting
the message to me. Is that clear?"

"Wouldn't it be simpler if I just asked you the question?"

Again the enigmatic smile. "But then you would not believe
that I have the power to read what is inside you without being
told."

I wrote on the piece of paper, "Will I always be a homosexual?" Then, following her instructions, I folded the paper and
put it under the crystal. But my skeptical side simply refused
to sit back and concentrate. Not for the last time in encounters
with my saviors, my rebellious side abruptly took over. I peeked.
I saw Gemma take the piece of paper out through some opening
in the bottom of the table, read it, then put it back.

"Open your eyes now," she said. "You are indeed a very
troubled young man. Just as I had thought. But there is hope.
Your particular trouble can be cured. But you must *want* to be
cured"—a phrase I would hear often in the years ahead.

"What do you mean?"

"I mean, you must give yourself up wholly to the cure. You
must leave your old life, at once, and join our gypsy family so
that I can be constantly by your side."

"Join your gypsy family?" The full absurdity of what Gemma
was suggesting was clear. And yet, I *was* tempted—though I'd
seen her trick with the paper, though my skepticism was entirely
to the fore. I can still feel the powerful impulse within me to
do exactly as she suggested. *Anything* to relieve the burden.

At least I was able to delay the decision. Fumbling toward the tent opening, I told Gemma I would have to think about it overnight, that in all likelihood I would do as she said, but that I first had to make "certain arrangements." As I walked out of her tent back on to the midway, she whispered gently, "It is your one chance for happiness"—another prediction I would hear often in the years ahead.

In the upshot, I did not appear at Gemma's tent at dawn, carrying my worldly goods. I went to Yale instead.

# 2

# EDUCATION

N INETEEN FORTY-EIGHT, THE YEAR I entered Yale as a
freshman, also saw the publication of Alfred Kinsey's
*Sexual Behavior in the Human Male*. The book proved a bombshell
on many counts, but particularly for what it said about homosexuality. According to Kinsey, 37 percent of adult American
men had had at least one orgasm with another man, the experiences co-existing in many lives with heterosexuality. The
incidence might be higher still, Kinsey suggested, were it not
for social constraints.

Others before Kinsey—notably Havelock Ellis and Magnus
Hirschfeld—had argued that homosexuality was a normal variant of human sexuality. But their views had long since been
eclipsed by the consensus within the American psychiatric establishment that, contrary to Freud, homosexual behavior *always*
represented pathology (a consensus reinforced by popular culture, exemplified by the negative images of gays in films).[1] It
was therefore in the nature of heresy for Kinsey to suggest in
1948 that erotic feelings for people of the same gender might
be a garden variety human impulse—rather than, as psychiatry
had insisted, the pathological response of a small group of clin-
ically disturbed Others.

Kinsey went still further. He argued that heterosexuality did not represent a biological imperative and that, in insisting it did, psychotherapists were functioning as cultural police rather than as physicians or scientists. The psychiatrists, predictably, responded with a mix of scorn and anger. Lawrence S. Kubie, a prominent therapist and author, commended Kinsey and his associates for the diligence of their research, but then loftily declared that only those experienced in clinical psychopathology (psychiatrists) could provide a reliable interpretation of "normality." And their judgment, Kubie made clear, had long since been rendered: homosexuality did not qualify.[2]

Adding his voice, Dr. Robert P. Knight—of Yale, my new home—declared that although the cold was also common in the American population, no one would be foolish enough to describe *it* as "normal." Another Yale professor, the zoologist George A. Baitsell, wrote plainly in *The Yale Daily News*, "I don't like Kinsey! I don't like his report; I don't like anything about it."

I arrived at Mother Yale's portals oblivious to the Kinsey controversy—though like most middle-class, white Americans, I had ingested psychiatric assumptions with my pabulum and was reflexively on Gemma's side, not Kinsey's. I was also very nearly innocent of sex. At age eighteen I was still a virgin; though with women, not for want of trying.

I had gone the whorehouse route while still in high school. It happened in Florida over one spring vacation. Three of us, with standard teenage bluster, had managed to badger each other into a local brothel. The madame, with the trace of a smile and just a bit too gracious, ushered us into a small sitting room, where four or five scantily dressed women were rocking slowly in their chairs; apparently they were enjoying their own kind of game. We sat down, covered with embarrassment, in the empty chairs. No one spoke. The women kept rocking, rocking. Finally, just as I felt I would bolt for the door, one of them broke into a laugh and said, "Okay, boys, time to choose. We can't spend all day."

I jumped up first (let's get this *over* with!), awkwardly grabbed the woman nearest me, and headed with her into a back room. She dropped her robe as soon as we got there and asked me what I had in mind. Everything, it seemed, had a different price tag, with "around the world" costing the most, a whopping twenty dollars. I told her I only had seven dollars, and showed her my wallet as proof; nobody was taking *me* around the world! She said for seven dollars she could only screw me (*only!* I thought).

She called me over to the bed, where I dutifully got on top of her and, as instructed, rubbed up and down against her body. My cock stayed resolutely limp. Sensing my rising panic, she put aside the rules of the price scale—though I wasn't to tell the madame or she'd catch hell—and blew me a little. To no avail. She said not to worry, that married men often came into the house and they couldn't get it up either. She promised not to tell my friends and, to aid in the deception, kindly put some ointment in the urethral opening of my cock, wrapped it in gauze, and snapped on a rubber band (could this really have been standard preventive treatment in the forties for VD?). With this outward proof of heterosexual grace, I later bragged to my friends about how great the fuck had been. One of the two, off-guard at seeing the gauze and rubber band concoction that I triumphantly displayed, confessed that he had no bandage on *his* cock; suspicion promptly deflected onto him as the "chicken."

The night of our high school senior prom, I tried to extend my reputation as a stud. I and my girlfriend Rachel, a "wild" girl by the measure of our crowd of "nice," middle-class kids, decided we would "consummate our love" on the night of the prom—and widely announced that momentous decision to our friends. They were properly aghast with admiration and anticipation. No one else had ever gone *that* far sexually.

The stage was carefully set. Following the dance, our crowd went for a late-night party to an apartment somebody's parents had vacated for the occasion. Fortified with liquor, we all began a heavy petting session on the floor of the darkened living room. Then, as if on cue, Rachel and I loudly excused ourselves and exited to the back bedroom—as everyone else held their breath. Again, I couldn't get it up, and again I lied to my friends. With Rachel's collusion, we explained to a groaning group of disappointed teenagers that Rachel had unexpectedly found she was having a period. For whatever reasons of their own, they went along with the subterfuge. But I sensed that the lie hadn't stuck, that I was "under suspicion." My hard-earned status as jock/intellectual—star of both the classroom and the tennis court—would, I felt certain, instantly succumb to my exposure as a sexual fraud.

Unwilling to admit, even to myself, my lack of lust for women, I kept trying to substitute will power. When the freshman prom came around at Yale, I invited a "known slut" as my date. Once more I announced in advance my plans for a hearty fuck, this time only to my best friend. And when I failed to follow through, I once more invented excuses—different ones to the "slut" (drunkenness) and to the friend (an elaborate tale of having come in my handkerchief to avoid the woman's—ever-present— period). Thereafter I stopped trying. My sister Lucile recalls that when she came up to visit me at Yale, I said to her, as I showed her around the campus, "Take off your coat, don't tell anyone you're my sister, and hold my arm." She obliged.

I was beginning to get the message. As far back as I could remember, I had been attracted erotically only to men, and my masturbation fantasies had always focused exclusively on them. Even as a preteen in summer camp I had had a "special friend." In the camp yearbook for 1940, my write-up described me as "one of Bunk 6B's twins. Many a night his counsellor came in to find Dubie [my nickname] sleeping beside his pal, Katz." And the last line of Katz's write-up poignantly posed the question, "What will you do if they ever separate you from Duberman?"

Two years later, the beloved Katz no longer sharing my pillow and, at the onset of my twelfth year, advancing rapidly on puberty, I organized my current bunkmates into a ritual we called "fussing." We would put a mattress at the bottom of the closet in our bunk and, through trial and error, developed a code question: "You feel like fussing?" If yes, we'd go into the closet, two at a time, and body-rub ourselves into pleasure. There was a definite hierarchy as to who got to go into the closet with whom (my first lesson in the tyranny of beauty, which the gay bars of later years were greatly to reinforce). Teddy and I, pretty blonds both, were much in demand, and on the occasions when we would haughtily disappear into the closet *together*, the bunk would be ablaze with sexual tension.

Psychiatry in those days dismissed such boyish antics as altogether natural, an expected, even necessary prelude to achieving "adult" (heterosexual) identity. But in my own case, the psychiatric prediction had not come true: my attraction to men had not disappeared over time. I nonetheless refused, tenaciously, to put the obvious label on myself. That would have been tantamount, given the current definitions of the day, to thinking of myself as a stunted human being, one whose libidinal impulses had been "arrested" at the stage of early adolescence. I still remember the overwhelming shame I felt when I came across a *Life* magazine picture gallery of "criminal types" and saw that the one labeled "the homosexual"—a sweet, pretty blond—looked *exactly* like me.

All through my undergraduate years at Yale I steeled myself against looking for sex, sensing that the only kind of experiences I would be drawn to would force on me a self-definition I was not ready to accept. I was protected by the notion, standard for isolated, young homosexuals in those years, that there were so few of us and we were so desperate to guard our secret, that no places existed where we could meet each other. But then one day an undergraduate friend offhandedly warned me to stay away at night from the Green (the large park abutting the Yale campus): "It's a hangout for fairies." I was shocked—and thrilled.

That very same night, having gotten myself so drunk I felt conveniently muddled, I headed toward the Green. It was dark and looked empty, but as my eyeballs focused, I saw a very fat, middle-aged black man sitting quietly on a bench. I sat down on the empty bench opposite him. After a minute or two, he started whistling softly, tantalizingly in my direction. Fueled by liquor, I got up, reeled my way over, and stood boldly in front of him. He started playing with my cock, then took it out of my pants. Wildly excited, I started to fondle him.

"Do you have any place we can go?" I whispered importunately.

"Nope. No place."

Suddenly I heard laughter and noise coming in our direction. I was sure it was some undergraduates—and equally sure we'd been seen. Zipping up my fly, I ran out of the park, ran without stopping, panicked, hysterical, ran for my life back to my dorm room. I stayed in the shower for hours, cleaning, cleaning. I actually washed my mouth out with soap, though I hadn't used my mouth—other than to make a prayerful pact with God that if He let me off this time, I'd never, *never*, go near the Green again.

The panic lasted for days. By the end of the week I was back on the Green, drunk again. This time I let myself get picked up by one of the cars cruising the area—and let the driver give me a blow job in the backseat. He was expert and it felt delicious. But perhaps because I let myself actually touch his penis, I went back to the Green only two or three times after that, when the urge for contact overwhelmed my controls; and only once after that did I let myself get another blow job. Then, in my junior year, drunk and desperate, I groped another equally drunk twenty-year-old outside a fraternity house—and barely escaped a nasty fight. Except for a single clouded experience in New York City—where I met someone in Grand Central Station, but then, in the hotel where we went, felt too uneasy to go through with it—that was about the sum of my sex life until age twenty-one. Two blow jobs, two panic attacks.[3]

I graduated Phi Beta Kappa from Yale and near the top of my class. It was clear where I was going to find applause and the self-esteem that purportedly follows in train. I had all the important traits for a successful life in scholarship: a huge capacity for isolation (to endure all those mandated hours alone in the archives), a deeply compulsive and perfectionist nature (to persevere in tracking down every last fact), and a well-developed sense of fairness (to prevent me from reducing complex evidence to cartoon heroes and villains).

The particular appeal of history as my chosen field for scholarship hinged somewhat on my relish for having the last word but was more centrally related to the need (which I could not have articulated at the time) to find some balance for a life heavily tipped toward the present and almost devoid of personal memory. It was as if, in my own life, I had an enormous black-board eraser suspended down my back to the floor, which, as I walked, instantly erased all trace of my footsteps. To compensate for that blank, I could turn to the comparatively painless collective memory we call history.

In blocking out my own past, I was following the example of my parents. Both of them, but especially my mother, seemed to regard any lingering on yesterday as an encumbrance to getting on with today, the source of useless anguish rather than useful experience. My mother was second-generation Austrian-American, but neither she nor her parents ever passed on to me family tales they may have heard about life in the old country, and certainly no one made reference to upholding a Jewish religious tradition in which they themselves had been barely schooled. My mother's family, with their determined lack of interest in all that had preceded, seemed hell-bent on outdoing the citizens of their adopted country in the national trait of present-mindedness. It was part and parcel of their determination to conform to mainstream values. But whereas my father, a Russian emigrant, submitted with gratitude, my mother did so with an underlay of resentment.

My mother, like her two sisters, was urged to go straight from high school into secretarial and sales jobs—to "go to business," to meet eligible men, to assimilate as fully as possible into the American Way. That driving passion to become just like everybody else predestined my mother to a traditional life as wife and mother, although her striking beauty, high spirits, and intelligence might, in a later generation, have led to a vividly asserted specialness. And she passed the goal of fitting in down to her son, along with the high spirits that would keep us both in a state of repressed rebellion, and this side of total capitulation. My athletic carriage would help me conceal my sexuality as successfully as my mother's feigned ordinariness had masked her own instinctive strength.

My father, more than ten years older than my mother and mad about her when they first married ("Marry him, Josie," her mother had urged, "he'll be a good provider"), was far more obviously foreign. One of seventeen children born to peasant parents who worked on a large farm in the Ukraine, his was the only Jewish family in the area. The epidemic of pogroms in Russia in the early years of the twentieth century made survival, not assimilation, the paramount issue. Passing reference was once or twice made by my father's sister to narrow escapes from the Cossacks, but no elaboration was ever forthcoming.

Though my father had little formal education, he had risen, while still a teenager, to the rank of foreman. But in his early twenties, he was drafted into the Russian army, decided to desert, somehow made his way to Hamburg, and in April 1913, age twenty-two, took passage to the United States. I know that much only because I have his boarding pass and his naturalization papers framed on a wall in my apartment. All that I ever heard from my father himself about his early life as an immigrant in New York—single, without money, contacts, skills, or English—amounted to no more than an occasional passing reference: he had lived in a furnished room with the elevated subway screeching by outside his window; he had somehow learned the cutter's trade; he had gotten his first job in a garment factory at a salary of seven dollars a week; he had quickly learned English and risen, again, to a foreman's job.

My father was, if anything, more mum when I was growing up about the details of his past life than my mother was about hers. And perhaps in part because she discouraged him from dwelling on his background. After he saved enough money to bring over his aged father, two brothers, and a sister from Russia, and helped them resettle in Brooklyn, my mother made such martyrlike noises whenever a visit was suggested, that contact became attentuated. Occasionally my father would sneak off to see his family on his own, just as, giving in to an occasional surge of nostalgia for his religious roots, he would sometimes slip out alone to attend services in an orthodox *schul*.

The family, however, attended services in a reform synagogue, and even then, infrequently. Starched and bedecked, we would, like other "Yom Kippur Jews," show up only for the High Holidays. Even then, no one (though perhaps my father, secretly) expected the children to sit through the entire service. We were free to escape after a brief half hour or so and would noisily play and shout in front of the synagogue, oblivious to the significance of the rituals taking place inside and to the possibility that some of the congregation might consider our antics disrespectful.

My family was as apolitical as it was areligious. The watchwords were the standard immigrant ones: making a good living and protecting the family from a hostile outside world. No energy or inclination remained for civic involvement of any kind. Beyond considering Franklin Delano Roosevelt a god ("He's good for the Jews," my father said), no politician or cause ever elicited any enthusiasm much beyond my mother's later remark that she voted for Eisenhower "because he looked like my father." After carefully saving his money, my father and a partner had been able in 1925 to open a dress manufacturing company, "Horwitz & Duberman." When it began to prosper in the thirties, he was hit with a strike, and I remember him saying, "I don't care how long it takes. I've got more money than they do and I can wait them out." My father was a generous, well-liked employer, yet he could never muster sympathy for anything so "un-American" as the trade union movement.

In 1920 he became a citizen, and in 1923 he married my mother. My sister, Lucile, was born in 1926, and I came along in 1930 (when my father was nearly forty). By then, "Horwitz & Duberman" was doing well enough for the family to afford a comfortable, though modest apartment on Broadway and Eighty-second Street. A beautiful infant, I was my mother's adored favorite, pampered and perambulated. My father settled for an occasional chuck under the chin or bounce on the knee. His indifference greatly pleased my sister, allowing her to settle quickly into surrogate motherhood, ordering me to drink *her* unwanted glasses of milk as well as my own, allowing me to hold her regal train during dress-up, refusing to speak to me when I failed to address her as "Princess." Despite the odds, and although our relationship would always have tumultuous interludes, she and I became close friends. When the unwelcome realization of my sexuality finally dawned on me, it was to Lucile, not my parents, that I would confide and turn for counsel. Supportive, she even accompanied me on some of my earliest tours of the gay bars.

My mother had taken great pleasure in my academic accomplishments, but when I told her that I intended to go on to graduate school, she protested. My father seemed not to care, about graduate school or about much of anything. He had long since fallen out of love with my mother, and she, energies and talents thwarted, had become more and more the termagant, nagging and voluble. My father turned to golf—we had become prosperous enough to be living in Westchester and to belong to a country club—and at home, he clung to a strategy of protective silence. But my mother egged him on to have a talk with me about my "disastrous" plan to "bury myself in a university." (Her terminology was not far wrong; I *was* eager to bury myself.)

He dutifully told me he would be disappointed if I did not take over his business someday, and predicted that, having been brought up in comfort, I would soon come to regret not having much money. It was mostly *pro forma*. I thanked him for his concern. He wished me well. My mother accused him of having bungled the talk. And I headed up to Harvard to get a doctorate in history.

From the first I prospered. Unlike most of my fellow graduate students, who within months were lamenting their fate (my youth! my beauty!—squandered over musty texts!), I was serenity itself. Nothing pleased me more than *not* having to squander my youth in pursuit of wine, women, and song. I had found scant pleasure in the touted joys of the flesh—and a plethora of it in the praise I had won for the quality of my mind. Solace lay in the library, not the bedroom.

The more secure I became in my status as an intellectual, the less gloom I felt about being—as the psychiatric establishment then insisted—a disabled human being. I did implicitly accept the culture's verdict that I *was* defective, but could now somewhat circumscribe the indictment; I no longer felt *wholly* unworthy—merely crippled in my affective life.

Now and then I even had an inkling that the psychiatric depiction of homosexuals as disordered and diseased people might be suspect. After all, unless one was prepared to argue (as I sometimes was) that pathology is itself the enabling ingredient in human accomplishment, then something seemed wrong with the characterization; how could a "sick" young man like me be functioning with as much clarity and insight as my Harvard professors assured me I was? My psychic confusion hardly lifted as the decade proceeded and the country's blanket and vehement (one might now say pathological) rejection of political and personal nonconformity deepened in tandem.

If anything like self-acceptance was light years off, my academic achievements had begun to provide me with a base of self-esteem from which I could begin to venture out. It became possible to explore my sexuality, however tentatively, without the overwhelming fear that failure with women (or success with men) would entirely obliterate me.

I've forgotten how I picked up the information, but I wasn't at Harvard more than a few months when I heard there were two gay bars in Boston, the Napoleon ("a collegiate crowd") and the Punch Bowl ("down and dirty"), as well as one or two more that, on the right evening, could be interestingly ambiguous. Slim pickings by today's standards, but for me, having lived so long in isolation, it sounded like a cornucopia. Later on, as my contacts and confidence grew, I would explore the two spots available in Cambridge itself: the riverbank in front of the residential colleges, where I once spotted one of my professors in the bushes and discreetly moved off; and the Commons, less appealing because townies looking for trouble rather than sex hung out there, and because whenever I did loiter under one of the historic elms, I couldn't shake my mother's ancient injunction *never* to walk through a park alone for fear of the sick people who lingered within; I had *become* the person my mother had warned me about.

During my first year in graduate school, I went almost exclusively to the comparative safety of the Napoleon. It was located in the then-derelict Back Bay area, not far from the Statler Hotel, down an obscure side street where few people wandered. There was no sign (if my memory holds) on the door of a brownstone that seemed indistinguishable from its seedy neighbors; and even after one knocked, discreet inquiries, along with a full visual assessment, took place (the point was to screen for plainclothesmen, not beauty) before entry was granted. Once you were inside, the range of amenities was surprising: two floors, with hatcheck, piano bar (*de rigueur* in the show-tune fifties), and a mostly jacket-and-tie crowd content to conform to the management's efforts at upscale elegance.

On my very first foray, I met a fellow graduate student and, unwilling to jeopardize my miraculous good fortune, agreed to go home with him that same night. Since my roommate was out of town for the weekend, "Ray" and I had sex in my dorm room. Perhaps *because* it was so pleasurable, I thereafter avoided him like the plague, rushing in the opposite direction whenever I caught sight of him on campus. Finally he cornered me one day: "Look—can't we be *friends* at least?" Caught somewhere between hysteria and relief, I managed to mumble yes.

It was the beginning of a friendship that has lasted to the present day. And the beginning, too, of allowing myself to socialize with other gay people. Through Ray, I gradually developed a circle of friends, almost all of them graduate students like myself, and entered a subculture that blessedly brought me from individual isolation to collective secrecy—a considerable advance if one can understand, in this day where all furtiveness is decried, the quantum leap in happiness from private to shared anguish.

And anguish we did, though with saving interstices of campy hilarity and genuine camaraderie. Howard, loyal and thoughtful, taught us much about the possibilities of gay friendship, even as Billy, with his malicious tongue, schooled us to be wary of its limitations. Charles, a languid Southerner, provided much of the hilarity. He took every opportunity to refer to, and sometimes display, his enormous cock, which he assured us in dulcet tones, eyes lifted dreamily toward heaven, had become legendary south of Mason-Dixon. Nearing thirty, Charles took advantage of his seniority to lecture us twenty-two-year-olds regularly about the dire perils of the gay life* and the need *at once* to bind ourselves to a lover with hoops of steel as the only possible stay against despair.

Sharing Charles's view, in the couple-oriented fifties, that a lifetime partner was indeed essential for human happiness, we pressed him for an explanation of his own single state, offering the needling suggestion that perhaps an over-dependence on astonished praise for his remarkable member might have kept him from settling down with one, perhaps jaded fan. Charles would sigh loudly, call on Heaven to forgive our youthful philistinism, and regale us with Gothic tales about how the treacheries of Good Old Boys had turned him into a crumpled rose (an invaluable asset, he added, in his chosen field, the study of literature).

Ray and I were the specialists in anguish. Being Jewish— which is to say, inclined to feeling guilty about being alive and at the same time to feeling superior in suffering—predisposed us to the psychiatric notion of homosexuality as curse and apartness. (It was preferable, perhaps, to feel guilty rather than powerless.) As the most earnest and ambitious of our group, we were tormented by the notion that life's deepest emotions and

---

* Yes, we were commonly using the term "gay" that early; within the subculture, the self-designation "gay" became widespread by the late twenties.

highest prizes might be forever outside our grasp. We seemed to have but two choices: to conclude that psychiatry was wrong about us or, that failing, to accept our fate as diminished creatures.

We could do neither. Though the culture had taught us to think badly of ourselves, our families (not yet aware we were gay) had raised us as princes of the realm, entitled to all we surveyed. This flawed upbringing, which ordinarily would have doomed the little princes to lives of presumptuous arrogance, in our cases provided needed ballast; having been so valued at home, we could never *entirely* succumb (though we leaned) to the cultural view of us as disfigured and depraved. But the only integration of two such disparate self-images that we could manage in the fifties hardly made us candidates for serenity: we were pieces of shit around whom the world revolved.

It might have been easier had we *not* been intellectuals. Priding ourselves on being the kind of superior people who based their opinions on so-called objective evidence (rather than popular superstitions or slogans), we put our faith in social science, hardly doubting that its products were "value-free." And in the fifties, the evidence generated by the social sciences continued overwhelmingly to corroborate the orthodox view of homosexuality as pathology.

Kinsey's work had, to be sure, provided a notable, if disputed challenge to that orthodoxy. But most of the data that would later confirm Kinsey—the work, especially, of Evelyn Hooker, Thomas Szasz, and Judd Marmor—lay in the future. Only one significant book emerged in the early fifties to bolster Kinsey's minority views on homosexuality: *Patterns of Sexual Behavior*, by the anthropologists Cleland Ford and Frank Beach. Using data from the Yale Human Relations Area Files on seventy-six cultures, Ford and Beach concluded that nearly two-thirds of those cultures sanctioned, and in some cases mandated, some variant of homosexual activity. But Ford and Beach also concluded that in most cultures homosexuality was considered inappropriate for *every* stage of life, and in no culture was it the sole form of sexual activity for adults.

Since Ray and I were, and had always been Kinsey 6's (exclusively gay), and since we had trouble seeing the bright side of anything, we looked on the Ford and Beach data as mostly negative confirmation of our benighted status. We even managed to twist it into a new instrument of self-torture; in portraying homosexuality as a "stage"—of adolescence, that is, not adulthood—the anthropological evidence (we decided) seemed to confirm the psychiatric view that "fixation" at one stage of development precluded progress to the otherwise natural culminating point of human maturation: heterosexuality. We would never, it seemed, have "complete" lives; we would always be some un-grown, truncated version of humanity.

That the conclusion did not overwhelm us was attributable partly to our upbringing (which had stored in us an irreducible amount of self-regard that transcended intellectual debate); partly to our confidence in our intellectual abilities (perhaps all great minds, or talents, we would argue, were housed—nature's way of balancing out traits—in otherwise deformed personality structures); and partly to the fact that we had found solace in a community of like-minded souls and, in the shadow of the hangman, were managing to have a fair amount of fun with our lives.

My trips to the Napoleon had quickly given me some much-needed sexual experience (though my inhibitions remained multiple) and then, within a few months, an introduction to the still more threatening world of romance. One night in the Napoleon, I ran into a classmate from Yale. We had barely known each other as undergraduates, since I was an ardent student and "Rob," as befitted his society lineage, had ardently steered clear of scholarly associations. But in Boston, where Rob had returned after graduation to be near his family, he and I were on a somewhat more equal footing. He was far more sexually experienced than I and also far more determined, from the first, on a love affair. To my skittish hesitations and withdrawals, he counterposed vigorous courting and glamorizing visits to family estates. The most memorable was a trip to Grandmama's Manhattan triplex.

A formidable dowager well into her eighties, she was—Rob was quick to tell me—Herbert Hoover's longstanding bridge partner (expecting him to say paramour, I was puzzled at the triumph in his voice). She received us in her library, seated unmoving in an armchair, dressed in a full-length black gown, a mass of snow-white hair framing a still beautiful face. After allowing the exchange of a few rigorous pleasantries, she had the butler show us into an upstairs bedroom so we could change into "appropriate" clothes for the evening.

Properly dazzled, I told Rob I "probably" loved him. He responded expansively by letting me fuck him for the first time—in the shower, itself a new experience. But I resisted his badgering insistence that I pronounce it the "best fuck" I had ever had, though I had had precious few. I had stretched my limits far enough for one day. My father's peasant stubbornness asserted itself; bristling at the hint of *droit de seigneur*, I told Rob the fuck had been "okay."

Rob and I called ourselves "lovers," but the affair was a good deal less profound than that, and the actual lovemaking was sharply circumscribed. It wasn't simply that I was a novice. I was also deeply bound by sex role conventions and by the determination—if I *had* to be gay—that I was going to be a manly (that is, "acceptable") version. None of this, of course, was consciously worked out; I simply performed according to the cultural script then dominant—though finally, of course, it's mostly a mystery as to who adopts which social cues and why.

A "real man," as we all knew in those years (and as many continue to affirm), was unyieldingly dominant, the penetrator, the aggressor, someone who took *only* the active role in bed. To help reinforce this neat paradigm, all sexual acts were conveniently labeled "active" or "passive," and those qualities were presumed intrinsic to the acts themselves. Thus, giving blow jobs and getting fucked were innately passive, female activities; getting blow jobs and giving fucks were active and male. There seemed no understanding at the time—and precious little since—that the muscular contractions of the throat, anus, or vagina, could, by several definitions, be considered "active" agents in producing any cohabitation worthy of the name—to say nothing of the psychological truth that s/he who sets and controls the scenario is, regardless of the nature of the scenario, the true "actor."

I was somebody who got blow jobs and gave fucks. For most of the few months I was with Rob, I was "trade"—I let him blow me. The boundaries suited us both; they assuaged my guilt by reinforcing my "masculine" image, and they fed his preferred view of himself as seducer and guide to the uninitiated. It wasn't until several years later that I could even begin, at first in fantasy, to acknowledge a desired role reversal; only rarely could I put the fantasy into action. By the late fifties, with a vocabulary and set of attitudes perfectly attuned to the times, I summarized my anxiety over those rare role reversals in a diary entry:

> . . . last weekend in New York I met a guy named Lou in the Big Dollar [a gay bar] and went home with him. Rugged Italian type, one-track-mind sexually—wanted, deliriously, to fuck me. His persistence excited me. It brought out all my passive desires—to be used, possessed, overpowered; which only occasionally come to the surface and which I act on rarely. I was tempted to give in this time, but controlled the impulse by telling myself what I knew was true—that the fantasy of being "taken" was more exciting than the actuality and that the subsequent psychological upset, plus the worry over disease, would far overbalance the slight pleasure. I wonder what lies behind the fantasy in the first place. I present an exterior of manliness, and in much of my actual sex life, play the dominant role, but there is a parallel and conflicting desire in me—sometimes very strong—to be passive sexually. In some complicated way I think all my homosexual activity is an attempt (among other things) to identify with a masculinity I never was sure I had. Being entered by a man is perhaps the most direct way of incorporating and absorbing that masculinity. And yet when I do allow myself to be "browned" [the genteel gay euphemism in the fifties for getting fucked] I almost never receive physical pleasure from it; that comes instead from assuming the opposite role—from browning others. But the fantasy remains strong: to be possessed by—and thereby to possess—a real man and his qualities.

The acknowledgment of more than one set of desires would make me a possible conscript, years later, to the sexual liberationist ranks. But those armies were not yet forming, and in the fifties, my identification with "real men," and my penchant for easy moralisms and impulsive self-recrimination, made it likely instead that I would be drawn to the messianic certainties of psychotherapy. Especially since the affair with Rob soon disintegrated. Though I did the leaving—too inconstant in my self-regard to bond for long with someone so unvaryingly enamoured of me—I felt the loss. Rob's steady adoration had kept my introspective gloom in check; now, in the wake of a "failed relationship," it burst out anew.

I suppose I might have rushed right then and there into a psychiatrist's office. But one unpleasant memory and one wondrous new experience delayed that outcome for several years more. The memory was from age fifteen, when my parents had sent me to my first therapist. Knowing nothing of my sexual orientation, the "cure" they had sought was for my mysterious silence around the house (the mystery is less dense in retrospect; I was trying to avoid scrutiny and detection, the sense already having dawned in me that I had a desperate secret to hide). Monosyllabic at home, I was exuberantly verbal outside it, a gregarious leader among my friends. My parents knew that, deplored the contrast, blamed me for it, decided a therapist could "fix" it.

I saw the therapist for a few months, but never told him about my sexual attraction to other boys. I instinctively distrusted him, perhaps because of his paeans to the wonders of family life and filial duty, and his insistence that if I would regularly embrace my mother and tell her I loved her, all would come right. Once, in recounting a dream, I came perilously close to telling the therapist more than I intended. Masturbating to a homoerotic fantasy in a room enclosed by glass walls, I was terrified that people in nearby buildings would see what I was doing and discover the truth about me. "Which was what?" the therapist asked. "Dunno," I replied, quickly recovering my protective monosyllabism.

That happened seven or eight years before I met Rob, but the memory slowed my progress to the psychoanalytic couch. Anyway, I told myself, the failure of a mere affair was hardly sufficient proof that, as psychiatry would have it, I and all homosexuals were incapable of forming satisfying relationships. After all, even heterosexuals had brief, inconsequential affairs. And besides, the several good friendships I had formed of late certainly seemed to argue for my capacity to connect well with others.

But far more convincing proof of my intactness—and my lack

of need for therapy—came along within a few months of the breakup with Rob: I fell in love. Nothing did more to make me willing to take on the onerous burden of a homosexual identity and to resist the psychiatric notion that *only* malediction would be my lot. Love felt a lot more like relief and joy.

# 3

# LARRY

H OW TO DESCRIBE "LARRY"? Thirty-five years of sea change
have intervened, repositioning the memory at every turn,
smoothing over the jagged ups and downs of our years together
to a hazy sweetness.

We met at the Napoleon, a few months after I broke up with
Rob. Larry was twenty, three years younger than I. He lived
with his devoutly Catholic, working-class Irish family in Canton,
a suburb outside of Boston, commuting every day to a clerk's
job with Filene's department store (from which he gradually
worked himself up to be a buyer). We were different in many
ways besides class status. Larry was muscular and compact in
build, low-keyed, intense, essentially nonverbal. He was my somatic ideal, I was his intellectual one; he helped me learn about
my body, I helped him learn about books and ideas.

Though our differences were in some ways deeply nurturing,
allowing us to open up new worlds for each other, we worried
from the beginning that our pervasive differences in background, education, and temperament would ultimately overwhelm our passionate feelings of attachment and our sense that
we did, profoundly and illogically, belong together.

We were expected to worry. And about much more than
temperamental differences. Two people of the same gender,
the culture had taught us, were not meant to spend their lives

together and, should they be foolish enough to try, would soon learn that Nature intended otherwise. As if that conviction was not debilitating enough, we also had to cope (as did heterosexuals) with the then-current cultural nostrum that when two partners were *really* meant for each other, neither sexual arousal nor emotional commitment ever flagged; health was defined as the absence of desire for more than one person, or at least the need to act on the desire.

Larry and I didn't vary from the acceptable pattern for about two years. From the beginning, young and hot, our eyes strayed constantly. But we were under several spells—the mainstream American injunction to be faithful, love, and the fear of losing love—and they held our hormones in check. Charles constantly told us, his voice resonant with campy amazement, how *incredibly* lucky we were to have found each other and what *utter* ingrates we would be should we *ever* do *anything* to jeopardize our good fortune.

Properly chastised and warned, Larry and I scarcely dared think about outside sexual contacts, dutifully concentrating instead on the seemly issue of whether we should or could live together. Since we were both scraping by financially (I was now self-supporting, or at least trying to get by with minimal family assists), moving in together seemed a pipe dream for the time being. This was an impasse that carried with it some relief for me, since I still felt ambivalent, even if less so under the trance of love, about settling down as a now-and-forever homosexual. We made do with weekend overnights in my single bed (by 1954 I was a resident tutor in Adams House, with far more privacy than when living in the graduate school dormitory).

But by 1955, after Larry and I had been together for two years, amorous zest and fantasies of eternal togetherness began, in tandem, to fray a bit. As they do, of course, with most couples, romantic intensity inevitably mutating (when the couple is lucky) into a more routine and comfortable domesticity. It's also commonplace for partners to view any erosion in erotic excitement with alarm, as a forecast of ultimate disaster. But the forecast seems more ominous still when the couple consists of two gay men—who have been forewarned of their incompatibility and told that sex was all they cared about and were good at anyway.

Larry and I continued to feel considerable passion for each other, but since it was no longer automatic and constant and now seemed to follow arguments rather than forestall them, we nervously wondered how much of a future we could count on. The more we wondered, the more prone we became to elevating garden-variety disagreements into the equivalent of Doomsday. And so we began to hedge our bets, slacken our commitment. (If it was only a matter of time before we broke up, maybe we ought to start looking around now for likely replacements?) Both of us, but I more than Larry, began having sexual adventures on the side. This deviation from the monogamous norm, in turn, further convinced me of my incapacity—generic, so long as I remained homosexual—for intimacy. Hadn't psychiatry long warned that homosexuals were condemned, by the very nature of their illness, to flee from relatedness to promiscuity?

Even if the culture had been supportive, Larry and I might have broken up; some of our differences, after all, did not bode well for the kind of long-term commitment that feeds best on companionable similarities of temperament and interest. But for straight couples, social values serve to counteract problems in the relationship; the high premium placed on heterosexual pair-bonding and family life provides plenty of brownie points and self-esteem for staying together. For homosexual couples, social values serve further to underscore, rather than counteract, interpersonal difficulties; being called "sick" and "degenerate" hardly gives one the needed psychic support for sustaining a relationship.

I began thinking once more about psychotherapy, thinking about "conversion" as my only hope for a happy life. Ironically, it was just at this time, the mid-fifties, that Evelyn Hooker began her research study of *non*-patient homosexuals, began to amass the counterevidence needed for challenging the notion, under which I (and most of the country) then labored, that homosexuals were sick people in need of treatment. Orthodox psychiatry had based its negative conclusions about homosexuality on studies of people who had come to therapists for help or on captive populations in prisons and mental hospitals. With a grant from the National Institute of Mental Health in 1954, Hooker matched thirty homosexual men with thirty heterosexual men, screening both groups for manifest pathology, and then subjecting the remaining candidates to a variety of projective tests. Two-thirds of both the heterosexual and homosexual men were judged (by outside evaluators, as well as by Hooker herself) as having made an average adjustment or better—and, significantly, the two groups could not be told apart psychologically.

In her later studies, Hooker would also find that far more homosexual men than earlier believed did manage to maintain long-term love relationships, despite the constant fear of public exposure and despite the culture's strenuous efforts to stigmatize those relationships. Indeed, Hooker would ultimately single out stigmatization as itself the prime cause of what pathology did exist in homosexuals.

In her first article, published in 1957, Hooker summarized her findings up to that point:

> . . . personality structure and adjustment may . . . vary within a wide range. . . . What is difficult to accept (for most clinicians) is that some homosexuals may be very ordinary individuals, indistinguishable from ordinary individuals who are heterosexual. . . . Some may be quite superior individuals not only devoid of pathology (unless one insists that homosexuality is a sign of pathology) but also functioning at a superior level.[4]

These suggestions provided a striking challenge to the dominant psychiatric view that homosexuals were a homogeneous group, bound together by dysfunction and neurosis. Hooker's series of articles would grow in influence over the years, but the initial one in 1957 appeared in the specialized *Journal of Projective Techniques*. Neither my friends nor I read technical journals in psychology, and it would be another decade before I heard a word about Hooker's findings. Indeed, by 1957 I was paying regular visits to a psychotherapist whose views of my "condition" were precisely of the kind Hooker was attempting to counteract.

I began seeing "Dr. Weintraupt" in late 1955, after the spiral of recrimination and reconciliation between Larry and me had come to seem hopelessly circular. These were the years when— for the privileged, particularly those living on the Eastern Seaboard—the decision to enter therapy seemed logical and valid.

In a culture that had grown apolitical and conservative, analyzing the inner life had become a primary, praiseworthy enterprise. For intellectuals and egotists especially, it was the elective choice of the moment, *the* certified path to self-knowledge.

From the first Weintraupt advised me to give up the relationship with Larry. Until I did, he warned, any real progress in therapy would prove impossible. The drama of our interpsychic struggle, Weintraupt insisted, had become a stand-in for the more basic intrapsychic conflict I was unwilling to engage—the conflict between my neurotic homosexual "acting-out" and my underlying healthy impulse toward a heterosexual union.

I resisted—not so much Weintraupt's theories, as his insistence on a total break with Larry. I accepted the need, but could not summon the will. I spent therapy hour after therapy hour arguing my inability to give up the satisfactions of the relationship—neurotic and occasional though they might be, and though my future happiness might well hang on their surrender. I resisted so hard and long that Weintraupt finally gave me an ultimatum: either give up Larry or give up therapy.

I turned to my friend Ray for advice and comfort. "I'll never find anyone as sweet or loving or loyal as Larry," I wailed over coffee cups and wine glasses. "If I give him up, I give up the best person I'll ever find."

"The best man," Ray would correct, his tone mournfully tentative, sharing all my doubts about a possible "conversion" at the advanced age of twenty-six.

"But do I have any choice but to try? After all, it hasn't been any bed of roses for Larry and me lately. And it can only get worse from here."

Dutifully leaping to the other side of the argument, Ray would halfheartedly say something about the value of "a bird in the hand." That would prompt me to defend the need to push ahead, against all odds, into the risky unknown. Which would lead Ray to a disdainful reminder that we were dealing with a real-life relationship not a soap opera. Which would cause me hastily to launch into a stringent intellectual assessment of psychoanalytic assumptions—which we would then reluctantly conclude were probably true, though unpalatable.

The dialogue and commiseration continued for weeks. Finally, torn with anguish and self-doubt, I decided I would *try* to give up the relationship with Larry, try to cast my lot, as Weintraupt had long urged, on the side of "health." But in the privacy of my diary, I went on lamenting and rethinking the decision, inadvertently revealing along the way how fully I had internalized the culture's homophobic biases:

*August 29, 1956*
God I miss Larry. How I wish he were here tonight waiting for me in bed, sweet, affectionate . . . and yet I can't really settle down with him. I have no confidence in our building any sort of a life. . . . Is any genuine commitment between homosexuals possible?

*September 2*
. . . went to the bars . . . Larry was safely on the Cape [vacationing] and couldn't *directly* prick my conscience ("You supposedly gave me up for analysis, and here you are a month later cruising in the bars") . . . Got quite drunk and came home with a youngish guy who I thought would be a good fuck. But he was lousy in bed—inexperienced physically, inane in every other way . . . After two hours of nonerect activity, we finally managed an orgasm. I was afterwards completely repulsed by what I'd done; this absurd compulsive intimacy with an anonymous body—and a disappointing one at that (which is perhaps why I'm so righteously repulsed).

He left early this morning. I've been moping around ever since. Came very close to rushing off to see Larry on the Cape. It's extraordinary how "right" seeing him would make everything. But I've yielded to this too many times before, and always without lasting satisfaction. It's been a full month now since we've seen each other—I've *got* to hold off—I *cannot* form any lasting relationship with him—why, I'm not sure— but this I do know, that it won't work, and I must give him a chance to free himself.

*September 3*
The great drought is over—with the usual awful results. Last night Larry called. I was so glad to hear from him, and

under almost no pressure, agreed to meet him . . . eventually I was talking drunkenly—meaning it all—about giving up the analysis, about missing him terribly, etc. And finally, sex. As miraculous as ever, and followed, as ever, by panic over what I had done and remorse over what I had said.

Will it ever be resolved? When I see him I'm lost; and I can't seem to stop myself from seeing him. Yet it's never enough. Could I really give up the analysis and accept my life as it now stands? Also impossible . . .

*September 4*

Nervous about having to tell Weintraupt what happened last night. Half hoping, like a renegade schoolboy, to be "dismissed." But I was unable to goad either him or myself into it.

The confessional did me good. And now, I suppose, the usual drifting till the next crisis. What of all the promises I made to Larry last night? Today I consummate the immorality by not even calling him. What else can I do? If I call, I merely reestablish a lifeline that consists of half-promises that always remain unfulfilled, and yet always remain. If only I could know that after my physical and neurotic needs are spent, there's still something left for us to live on. I sometimes think there is—but Weintraupt had thrown so many of my feelings into doubt and confusion, I can't even be sure of "sometimes." And so I'll continue to drift; trying not to call—hoping he'll call me; continuing to go to Weintraupt—planning imminently to quit.

*September 7*

Just back from the bars. Larry was there and we mooned around each other—with intermittent snarls—all night. Curse Weintraupt and my bloody fine powers of resistance! I'm so sick of considering consequences, "looking ahead"—to what? To a question mark, to the bare possibility that I may someday be able to marry and have children.

1:45 a.m.: Larry called a few minutes ago. "Can I borrow your car to get home?" "Sure, I'll meet you at the gate [of Adams House] in 2 minutes". And at the gate he looked—so beautiful. Then he cried and said he loved me and swore he'd never "bother" me again. How the hell can I resist? I asked him to come upstairs. He hesitated and said he was tired of "taking the blame." We went through this 3 or 4 times. Finally, in a pique at his stubbornness, I walked away— half expecting and more than half hoping to be called back. But no, he let the gate close . . .

*September 8*

I'm like a stupid child who can't profit from experience. Larry returned the car during the afternoon and I invited him up, although I was playing cards. He slept while we played and then when the others left, I woke him, crawled into bed, caressed him—and that was that. I simply made no effort to resist. Why invite him up in the first place? Why not wake him hurriedly? . . . No, none of those sensible things. Attraction, tenderness, wonderfully passionate sex—and then the usual regret over the destructiveness of my lust, both to Larry and to my analysis.

*September 10*

I quit the analysis this morning. After months of indecision, the final action was almost unexpected. I told Weintraupt about last night with Larry—and about a dream in which my "auditing" a course evolved into a symbolic reenactment of my attitude towards the analysis—i.e., an onlooker, an auditor, rather than a participant. From there it was only a step to being told my attitude made the analysis circular and endless; and since in honesty I couldn't swear that I would be able to change it, it was mutually agreed that it would be best to stop. Yet having made the decision, I can't accept it. Accepting it means accepting my life, being satisfied with it. And I can't . . .

I told Larry immediately about my decision to quit therapy, and we met for a serious talk about our future. We began the evening by having sex ("How great not to follow it," I wrote in my diary, "with panic and guilt"). Then later, over dinner, I told him that the best I thought I could manage would be a part-time relationship, no strings attached. I was happy, I said, for us to go on seeing each other—if he was—but no longer thought an exclusive relationship would work, explaining (as I

wrote in my diary) that "I remain incapable (don't all homosexuals?) of finding satisfaction permanently with one person."
Larry, an accepting stoic by nature, and extraordinarily tolerant
of my mercurial shifts, asked for no further details or explanations and simply agreed henceforth to a loose arrangement
between us.

But in a real sense, therapy had already poisoned that well.
Weintraupt's certitudes about the hopelessness of homosexual
life managed to underscore all my pre-existing doubts about
my—or any homosexual's—capacity for love and commitment.
Like most homosexual couples in those years, Larry and I had
distrusted ourselves far too much to affirm what might have
been genuinely different, and creatively different, about a gay
relationship, to affirm (rather than apologize for) some needed
distinctions between emotional and sexual fidelity. Instead we
had invested our energies, as well as our hopes for certification
as *bona fide* human beings, in conforming as closely as possible
to the mainstream norm of what constituted a healthy union—
meaning now-and-forever monogamy. Not the least of the sab-
otages the conformist fifties committed was to instill the notion
that "different" was the equivalent of being "disturbed" and, in
the case of political nonconformists especially, "dangerous."

But being declared an unfit candidate for intimacy released
me, ironically (though the irony escaped me at the time), better
to enjoy the pleasures of the flesh. I was a horny young guy
who had never before had license to explore the nonmonogamous urges of his body; being certified as "sick" hobbled my
confidence but liberated my libido. I even had the occasional
inkling that in breaking away from Larry I was *using* the insistence of orthodox psychiatry that I was incapacitated for love
to justify some unorthodox and overdue sexual adventuring that
the culture would sanction only for those lost souls unable to
partake of the *real* satisfactions of monogamy.

I now began to roam with a vengeance, as if—being a dutiful
creature of the culture—determined to live out Weintraupt's
prediction that only therapy could have saved me from a life
of random, disconnected promiscuity. I even called an old friend
in New York City and asked him to meet me one night for a
tour of the hot spots. We started decorously enough, with dinner
at the East 55 restaurant, which, daringly for those years, openly

catered to a homosexual clientele. I reacted to the scene with disdain. "The place was filled with babbling queens," I wrote indignantly in my diary, "who, because they can afford to spend $5 on a dinner, feel they are also entitled to talk at the top of their lungs." It was one thing to accept one's fate as a homosexual, another to be queer; I wasn't about to identify with any of that " 'girl' crap." But I did have the limited grace to add in my diary, "Oh why criticize—I suppose the sick should stick together!"

From there it was down to Lennie's, a gay bar in Greenwich Village. I spent most of the evening talking to a redhead from Toronto named Rick and ended up in bed with him. Disappointed in the sex, I drew a self-lacerating moral in my diary: "Perhaps I purposely single out those to whom I'm only marginally attracted—thus ensuring disappointment. A way of punishing myself? Of preventing any further involvement?" When I attended a straight friend's wedding that same week, I enviously compared the contentment I chose to see all around me ("wives bearing, husbands beaming," I wrote in my diary) with my own empty life. But I was not yet wholly brainwashed: "Perhaps I mistake it," I added, "and am merely romanticizing."

I alternated between fits of remorse over quitting therapy ("throwing away my one chance at health") and self-recrimination over my inability either fully to commit or fully to withdraw from the relationship with Larry. He, within a few weeks, tried to bring matters to a head by putting a ban on our having sex ("We've got to try to form a new kind of relationship—friends, since lovers hasn't worked; and occasional sex with each other is merely postponing the adjustment"). Larry said he still preferred going to bed only with me, but rather than settle for occasionally, he had decided he preferred never—knowing the thought of never would frighten me more than him.

Having no choice, I agreed that we would stop having sex together, and went back to my routine of bar-hopping. But Larry himself proved unwilling to stick to the agreement, and within three weeks, at his initiation, we were back in bed. Within a week after that, we accidentally ran into each other at the Punch Bowl (the Napoleon had now become too buttoned-up for my taste). Sensing I had my eye on someone else and was reluctant to leave with him, Larry angrily vented his frustration at our on-and-off gyrations. I told him (as I wrote up the exchange in my diary that night): ". . . I hate tormenting him and yet I am incapable now of changing my insane pace of promiscuity. I said I'm useless to both of us. We agreed not to see each other any more."

The "insane pace" turns out, on rechecking my diary, to have amounted to one sexual experience in two weeks. Maybe I was exaggerating to help Larry break our stalemate. More likely, I *felt* such a pace to be insane. In forsaking the certified One-Person-Now-and-Forever model of health, I saw myself as descending into an iniquitous pit of promiscuity. Although sleeping around gave me quite a bit of incidental pleasure, it was circumscribed by guilt.

After one sexual encounter, I wrote despairingly in my diary: "I tell myself how meaningless this anonymous cycle of body and body is, but I continue to repeat it; partly, no doubt, because of the necessity to keep proving myself, but also because the means of forming a healthier, more complete relationship are slight." Another evening, having successfully maneuvered someone to bed whom I had long found attractive, and although sex with him had been enjoyable, I felt compelled to atone: "My revulsion is working overtime. All sorts of resolutions. Eager for work—never going to waste time bar-hopping again, etc. No satisfaction there anyway. All set for a return to analysis; must have a wife and family, only possible things that matter."

But I was not yet ready to give therapy another go. I was willing enough to label my sex life neurotic and compulsive, but felt myself powerless to change it: "I can neither give up my homosexual activities, nor devote myself guiltlessly to them. Paralyzed on the one side by desire and on the other by knowledge." Besides, as was soon to become clear, Larry and I were not yet finished with each other.

Despite having broken off forever, within a short time we were again having sex. This time, more than a little exhausted at all the reformulations, we avoided cementing a pact of any kind and simply let our meetings take what shape they would. By now I was nearing completion of my doctoral thesis, and both Larry and I knew that within a year I would be leaving the Boston area for a full-time teaching job. We no longer had any expectation about sharing our lives in the future—though there would be occasional pangs of longing and regret for several more years, and for several decades (for we did stay in touch) unexpected surges of deep feeling for each other.

When I took up my first teaching job at Yale in the fall of 1957, Larry and I still occasionally alternated weekends in Boston or New Haven. Saying good-bye to him after one of them, I remember tears gushing from my eyes, wondering bitterly why I let myself acknowledge the full depth of my feelings for him only when I safely knew it could be indulged infrequently. As I wrote in my diary, "If I don't love him, why did I cry so painfully when it came time for him to leave? If I do love him, why has our relationship fluctuated so wildly the last few years? A riddle I long since gave up on. Anyway, it's awful being alone again . . ."

It was so awful that within a few weeks of arriving at Yale, I decided I had to go back into therapy.

# 4

---

# YALE

I HAD ARRIVED IN September 1957 with a recently diagnosed ulcer to accompany my generalized misery at separation from Larry and from the group of friends I'd made in
Cambridge. The doctor put me on baby food and sternly warned
me against "too much stress" in my life. The baby food soon
quieted the ulcer, but telling me to reduce stress was about as
helpful as telling me to become somebody else.

I rented a small attic apartment out on Whitney Avenue,
about ten minutes from the campus, fixed it up as much as my
$4500 salary (top dollar in 1957, even for a Harvard Ph.D.)
would allow, and tried to get used to cooking solitary hamburger
dinners. But lonely and unsettled, I quickly fell into depression.
The challenge of full-time teaching (I had been a part-time tutor
at Harvard) helped absorb much of my energy, but added its
own set of insecurities.

Not yet knowing that incoming students can be as terrified
as even their most unseasoned instructors, I literally choked up
with nervousness on meeting my first class. By busily writing
my office hours on the blackboard, calling the roll, and re-
arranging the seats, I bought enough time to recover my voice,
but not to remove the tremor in it. In my diary, with almost
reflexive self-recrimination, I sternly told myself that my "in-

secure" personality would keep me from ever achieving a truly
natural classroom manner, but that I had the obligation at least
to aim for the next best thing: "to avoid overt affectations and
to prevent my neuroses from concentrating on the glorification
of 'Me' rather than an illumination of the materials." My ulcer
greatly enjoyed those hectoring sentiments.

I did have a few friends left over from my undergraduate
days at Yale, when I had gotten friendly with two or three young
faculty members. One of them, Henry, a Southerner by birth,
now had a sumptuous set of bachelor digs in Silliman, a Yale
residential college, and he sometimes invited me to his elegant,
closeted dinner parties. The china was Wedgwood, the music
Mozart, the mood urbane, the banter clever, the politics
conservative.

This was the year of Little Rock, when a brave group of young
black students tried to integrate their local high school, and the
controversy so gripped the nation that even Henry's genteel
dinner parties were occasionally disrupted. Henry himself, losing his characteristic lassitude, would argue heatedly that the
South (meaning the white South, of course) "needed time," that
if let alone, it would gradually but surely proceed along the path
of integration. When some of us pressed Henry for evidence
that the South, having been "let alone" for almost a hundred
years, had in fact made progress in that direction, he would
grumpily insist that the process would only be impeded by "outside agitation."

The only alternate amusement in New Haven to mannerly
dinner parties was the Shubert Theater, in the fifties still a major
tryout spot for shows on their way to Broadway. I saw every
play that came through, glad for the chance to forget myself
and glad for the chance to vent my critical faculties on something other than myself. I filled my diary with harsh judgments:
Anouilh was a "brainless and frivolous old queen"; Helen Hayes
an "All-American Grandmother"; *The Country Wife* was "tedious
and static"; *J.B.* "oracular and dreadful." The judgments may
have been shrewd enough, but the amount of acid invested was
suspect—as if eating away at my belly could not occupy the half
of it.

I needed an outlet other than closet theater criticism or complacent dinner parties. I needed sex and companionship. But on arriving in New Haven I had taken the veil, had sworn I would never set foot in any of the three bars—George & Harry's, the Taft Hotel, and Pierelli's—known to be at least intermittently gay. There were good reasons, even beyond my usual self-punitive ones.

For it was in just these years that the Smith College scandal broke: several male faculty members were convicted in court of the crime of passing to each other "pornographic" materials (which in the fifties mostly meant muscular models posing awkwardly in Roman togas). Newton Arvin, the famed literary critic, already having had several emotional breakdowns and terrified at the pending scandal, was rumored to have implicated the others by turning over his diaries to the state police. Two young faculty members were dismissed, their scholarly careers ruined.

Attitudes at Yale, it soon became apparent, were no more advanced. In the late fifties a young faculty member (and friend of mine) responded to a student's verbal pass at a drunken party with something more than that—versions varying from a direct grope to the whispering of sweet scatalogical nothings. The student ran screaming (literally) into the night—and the next day, into the dean's office. Adopting what some, in that fiercely homophobic time, insisted was a humane line, the Yale administration hinted to the miscreant faculty member that if he would deny the student's story as a fabrication, the incident would be hushed up. He refused, reluctant to demean his own nature— hardly a common response among homosexuals in those years. The administration affected regret at such "foolish bravado" and, declaring it had done everything possible to save the faculty member from his own recklessness, fired him. He never got another academic job. Nor, in fact, did he ever seek one, preferring to run a boardinghouse (which he does to this day) rather than live among the conventional prudes of academe.

So there were real reasons for staying out of the New Haven bars. Since none of them was exclusively gay, it was all too likely that on a given night some straight undergraduates, utilizing New Haven's few options for a wild time on the town, might happen into them—and the next day carry to the dean's office the news that the new instructor was a queer. I decided it was safer, whenever celibacy or isolation proved too much for me, to take the hour and a half drive down to New York.

It was time, I reasoned, to return to therapy. I didn't want (as I wrote in my diary) "to start the pain and upset of analysis all over again," yet felt I had to. At twenty-seven, my career was moving along well but my personal life seemed a shambles. I'd moved away from my friends and lost my lover, had developed an ulcer, felt mostly blue, occasionally manic, never peaceful.

The therapist I chose this time was "Dr. Albert Igen," a professor of psychiatry at the Yale Medical School. I liked him immediately. Low-keyed and compassionate, he refrained from pompous pronouncements and optimistic predictions alike, telling me that for the sake of a "sounder adjustment" we should indeed work to change my sexual orientation, but that there was no guarantee of success. "It will largely depend," he solemnly told me, "on your wish to change. The ultimate rewards will be great, but since the process of change is fraught with frustration and difficulty, you must greatly *want* that change in order for it to happen." We agreed on three sessions a week, at twenty dollars a session. That was difficult for me to manage financially, even with occasional help from my parents. In asking for that help, I told them I was going into therapy to resolve a few "marginal issues" in my life.

Igen's tentativeness, in happy contrast to Weintraupt's certitude, seemed to me an encouraging sign. Yet the day after I met with Igen, I felt unaccountably depressed. Perhaps I sensed—certainly it was not conscious—that in the guise of self-improvement I had in fact inaugurated yet another round of self-sabotage. By that evening my stomach was rumbling away, and on impulse—psychiatry would have said "in resistance to the commitment I had just made to health"—I decided to tour the New Haven bars. As I wrote in my diary, "So I risk my job—I'm sufficiently depressed not to care. If I could stand still and *understand* the depression . . . I'd no doubt be better off. But homosexuality has been a channel—*the* channel—for so long that it's easier to keep running."

When I reported the excursion to Igen, he said he agreed with Weintraupt—though Igen employed a mournful rather than peremptory tone—that change would come only if I proved willing to sit with my "problems," working on them slowly and deliberately in therapy instead of "acting them out." I said that I had tried all that before, with Dr. Weintraupt, and that the strain had proven intolerable. Igen's response was temperate: "You are now older and wiser, better able to withstand the need for instant gratification. Besides, the injunction from your therapist now coincides more exactly with what you feel within. In your healthier moments, you *know* that your sexual compulsions are destructive and should be resisted. But the decision to resist must, of course, be yours."

Perhaps because he didn't press me for an immediate commitment to celibacy, I said I would try, though I wasn't feeling optimistic about my chances on either side of the equation. As I wrote that night in my diary, "The prospects of a lasting homosexual relationship are too slim for me to get much comfort from the possibility; and a satisfying heterosexual relationship is still so remote that I can barely even wish for it. But perhaps either luck in the first area or Dr. Igen in the latter will make one or the other come true. In the meantime, I remain skeptical and unhappy."

I sat still for a whole month. Then Dr. Igen told me he had to have an eye operation and would be out of the office for four or five weeks. I cried a little, possibly with relief, told him I would *try* to hold the fort but didn't see how I could do that without having the support of continual therapy sessions. He said again, this time with more than a trace of impatience, "That decision is yours."

I ended up in New York that weekend, going to Everard's, the gay bathhouse, two nights in a row. Ray had recently introduced me to the place, and I had quickly developed a hate/love attitude toward it. I hated the squalor of its filthy corridors, the surliness of its attendants, feared its invitation to abandonment. I loved its animal anonymity, the absence of all pretense at verbal prelude or gradual seduction, the easy opportunities for voyeurism and exhibitionism (in which I rarely let myself indulge), the constant changeover in the players, the plethora of opportunities (knowing a hand pushed away here would be welcome there), disconnected bodies unapologetically pleasuring each other in alluring disregard for every staid convention. I loved *and* hated the unnerving challenge to my moralistic training in denial.

Ray was even more of an afficionado of the baths than I was. He would come in from Boston and I from New Haven, and we would meet in New York for dinner and then proceed together to Everard's. But we were careful not to continue our chatter once inside; not only did it detract from the desirable image of stolid backwoodsmen that we cultivated, but it would draw stern looks of disapproval from the other patrons, deeply offended that so trivial a pursuit as *talk* was impinging on the high seriousness of *sex*. Sometimes I patrolled the passageways till dawn, unable to tear myself away from the prospect of the hunk I had spotted three hours earlier reappearing; and yet, no matter how tired or inflamed, never able fully to let go, never able to participate in the orgiastic doings of the steamroom. Everard's capsized but did not sink my ingrained, careful scenarios of what was permissible sexuality.

In April 1958, at the end of my first year of teaching at Yale, I was elected a resident Fellow of Silliman College. That meant luxurious quarters—a five-room apartment, complete with an oak-paneled study, daily maid service, and free meals in the college dining hall. It also meant greater integration into the academic community. I felt uneasy about moving into the midst of the well-bred, closeted life of Silliman's bachelor fellows, with their endless rounds of drinks and dinner. Measured against such mainstream rituals and sexless lives, I felt myself a rebel by comparison. My priorities were work, therapy, and time to make trips to the bars and baths of New York, and from the first I put myself on guard against too great an involvement with Silliman's consuming social life.

But some of the resident faculty were pleasant people, at least for an evening, and besides, I felt grateful to have been taken out of my Whitney Avenue attic and deemed a presentable member of society. So now and then I joined the tasteful proceedings—and indeed felt much the better for it. Within just a few months of taking up residence in Silliman, some of the gloom and anxiety that had been haunting me fell away. I had even given an eggs benedict Sunday brunch for twelve.

As my spirits lifted, so did my libido. I became a regular in New York on weekends, sometimes staying with my parents (who lived in suburban Mount Vernon), sometimes with "Harry," a boyhood friend I had re-met in a bar. Harry had been drummed out of the State Department earlier in the fifties, losing a promising career to charges of "moral turpitude."

He would never discuss the particulars, but Harry was in fact one of hundreds, perhaps thousands, hounded out of government service throughout the decade. Columnists like Lee Mortimer of the New York *Daily Mirror* issued dire warnings that a homosexual epidemic was sweeping the nation, spawned by Communist agents determined to sap the national strength. Lesbians were said to be already in control of the WACs and WAVEs, and were organizing the high schools. Ten thousand homosexuals had purportedly honeycombed federal agencies, undetected by the FBI.[5]

Senator Joe McCarthy took up the theme of the "homosexual menace" to national security and made it an issue throughout the decade ("Hell hath no fury," went a common underground quip, "like a closeted gay"). It was widely agreed in the press and in government circles alike that homosexuals *by their nature* were unfit and unreliable public servants. As one Senate report put it, "Those who engage in overt acts of perversion lack the emotional stability of normal persons," and the "indulgence in acts of sex perversion [then further] weakens the moral fiber of the individual"—thereby causing him to be more interested in seducing fellow employees than in performing his job, and making him easy prey to the blackmail and blandishments of foreign agents.[6]

Having been branded a "sex pervert," Harry devoted himself to claiming all its sybaritic benefits. Joining his family's prosperous business, he commanded a large salary and spent by far the greater portion of it on conspicuous consumption—notably on luring pretty blond boys to his side. I sometimes tagged along on Harry's search-and-destroy missions around the city, torn between gratitude for his largesse and resentment at his seemingly endless supply of gorgeous young men.

I was doing okay myself, but had to work harder at it. The Grapevine became my bar of choice. It was the liveliest gay spot in the city in the late fifties, patronized by lesbians as well as gay men, and a forerunner of the seventies discos, which thought themselves *sui generis*. Indeed one of my diary entries from April 1958 reads like a press release from the disco-queen delirium of twenty years later: ". . . absorbed and yet released in a concatenation of emotions, bathed and abetted by the heat and excitement, the stimulation of the liquor and the music." We would, like those who came later, dance till dawn, pour comatose out into the streets, suffer gargantuan next-day remorse (which in the seventies purportedly gave way to mere exhaustion).

I had several mini-affairs and an occasional one-night stand. My romanticism would infallibly elevate the former into eternal matehood, and my guilt would discredit the latter as "wild indulgence." Between yearning to connect and the conviction that no homosexual could, I had trouble enjoying any experience for what it actually was. But then I met "Billy," and it seemed for a while as if all had come right.

We met in Cherry Grove, the gay watering hole on Fire Island. With Harry and his blond bombshell of the week, I had rented a cottage for the Memorial Day weekend in May 1958. It wasn't my first trip. Ray and I had ventured out there a few times before, astounded at the brazenness of the place and keeping a gingerly distance from the open-air orgies at the meat rack. (The straight couple in whose house we had rented an overnight room exempted us from the goings-on with a warning to beware the "fairies" prowling the boardwalks at night.)

There was no electricity in Cherry Grove thirty years ago, and the gas lamps cast a romantic glow, even as they kept the boardwalks desirably dark so that quick sex or smooching in the entryway to a house was possible. But the darkness also meant danger. Toughs from Saville would come over on the ferry for an evening's sport at Cherry Grove. That meant either staring bug-eyed at the queers or assaulting them—preferably on the boardwalk at night after luring someone to an isolated corner with a horny wink or gesture. When Saville teenagers weren't threatening the vacationers, plainclothes police were; the prototypically burly men lumbering along the boardwalk in their simulated casual clothes might have amused the natives more if they hadn't known that any sign of open affection toward a friend or lover could land them in jail.

Though Cherry Grove had been known since the twenties as a gay resort, dancing in the hotel pavilion at night was a far more sedate affair in the fifties than the happily unbridled scene of later years. Nor was it any less restrained in Fire Island Pines, a second, "upscale" gay community that developed during the early sixties. There, same-gender dancing was forbidden, and an employee was stationed on top of a ladder with a flashlight to enforce the rules. As a dodge, we would sometimes commandeer a lesbian friend or a female bystander from one of the yachts tied up in the basin for an evening's ogling; if two men were dancing with a woman, all three were then allowed to touch—intimations of group sex, unlike same-gender sex, concerned the authorities not at all.

These were the years when the cult of the body had not yet been hallowed. The parade up and down the Fire Island beach was no less relentless than now, but thirty years ago the sight of a perfectly muscled form was still an event, able to elicit murmurous beach-blanket sighs rather than the bored stares or impolite putdowns ("If only his weenie were as big as his pecs") that became standard in later years.

I kept my own parading to a minimum. Looking at pictures of myself then, I can now see that I had a strong, well-proportioned physique, but I had never consistently believed it. As a teenager I had used an ankle-length terrycloth robe for concealment when at a swimming pool, stripping down for a quick dash into the water only when no one was looking. Even with my lover Larry, I had had trouble letting myself be fully seen. Always body shy, embarrassed by display—symptomatic, doubtless, of my stuttering discomfort with all things gay—I felt far more comfortable talking to someone in a bar than trading body signals on a beach.

The routine—all the routines—of Fire Island were familiar to me by the time of that 1958 Memorial Day, and I told myself not to expect more than a pleasant few days in the sun. But by Friday evening I was already feeling disgruntled. The crowd seemed too flamboyant that weekend for my inhibited tastes, and I told Harry I would probably go back to New York in time for Saturday night barhopping.

Before turning in late Friday I decided to take one last look in Duffys, the Cherry Grove bar. Billy was there, having just gotten off the ferry a few hours before. The physical attraction was immediate and mutual, and that night we took a blanket out on the beach and had sex. That, I thought, was that. We said we'd look for each other on the beach the next day, but I felt no particular urgency. On Saturday I avoided the back-and-forth parade until late in the afternoon, when I finally wandered over to Billy's blanket. Desultory chitchat soon became charged, and I decided to cancel my plans to leave for the city. By Sunday I felt possessed, wildly attracted, committed for life. Billy maintained more of a distance, yet agreed to plans for the following weekend in New York.

Dr. Igen tried to calm me down. He said the intensity of my reaction, and especially my fear that Billy wouldn't reciprocate my feelings, suggested an archetypal drama only incidentally related to Billy himself. With prodding, I supplied the archetype: my father. A sweet but distant man, he had met my attempts at closeness, as a child, with vague indifference. I would produce that same unhappy outcome with Billy, Igen warned, unless I worked hard to understand and control my impulse to bind him to my side. But this was no time for caution, I protested. Having finally met someone I felt I could care for, didn't it make sense to let my feelings be known and to pursue them? Hadn't I in general been too cautious with my life, working my way methodically through the academic traces, dutifully churning out the required doctoral thesis, quietly following the rules for institutional success?

Perhaps, Igen replied. But I had the cart before the horse. The cure for feelings of professional sterility was not a half-baked leap into emotional turmoil. My current concentration should be on my therapy; until I resolved my conflicts, I could not hope to improve either my professional or my personal life. There was real merit to Igen's argument, as my stormy relationship with Billy would prove. But Igen never saw (or acknowledged) that some fair portion of my conflicts arose from therapeutic assumptions themselves about the pathology of homosexuality, and that it was the cautious climate of the day, rather than the needs of an individual patient, that dictated his automatic suspicion of risk-taking of any kind.

I didn't see any of that either, of course, and in my diary dutifully parroted Igen's wary views: "To make any radical changes in my life without first securing my emotions, would in all likelihood be only exchanging one set of discontents for another." Yet I refused to bow entirely to prudent advice (a rebellious underside would always prove my saving grace). To counteract my feelings of discontent with the world of scholarship, I "daringly" decided not to spend all of my free time converting my doctoral dissertation on Charles Francis Adams into a full-scale biography and to use some of it to explore my long-standing impulse to write a play. In my late teens I had toured with an acting company, and although, at parental urging, I had given up the idea of making the theater my career, its appeal had remained.

I also decided, despite the odds, to pursue the affair with Billy. He was a sweet man. It seems right to fall in love with goodness, so long as one remembers (not easy for those of us socialized to be men) that goodness is not an aphrodisiac, and can desist from blaming the relationship or oneself when comfort displaces passion. That was even harder to manage in the fifties, for the emphasis then was on the inseparability of love and sex, on their happy and perpetual union. After the first few months of absorbing ecstasy, Billy and I lapsed into a reciprocal affection that made me feel peacefully connected—but not particularly turned on.

We both viewed the decline in erotic excitement as a negative judgment on our prospective compatibility and for the next six months tried to figure out whether we could salvage domesticity by sacrificing monogamy. Agreeing that complete fidelity was impossible anyway, since males (we had been taught) were promiscuous "by nature," we tried giving each other a loose rein except when together on weekends. It didn't work. Even though neither of us in fact roamed very far, I couldn't shake the notion that a roving eye signaled cosmic disabilities. Ten months after we'd met, Billy and I threw in the towel.

By winter, I had a second ulcer. Dr. Igen used it to sound his old themes with new urgency. After nearly a year and a half of therapy, he said, it was time for me to take hold. The failure of the affair with Billy should have conclusively demonstrated to me, Igen said, the futility of investing my hopes for sustained intimacy in a homosexual relationship. It was time to look elsewhere, time to close the "escape hatch," confront my underlying anxiety, move toward a heterosexual adjustment.

My assent was less automatic this time around, a rudimentary resistance apparent in the tone I took when pondering Igen's near-ultimatum in an April 1959 diary entry:

> I haven't as yet really resolved in my mind whether I want to make the "grand effort" or, instead, give up the analysis. No small part of my discontent has sprung from the tension which analysis itself has set up. For six years now I've been made ever more aware of the difference between the way I act and the way I *should* act. I've never attempted what possibly could be a satisfactory homosexual adjustment because I've never been sure that I had to settle for that. If I once decided that I was unwilling—perhaps unable—to give up my drives and go through the prolonged agony necessary for a "conversion," then I would be forced to accept my present condition and make the best of it. Once the frame was definitely established, I could work within it toward a reasonable adjustment.

I was still using words like "settle" and "condition," and I quickly went on in the diary to disavow my own rebellious thoughts:

> On the other hand, I recoil from the finality which all this implies. I'm too aware of the inadequacies of homosexual life, of the limited relationships and the emotional constriction, to willingly consign myself to it. And if there are serious difficulties now, how much more intensified will they be in ten years, when my physical attractiveness has faded. Perhaps the situation is literally insoluble.

If the end result was familiar capitulation, I had at least flirted with the notion that society—and its creature, psychotherapy— was as much or more responsible for my unhappiness as any inborn disability. I was picking up, almost imperceptively, some new breezes just beginning to stir the claustrophobic cultural air.

For by then, the late fifties, a *bit* more tolerance for nonconformity had accompanied the gradual easing of international Cold War tensions. To Evelyn Hooker's now-mounting number of articles portraying a contented segment of the homosexual population never previously visible to orthodox psychiatry, were added the psychoanalyst Thomas Szasz's first essays. Szasz charged that classifying homosexuality as pathology was paradigmatic of psychiatry's long-standing error of equating "differentness" with "disease."[7]

In late November 1958, radio station KPFA-FM in Berkeley, California, sponsored a two-part program called "The Homosexual in Our Society" (alas, I didn't hear the show at the time; I only learned of it some twenty years later, when I came across the transcript while doing research at the Kinsey Institute). During the broadcast, the psychiatrist Blanche Baker denied that homosexuality was "a neurotic problem," insisting instead that it was "more a basic personality pattern reaction, just as some people prefer blondes and others prefer brunettes. . . Now, that doesn't mean that homosexuals may not become neurotic. I think that they often do, because society is so hostile to them. . . . They are subject to a great many pressures and a great deal of unhappiness." Baker further declared, and several of the other panelists agreed with her, that "homosexuality is one of the heritages from our mammalian ancestry. . . . We are dealing with something that is pretty basically part of our human heritage and that we have been trying to stamp out. My emphasis is: let us accept it and develop the wonderful things associated with it. Because so many homosexuals are very versatile, gifted people, and I feel that society should make them proud members, and that giving encouragement brings out much in the way of hidden resources."[8]

Public discussion of homosexuality was rare in those years, and supportive, nonjudgmental discussion almost unheard of. The representative voice in psychiatry in the fifties was Edmund Bergler, not Blanche Baker. Bergler was as extreme in his denunciatory rhetoric as he was sanguine in his predictions of cure. Claiming to have analyzed dozens of homosexuals, he found them *all* supercilious, megalomaniacal, and wholly unreliable as human beings; yet he also claimed a 99 percent cure rate as a result of having resolved preoedipal oral fixations.[9]

(Wardell Pomeroy, Kinsey's co-author, hoping to put an end to such false claims, once challenged psychotherapists to produce a single patient whose actual sexual orientation—as opposed to external behavior—had changed; no one accepted the challenge.)

In describing his homosexual patients, Bergler adopted an abusive, scornful tone that bordered on professional incompetence, characterizing the "great percentage" of them as, among other things, "swindlers, pseudologues, forgers, lawbreakers of all sorts, drug purveyors, gamblers, pimps, spies, brothel-owners, etc." Yet Bergler's fellow therapists frequently quoted from his work, covered him with honors—and never once rebuked him for the transparent, disabling anger he freely vented against those who had entrusted themselves to his care.

Alas, I can't exempt myself from that company. Though it deeply embarrasses me to admit it, I once wrote Bergler (I think it was after reading his 1956 best-seller *Homosexuality: Disease or Way of Life?*) asking for his help—a measure, I suppose, of my desperation. Bergler wrote back to say he would consider taking me on as a patient when and if I moved to the New York area. By the time I did, fortunately, I had accepted other (not necessarily more trustworthy) guides.

Police departments, no less than psychiatry, remained immune in the fifties to the humane views of the maverick Blanche Baker. Indeed, there was a surge in police raids on gay bars, and an ever-present danger developed of being entrapped by plainclothes detectives on the street. In New York, under the prodding of the virulently homophobic *Daily Mirror* columnist Lee Mortimer, a citywide series of roundups in the late fifties kept us in a state of constant jitters. We went to the bars anyway—courage in those years took unfamiliar forms—but when we did, my friends and I always carried with us the name of one of the three lawyers who specialized (to their own great profit) in getting arrested homosexuals out of jail; they knew whom to pay off and how much to pay them.

Much of the credit for whatever new attitudes were being forged in those years belonged to the Mattachine Society, a tiny male homosexual emancipation movement founded in 1951 in Los Angeles, which then spread to several other cities. Mattachine insisted that homosexuals, far from having anything to apologize for or regret, represented a unique subculture with much of value to contribute to the human family as a whole. Initially, Mattachine was doubly subversive: not only did it describe homosexuals as an oppressed minority "imprisoned within a dominant culture" and call for militant, collective action for its liberation, but it did so in the context of a sophisticated left-wing analysis of class exploitation.[10]

The socialist orientation of the original founders soon proved too much for most of Mattachine's members. Joining a fringe organization designed to improve life for a despised minority was courage enough for them; employing Marxist analysis seemed suicidal at a time when Senator McCarthy was at the height of his influence and the country awash in anti-Communist hysteria.

The ranks of Mattachine—never more than a few hundred—buckled and split. Leaders of the opposition declared that homosexuals were *not* different from heterosexuals in any ways that mattered, did *not* form a separate subculture, did *not* have any sympathy for left-wing politics. They rejected the notion of militant collective action as an appropriate means for improving the lot of homosexuals, instead insisting that a continuing reliance on the "experts" was the best hope for changing social attitudes. Mattachine's chief goal, the opposition said, should be full integration into American life (and full acceptance of its values), and its main energy should be devoted to "aiding established and recognized scientists, clinics, research organizations and institutions . . . studying sex variation problems."[11]

The left-wing founders of Mattachine argued that this amounted to an abandonment and betrayal of all that was special in the identity of the homosexual community, unconditional surrender to a conservative social creed, relinquishment of the future to those very social scientists and therapists who in the past had been instrumental in forging homosexual oppression. They argued in vain. By the mid-fifties, Mattachine had fallen into the hands of the cautious assimilationists, and the Daughters of Bilitis, the fledging lesbian organization begun in 1955, pursued its work in the same prudent spirit. Something of the movement's original militancy was kept alive in *ONE*, the Mattachine's magazine, henceforth run as an independent publication. But it would not be until the late sixties that an affirming, assertive spirit would again gain currency.

Locked away in my Ivy League tower, I heard nothing of this internecine warfare among a handful of people on another coast. Even if I had, it's doubtful I could have digested the news—I was too wedded to psychiatric dogma, too absorbed in my own tightly circumscribed routines, trying to get laid or trying to stay away from getting laid, ambivalently pushing ahead on a scholarly career I found only intermittently engrossing. Ironically, the one aspect of Charles Francis Adams's biography, on which I dutifully continued to work, that did capture my interest was his involvement in the antislavery movement. I strongly applauded his commitment to organized protest on behalf of the oppressed—yet never drew (at least not consciously) what later would seem the obvious analogy of the need to struggle on behalf of my own liberation. I did not yet know I was imprisoned.

Ray was beginning to get an inkling. He was living in Paris in 1959, completing a book on Balzac. Struck by how differently his gay friends in France regarded themselves, he wrote me an anguished letter:

> . . . suddenly all that psychologizing [Ray, too, had long been in therapy]—why homosexuality is a dead end, why one can't be happy or really creative in it, etc.—however *true* it probably all is, just seems to me like an intellectual defense that helps to make me feel superior & not really involved in the more *direct* disadvantages of living that way: rejections, disappointments, etc. Whatever pleasure and excitement & sometimes even better things that I get in living "that" way is more powerfully *felt* than all the depressing psychological distortions that I *know* are probably behind the whole thing. . . . Being around the French has helped me to that last conclusion. They're a terrifically *non*-psychoanalytic nation. . . . Their being gay seems not to be dominated by a constant sense of all they *can't* do because of that. In other words, I've come to wonder not so much about how neurosis cripples, as I've done until now, but rather about how, unless one is very far gone, there's still so much energy & possibility left

in the personality in *spite* of the neurosis. . . . The French guys I've met seem to me quite a bit healthier, & the reason is perhaps partly because they haven't been conditioned to brood about how they're sick. . . . I almost feel as if I've really never opened myself to living wholly as we are . . . taking some important chances emotionally, not always hiding behind a sense that this is really only a temporary aberration. . . . I really don't know if I'm going crazy or moving towards a more honest life. It's *terrible*, but one part of me feels that much of the therapeutic treatment of the last too many years has been one big ghastly lie. . . .

I wrote back in tentative support of Ray's revulsion against therapy and the self-paralysis it generated, but neither of us could sustain the protest. To do that, we would have had to challenge the assumption that homosexuality *was* a neurosis, and as yet we had gotten only to the point—which at that time we thought daring, possibly crazy—of wondering whether within those neurotic confines we couldn't hope to lead some truncated version of a decent life. Three weeks after his first letter, Ray was writing that he "already would like to qualify a good many of the things" he'd said, and we were again off and running—back to our therapists.

Late in September 1959, I finished my biography of Adams, and it was accepted for publication by Houghton Mifflin. That alone was reason to feel that I probably owed to therapy whatever good was happening in my life. What further convinced me was meeting a woman in whom I felt genuine interest.

"Nancy" was Canadian, was completing her doctorate at Yale in American literature, and was engaged to someone back in Toronto. We took to each other immediately. Sharing similar backgrounds—immigrant Jewish fathers who became financially successful; dynamic, native-born mothers who had never been encouraged to use their gifts and had turned querulous—we also had many of the same personality traits. We were ambitious, competitive, obsessive, complaining, and hard-working, and had articulate social charms that concealed far less tidy interiors. With temperaments matching right down to a shared penchant for self-dramatizing humor, Nancy and I were like brother-and-sister clones. Yet we never quite gave up the idea that we might become lovers.

For two years we danced around that possibility. In the back of my mind was Igen's voice, enthusiastically urging me on; in the back of Nancy's was her starchy fiancé's insistence on monogamy. Still, as she told me many years later, after she and her fiancé had long since married, she was "pretty sure" we would have become lovers if *I* had wanted to. I didn't, but I tried hard to coax the desire into being. We would have a few drinks of an evening in my apartment, turn on music and dance, kiss gently on the lips, and wait expectantly for my body to go into hormonal overdrive—which it never did.

My lack of interest deeply puzzled me. Without doubt Nancy and I were ideally suited, sharing values, open and warm in our affection, comfortable and trusting; we did love each other. It seemed downright unfair—a comment on the malign illogic of the universe—that such entire compatibility would not be blessed with a little usable lust. I tried not to think of friendship—knowing how rare it was—as a consolation prize for those who couldn't manage the main event. But focused as I was on my inadequacy as a lover, it was hard to feel grateful for my talent as a friend.

Dr. Igen kept the focus steady. He encouraged me to speculate about the source of my "unconscious resistance" to physical love with a woman. Though rarely theoretical, he made reference to a possible "breast complex" and asked me if I had reacted violently to being weaned. When I laughed and said I couldn't remember as far back as yesterday's movie, let alone my experiences in the crib, he replied, with a pained expression, that that too was part of the resistance.

Alarmed at how sulky he looked (would he tell me I was hopeless? would he give up on me?), I offered in quick substitution a lengthy speculation about how unlikely it was that a mother as devoted as mine would have weaned me prematurely and thus provoked my rage. His expression lightened a bit, and he took up the theme of my mother's devotion. "Yes," he said, "devotion embedded in control, devotion as a mask for seduction. Is it any wonder you have had difficulty ever since in entrusting yourself to a female? You're chronically angry at women and refuse to get it up for them. To enter a vagina is for you to risk being swallowed alive."

That brought us back to Nancy. I worried aloud about the morality—while working through my "resistance"—of "leading Nancy on." I recognized her own ambivalence about our sleeping together, but didn't that at least partly relate to the confusion she felt at my lack of desire? And wouldn't it be kinder and more honorable simply to tell her that I was sexually attracted to men, not women?

Igen would have none of it. He assured me that the real immorality would be to blurt out the truth about my homosexuality. "That would be a disservice to both of you," he would say. "After all, homosexuality may soon be a thing of the past with you, and to bring it up would be to sabotage any prospect for a different kind of future." Such optimism, as I turned thirty, seemed increasingly fanciful, but I wanted to believe him. After all, I had known other gay men who had married, who had functioned well enough sexually to have children, and who had seemed content. Their strategies for dealing with homosexual urges varied from secret trips to the baths to celibacy (extending, after a while, even to their wives). Why let the small matter of lust stand between one and the certified good life?

I eased my conscience about being dishonest with Nancy by periodically throwing out oblique hints. When, for reasons of her own, she turned a deaf ear to them, I occasionally became more explicit and once described in some detail a recent bar pickup in New York. Nancy treated the revelation as an isolated, even bold adventure, and we went on as before.

It wasn't until 1961, as she was preparing to go back to Canada, that I *insisted* she hear the full truth. Years later Nancy recalled in a letter to me how "*stunned*" she had been at the news: "I remember quite literally not sleeping for the next two nights, and being in a state of absolute internal tumult. It was all beyond my experience—and the more so because my emotions were engaged." She mulled over the possibility of staying on in New Haven, making me into something like a project, helping me to "break through" into heterosexuality. Doubtless Dr. Igen and his colleagues would have applauded her impulse; to this day the popular cure-all for homosexuality is (for gay men) "the love of a good woman" and (for lesbians) "a good fuck." But Nancy had sounder instincts and headed home to safer shores.

I missed her terribly. It was the summer of 1961, and I was at loose ends on all counts. My biography of Adams was completed and in press; the campus was deserted; and in August, Igen left for vacation. I did what I had to do: I started another book, a biography of James Russell Lowell, the poet-diplomat whose antislavery politics had long interested me. Yale had recently awarded me a Morse Fellowship, which meant no teaching responsibilities and full salary for the upcoming academic year.

I upgraded my car from third- to second-hand and headed out for a series of research trips. The largest collection of Lowell manuscripts was housed in Harvard's Houghton Library, and for most of the summer of 1961, I traveled back and forth between New Haven and Boston, abysmally lonely, burying my feelings in work, doing my best to keep to a routine as motorized as the road. When feelings surfaced anyway, I tried pouring them into poems—tormented, self-dramatizing, revealing something of the frantic paralysis I felt:

> I walk in a well-pressed suit
> and perfect collar
> yet hate the sun.
> It Christs out the truth
> and flays my suit
> till I scream.
> Not pain,
> but sensitivity to light

By fall, it felt harder and harder to force myself into the car and on the road. I was constantly tired, often on the verge of exhaustion, and my stomach churned with nausea. At first I thought I was getting another ulcer. But then I noticed my urine had turned dark and my stools light, and I decided it was time to consult a doctor. He put me straightaway into the New Haven hospital with a severe case of hepatitis—the worst, he said, that he had ever treated. "How in God's name," he wanted to know, "have you managed to stand upright, let alone drive back and forth to Boston and work all day in a library?" How indeed, I thought, when I couldn't even manage the lesser miracle of getting a hard-on with Nancy?

For a week or so, my liver tests failed to improve, and, as I later learned, there was some concern about whether I would pull through. In the upshot, I spent several months in the hospital and was finally released only on the promise that I would go to my sister Lucile's house outside of New York City and not set foot out of bed for another six weeks. Lucile had recently remarried and lived in a spacious house filled with the comings and goings of four exuberant teenagers. I was installed in an upstairs bedroom, coddled and confided in, made privy to all the dramas of everyday life I hadn't realized I'd been missing— and within two months was packed off back to New Haven, much restored in health *and* spirits.

But I was not entirely out of the woods. Painful sores appeared on my penis, so painful I nervously recalled biblical plagues and punishments. No, the doctor said, nothing so apocalyptic: "You have herpes simplex, a frequent aftermath of hepatitis. The sores will subside, but never disappear."

*"Never?!"*

"Once you contract the virus, you always have it in your system. But you can go for long periods of time without its being active."

In those pre-acyclovir years, no satisfactory treatment existed for herpes; one tried everything, including prayer. I began what would turn into a sixteen-month pilgrimage to dermatologists' offices in search of relief—after a while, in search just of hope. One dermatologist recommended constant "warm soaks," and for a month—until superseded by a later nostrum—I wandered the apartment with my penis submerged in a glass of warm water. I even got adept at talking on the phone, lips chattering away about my latest Lowell research find or departmental crisis, eyes fixed lugubriously on my flaccid, scab-flecked organ floating senselessly in its liquid bath.

It was now useless with a vengeance. Igen suggested that the affliction contained a message we needed to decode and an opportunity we needed to seize. The message, as we worked it out, had to do—surprise!—with my unconscious. Having despaired of my ability consciously to control my sexual acting-out with men, I had let my unconscious—in touch with my deep, continuing desire for a heterosexual adjustment—take over. Wondrously intricate in its workings, my unconscious had come up with a brilliant solution. It had created all at once an unarguable physical obstacle to sexual activity, a set of real physical symptoms on which I could focus some of my generalized anxiety, and an arresting symbolic visualization of my inner state—the sick penis as a representation of my underlying sense of worthlessness. It was now my job to carry this impressive subterranean achievement onto a conscious level, to accept and incorporate its insights as rational guides to behavior. If I succeeded in doing that, Igen triumphantly predicted, I would no longer have to hold on to the viral infection as a safeguard against future backsliding.

While I was still in the throes of this bewildering set of symptoms and injunctions, my biography of Charles Francis Adams was published to a fine set of notices, including the front page of *The New York Times Book Review*. Soon after came the announcement that the book had won the Bancroft Prize. And soon after that came an offer from Princeton for me to join its history department, with a raise in both pay and rank over what I had at Yale. The damage herpes had done to my ego seemed all but repaired. Igen expressed regret that I would leave therapy just when I was making "great strides" and, equating enforced celibacy with inner conversion, seemed "on the verge of a cure." But he agreed that the Princeton offer was too good to turn down. He wished me all the best and urged me to "stay in touch."

# 5

---

# PRINCETON

S̲O HERE I WAS at Princeton, fall of 1962, cock in a sling,
psyche on hold, students bright and stuffy, colleagues
pleasant and stuffier, career booming. I made the obvious
choice: to devote myself to what seemed most promising—my
work. I had courses to prepare, Ph.D. candidates to advise,
faculty meetings to attend, Lowell research to pursue. But just
to be sure no free time could emerge, I added several large,
new projects.

The careening events of the civil rights struggle—the lunch
counter sit-ins, the Freedom Rides, the emergence of the Student Non-Violent Coordinating Committee (SNCC), the voter
registration drives, the attempt by James Meredith to integrate
Ole Miss, the campaign to end segregation in Birmingham, the
murder of Medgar Evers—further ignited my interest in the
analagous antislavery crusade of the preceding century, an interest already well advanced by my work on Adams and Lowell.
Though I hardly knew it at the time, involvement with the black
struggle was serving as a channel (not a substitute) for working
my way into an awareness of my own oppression.

I decided to ask a number of leading scholars to write essays
for a volume designed to reevaluate the antislavery struggle. I
wanted to rescue it from earlier historical interpretations that

had been conservative and even racist in bias, had characterized the movement as unnecessary and its adherents as meddlesome fanatics. (The volume eventually appeared as *The Antislavery Vanguard* in 1965.) I also started work on a full-length play, *The Martyr*, based on the life of Elijah Lovejoy, the antislavery editor. To plug any remaining leisure minutes, I accepted nearly all of the many requests that began to come my way as a result of the Bancroft Prize—speaking engagements, reviews for the New York *Herald Tribune*'s *Book Week*, scholarly articles for a variety of journals.

I knew that I was being (as I wrote in my diary) "almost desperately compulsive" about staying busy. But lacking compassion for myself, I didn't locate the desperation in feelings of loss or deprivation (of sex, friends, even the consolations of an occasional drink—the doctors having banned all liquor because of my bout with hepatitis). Rather, using the self-punitive formula Dr. Igen had encouraged, I saw my work compulsion as a pretext for not dealing with the "basic anxieties" that stood in the way of a commitment to heterosexuality.

"Some part of me," I wrote in my diary, "as my defenses crumble, is making a desperate effort to build the walls—the last wall—back up. I almost feel as if I'm a third person watching the two parts of my own being engage in struggle—the one pushing toward [heterosexual] health, the other desperately nursing the defenses. I know which I wish to succeed, occasionally I even feel strong enough to feel confidence in success. More often, I feel almost disinterested, which probably means that I am a little afraid to hope too positively. The struggle has been so long, and I am still so desolate, that I can hardly believe in a happy resolution. Yet I can accept even less easily anything other than that."

This same year of 1962 saw the publication of a book that confirmed all my self-doubts—and the psychoanalytic assumptions that had prompted them. The book was Irving Bieber's *Homosexuality: A Psychoanalytic Study of Male Homosexuals*, a work that was instantly hailed within the psychiatric profession and was regularly cited (and sometimes is even today) as authoritative. Contrary to Freud, Bieber *began* with the assumption, which he took as unarguable, that homosexuality was pathological. He denied that constitutional factors made any contribution to a homosexual orientation, insisting that it developed in boys entirely as a result of a particular family configuration—close-binding mothers, distant or hostile fathers. The orientation, however, could be reversed. Bieber confidently predicted, as Bergler had before him, that most homosexuals with a strong motivation to change could do so with the help of a knowledgeable therapist. Unlike Bergler, Bieber's study carried an official imprimatur: the New York Society of Medical Psychoanalysts had sponsored it, and the data on which it was based, though limited to 106 homosexual patients, had come from some seventy-five different psychiatrists.

Bieber's views (along with those of Charles Socarides, whose most publicized work appeared a few years later) dominated psychiatry for a decade, and beyond. *Homosexuality* was referred to widely and approvingly and was generally taken as a vindication of the profession's insistence that homosexuality was an illness—a treatable illness. Such views were grist for my mill. My own parents seemed classically to fit Bieber's prescription. My mother had indeed dominated the family unit and had indeed minimized my father, a sweet man who sought safety in detachment. And certainly every therapist I had consulted since age fifteen had peddled the very same notions Bieber seemed now to have authenticated.

It would be years before the deep flaws in Beiber's study would become apparent—to me and to others. Subsequent work has suggested that hostile/detached fathers do not "cause" homosexual sons; rather, sons who appear to be different from the standardized model can cause their fathers to become hostile or detached. It is now also possible to see that patients in therapy tend to internalize the values of their therapist, to parrot back the formula response—for example, about having had a poor relationship with their father—which the therapist himself has inculcated, and indeed to accept the therapist's definition of what a good relationship is.

Bieber's methodology, moreover, was badly flawed. Although his book won a research award from the American Psychiatric Association in 1964, it failed to make needed comparisons between the "health" of homosexual and of heterosexual men. And it was based on a limited and badly skewed sample: 106 men who were clinical patients (26 of whom had been diagnosed as schizophrenic)—in other words, a sample that was pre-selected for pathology and that wholly neglected the nonpathological homosexual population previously studied by Evelyn Hooker. Looking for illness, Bieber had found it; wanting to hear the message of pathology, psychoanalysis had written it.[12]

Subsequent anthropological studies, moreover, have amply demonstrated that the large majority of nonindustrial cultures sanction or encourage homosexuality among males (much less has been learned about females) in some form and to some degree, and that the family patterns in those cultures vary widely, rarely approximating the "binding mother/absent father" pattern that Bieber had insisted upon as causal. Clearly he had not isolated anything remotely like a universal variable with which to explain homosexual behavior.

Indeed, Bieber may have parochially chosen to emphasize "malfunctions" in father/son relationships in the West as explanatory precisely because neither he nor other analysts could (or still can) face up to Freud's insistence that we all have a bisexual capacity. In order to reject such impulses within themselves, these therapists may have needed to attack such impulses ferociously in others. The attack, as Dr. Lawrence D. Mass has suggested, may have been sharpened in a predominantly Jewish psychoanalytic establishment by the then commonly shared (and false) view that the Nazi hierarchy had been riddled with homosexuals. Unable, in any case, to tolerate the suggestion that the yearning for physical intimacy with one's own gender might be natural, the psychiatric profession found great comfort in Bieber's insistence that such impulses were the *unnatural* result of a "faulty" child-rearing pattern—that is, a pattern that did not conform to normative cultural expectations.

Much the same sort of response can be seen in the way white America gratefully greeted the Moynihan Report of 1965, which characterized the female-dominated black family unit as "pathological"—that is to say, not sufficiently and dutifully imitative of the patriarchal, nuclear family model that middle-class white America had pronounced "normal." Conformist cultures cannot tolerate challenges to social norms without risking challenges to existing patterns of political and economic power. Thus Moynihan found it preferable to focus on the presumed failings of the black family rather than view its structure as a creative adaptation to a social system that has been unresponsive to black needs.

Similarly, American psychoanalysis in these years was doing its dutiful cultural work of identifying and stigmatizing sexual nonconformity of all kinds. It had long since put aside Freud's original mission of challenging mainstream values in favor of winning acceptance as their guardian. Had American psychoanalysis been the legitimate heir to Freud's questing spirit, instead of its perverter, it might have been engaged instead in trying to understand such matters as why heterosexual Americans are such limited lovers, and why American men in particular are so emotionally constricted; in identifying and ameliorating an American sexual ideology that encourages its citizens to distort and deny the pleasures of the body; in examining the child-rearing practices that manage to destroy the capacity of most children (especially boys) to enjoy intimacy with members of their own gender. Psychoanalysis could have redefined the "problem" as: how did homophobia become central to our sexual ideology—and how can the majority of parents be taught to stop relating to their children in such a way as to diminish their affectional and sexual expressiveness? But psychoanalysts were bent instead on winning their stripes as good Americans. And thus "Science," even as it once more touted its objectivity, once more merely subscribed to, and reinforced, popular prejudice.

*The New York Times* in 1963 also lent itself to popularizing the Bieber line on homosexuality. On December 17 of that year it published an unusually lengthy article with the banner headline GROWTH OF OVERT HOMOSEXUALITY IN CITY PROVOKES WIDE CONCERN. Expressing the general alarm that homosexuality had become more visible—a more "obtrusive part of the New York scene"—the *Times* canvassed current opinion on homosexuality and ended by giving Bieber's views far more space than any others. And at the close of the article it quoted Socarides to the effect that the drive to win social acceptance for homosexuals was mistaken because "The homosexual is ill, and anything that tends to hide that fact reduces his chances of seeking and obtaining treatment."[13]

I myself, of course, was not much further along in 1963 than the *Times*. Burying myself in Princeton and in my work, I tried to steel myself to a life of isolation, tried to make the best of the "bad hand" dealt me, consoling myself for the lack of a "legitimate" affective life with the notion that through scholarship and writing I would nonetheless manage to make some contribution to the general culture from which I was effectively barred—indeed, *determined* that I would. Yet, I often felt locked into "deep feelings of aridity and hopelessness," convinced of "the derangement of the person alone" (as I once wrote in my diary). Casual acquaintances sometimes confused my situation with enviable solitude. Their eyes would grow misty as they talked about my good fortune in being able to live a life apart, to devote myself wholly to my work without the cluttering commitments of family life. These were invariably acquaintances suffering from writer's block or a bad marriage, and I had to check the impulse to shout, "Moron!—if I didn't have to expend so much energy fighting loneliness, I'd be writing *twice* as much as now!"

I felt puzzled and put out that others could confuse productivity with happiness or could fail to see that my chatty social skills were a cover for melancholy—in short, that they wouldn't acknowledge my pain. For I *needed* that pain. It was a substitute companion, a badge of superiority to counteract the otherwise omnipresent feelings of being deficient. Similarly, I had to insist, even to myself, that I performed prodigies of work *only* because I had such a surfeit of pain to kill. A real surfeit of pain, of course, is disabling, not energizing. And besides, I often *enjoyed* research and writing. Were that not the case, it's unlikely they could have served so well as anodynes.

If my discontent was not as pervasive as I sometimes claimed, it was sometimes more than work could absorb. Though I had inundated myself with deadlines and drafts, the urge to wander off to the big city in search of comfort kept surfacing. On one of those trips, in celebration of herpes being in remission and in defiance of my therapeutic "goals," I actually went to bed with somebody—the first time I'd had sex in fifteen months. In my diary I grudgingly acknowledged that the experience "was not unsatisfying. . . . It was good to embrace and be embraced, to lie next to someone, even though he was a comparative stranger. . . ."

But I had been taught that impersonal sex, even with a partner of the "correct" gender, could not meet *any* legitimate need (how many needs it does meet, of course, continues to be debated). And so I summarized the encounter negatively: "The sadness comes from performing acts of intimacy without the feeling of intimacy—compounded by the faint but still stubborn hope that going through the act would somehow produce the feeling. When, inevitably, it fails to, the sense of loneliness becomes more acute than it ordinarily is, for now I am stripped even of the illusion that sex can bring me—lovingly, truly—to another person."

It was sound, of course, to distinguish between casual and intimate sex—but not to denounce an ice cream cone for failing to be a lobster dinner. In denying that casual sex could ever, in any mood, offer me pleasure, I was setting myself up for automatic disappointment with my own experience, ensuring that such encounters could only be followed by gnawing melancholy; and then, because I could not entirely give up the gratification that managed to survive my own negative descriptions of it, I was building in a circular future of self-recrimination and penitence. But I was not ready, in the early sixties, to make the needed distinctions (ultimately, I would make too many, insisting that paid encounters with hustlers were *preferable* to the demands of matehood).

For a while I thought the answer for me might be to chuck it all—Princeton, academia, personal achievement, the purported life of the mind. As the black struggle for equality heated up, as hundreds of demonstrators were arrested in the Deep South in the spring and summer of 1963, the idea took hold in me that I should express *directly* the deep identification and commitment I felt to the civil rights movement, should become a full-time activist rather than a part-time scrivener pleading movement issues in the press. The impulse was short-lived. I was too invested in institutional success. I couldn't imagine any psychological safety outside it.

Then a middle way unexpectedly presented itself. After the success of my Adams biography, a literary agent in New York asked to represent me. Flattered, I nonetheless felt called upon to remind the agent that the scholarly works I intended to write would be unlikely ever to earn her a commercial nickel. As we were debating the pros and cons of representation, a Broadway producer asked the agency if it could suggest a writer to do a documentary play about the American presidency (the recent success of *The Hollow Crown*, a stage work about the British monarchy, had inspired the idea). The agency pushed my candidacy as an "eminent" historian with "some" playwriting experience (I had indeed completed *The Martyr*, primitive and unproduced though it was).

All parties met, liked each other, and agreed to proceed. But then, within the week, I had an inspiration: we should do the evening not about the American presidency, but about American blacks—the story of being black "in white America." Another meeting was convened, and I made an impassioned plea for a shift in gears. Nobody bought it. The producer thought "the black theme" too controversial, the agent thought it too uncommercial. But the notion had taken such hold within me that I refused to abandon it. I told them to find somebody else to do the presidency script; I was going to give my own idea a try. I hadn't intended an ultimatum, but it worked to that effect. Taking adamancy for authority, the producer reluctantly acknowledged that my idea might have some merit—but offered neither an advance nor a contract to help me explore it further.

I hardly cared. I felt certain I had come up with a good idea, and more—with an instrument for advancing social justice *and* my own salvation. I worked as if possessed and within three months had a completed script. Reading it, the agent relented, but the producer continued to hem and haw. Frustrated at the delays, I took Ray up on his suggestion that we treat ourselves to a holiday in Greece. Euphoric at having thrown over the traces by writing a play, I was ready to break loose in other directions.

The two weeks in Greece proved a revelation. *All* Greek men, it seemed, were bisexual! That is, for a price. The particular moment of truth for me came in Athens, as I was sitting alone one day on a bench in the royal gardens. A Greek paratrooper in full regalia, and conforming to fantasy specifications in all other regards as well, walked by and grinned fixedly at me. Covered with confusion (could his look really mean *that?*), I managed only a weak smile in return. It was all that was necessary. In a flash he was seated next to me on the bench. He knew not a word of English and I not a word of Greek, yet in short order we managed to convey sexual interest in each other. Within minutes of meeting we were barreling along in a taxi headed I knew not where, but nervously telling myself that it might well be the morgue.

It proved to be a seedy hotel in a part of town decidedly not touristy. For someone who had waited fifteen months in New York before having sex, this was changing pace with a vengeance. After a heated discussion in Greek with the concierge, which ended only when he pressed some money into her hand, the paratrooper led me up the rickety stairs, as melodramatic scenarios (the least of which was simple robbery) pressed me in their thrilling grip. Nothing sinister ensued; we had the most affectionate puppy-dog kind of sex, mutual and tender, capped by sighs of satisfaction and signaled plans for a repeat performance soon.

But then, as we were leaving the room, he gestured to the wallet in my pants pocket. So this is it, I thought, this is how they do it. I prayed that despite my untimely death, plans to produce my play would somehow proceed. When I held open the wallet to him, he picked out a five-dollar bill—probably less than he'd paid for the room—kissed me again passionately on the mouth and led us out of the room.

I was breathless with excitement when I reported all this to Ray an hour later. Clearly, I said, the five dollars was merely a symbolic point of old-fashioned honor, clearly he was a dear man, clearly we were in love, clearly I should bring him home with me to the United States. It took several hours, three shots of ouzo (and an ensuing fit of violent vomiting) before I could be persuaded that on the last count at least, I was misguided: Greek paratroopers, even when not in full regalia, were unlikely to be well-received in the drawing rooms of Princeton. Ray unkindly hammered the point home with a pointed reference to Tennessee Williams's novel *The Roman Spring of Mrs. Stone*, in which a repressed American spinster recklessly throws herself at the feet of some callous, passing gigolo. Okay, okay, I said, I would return to New York without him. I would solemnly recommit myself to ART.

My art, as it turned out, needed me. All had not gone well with the play in my absence. The original producer had balked, and a wealthy backer to whom the agent had sent the script had pronounced the second act weak. So all was put on hold pending revisions, and I was urged to do them quickly while interest in a production still lingered. To get my juices flowing again, the agent put me together with a young director, Harold Stone, who had liked the play and was eager to work on it with me. We proved a good combination. Our chemistries meshed, and together we quickly hammered out the needed changes. Reading the new version, the agent whooped, "You've done it!" by-passed the original, foot-dragging producer, and sent it to Judy Marechal, an Off-Broadway manager who, though still in her twenties, already had several hits to her credit. Judy read the play overnight, instantly optioned it, and announced plans to open at the Sheridan Square Theater within two months—by late October 1963.

Six frantic, joyful weeks followed, my troubles on hold, my fantasy dreams of escape and redemption seemingly within reach. I dutifully met all my classes and campus obligations, knowing that my mandarin colleagues had cast a disparaging eye (not unmixed with envious anger) on this most peculiar, most unscholarly, "theatrical venture." But I spent every spare minute at the theater, thrilled to be rescued from isolation, thrilled to be part of the warmth and camaraderie of a collective enterprise.

And it was that. Some of my later experiences in the theater amply confirmed the clichés about swelled and childlike egos, but not this first one. It went from the beginning as the storybooks might have written it—a concord of cooperation and good will. Having an unknown cast helped; everyone looked to the production as the dreamed-for break—and indeed it did launch Gloria Foster and Moses Gunn on their careers. Only Michael Sullivan (a brilliant young actor who later died of an overdose) displayed even a semblance of temperament.

Flamboyantly gay, Sullivan had arrived at auditions—to read for a variety of dignified roles that included Thomas Jefferson—dressed in assorted shades of mauve and sporting very large rings on all the fingers of one hand. He gave a brilliant reading, but we didn't dare hire him, fearing *his* reality and that of the roles he would be asked to play could not possibly coincide. But when none of the other auditions compared with Michael's, we called his agent and suggested he read for us again—this time more "appropriately" garbed. Michael complied, gave us a compelling reading, got the part—and thereafter had to be constantly watched to prevent the Sage of Monticello from reappearing as a twentieth-century drag queen.

In between rehearsals and script conferences, we met until the wee hours trying to brainstorm the perfect title (*In White America* was a late, contested entry), and to conjure up names of possible angels to help complete the funding. Judy had budgeted the evening at $12,500 (which today wouldn't cover a week's advertising costs), and with her relentless energy had rapidly raised most of it; for the remainder, she had conned some of the nonunion technical staff into accepting promissory notes. But a few days before opening night, I arrived at Judy's basement apartment in the Village to find her tearing her hair. "I don't see how we can open," she moaned. "The carpentry shop has refused to deliver the set unless I can come up with six hundred dollars by morning." By morning she had it. Not about to see my bright new dream foreclosed, I got an emergency loan from my mother.

On opening night I paced the lobby just as an anxious playwright should, but broke from the traditional scenario in order furiously to hush a late-arriving patron who was chatting away volubly to his companion even though the curtain had gone up. The patron's indignant look of surprise puzzled me—until one of Judy's assistants, pale with alarm, whispered in my ear, "You have just shushed Henry Hewes." Hewes was then the influential critic for the *Saturday Review*, and I became inconsolable at the hubristic doom I had called down on my own head. Repairing to the bar next door, I drowned my despair in proverbial shots of scotch.

The notices dispelled all gloom. Henry Hewes never did review the show, and the *Daily News* also refused, telling Judy the play was "incendiary." But the rest of the press was almost unanimous with praise. The play settled in for a long run (ultimately more than five hundred performances), and offers soon came in for publishing and amateur rights, for touring companies and foreign productions. Yet the commercial rewards remained marginal. For the first few weeks, despite the fine reviews, audiences were light, and even after they gradually built up through word of mouth, we rarely sold out on weekdays and never exceeded the break-even point by much.

But I got much more from *In White America* than a few thousand dollars in royalties. Offers of all kinds came in. Book editors wanted me to sign contracts on any subject of my choice; radio and television shows called for interviews; half a dozen universities inquired if I could be moved from Princeton; Carey McWilliams, editor of the *Nation*, invited me to become a regular contributor; Channel 13, the New York PBS station, wanted me to serve as an occasional commentator on the "cultural scene"; the *New York Times* invited me to review books and in December 1963 published an article about me so filled with puffery that it seemed written to a press agent's specifications (". . . a good-looking, earthy, knowledgeable thirty-three-year-old scholar," etc.).

But beyond all that, I got the sense of an expansive new life opening up for me. And beyond even that, the sense that I was really in pretty good shape, not the badly damaged, disfigured human being my disapproved sexuality had implied. With so much applause coming my way, my way didn't look so bad. I decided that I deserved to live in New York, where I felt comfortable and accepted, and to commute to teaching. Knowing how insular the Princeton community was, how shocked it would be at someone *preferring* to live elsewhere, I offered to resign from the history department and accept a teaching position at a New York university. The department assured me that a commuting relationship was workable (it would later change its mind) and in proof of its eagerness to have me continue on staff, gave me a tenure promotion to associate professor and a year's leave at full pay beginning July 1964.

My cup indeed runneth over. I moved to New York that summer.

# 6

---

# NEW YORK

M Y APARTMENT WAS THE first floor of a brownstone on Thirteenth Street in Greenwich Village. It had a fireplace in the living room, a nook of a study, and a cozy little terrace overlooking the neighbor's garden. The rent was a steep (for those days) $250 and friends tsk-tsked about extravagance. But in my high-flying new mood, I decided to go for it, silently promising to do my laundry in the kitchen sink. Within weeks came the double news that Princeton had raised my salary to ten thousand dollars and that *In White America* had won the Vernon Rice/Drama Desk Award as the best Off-Broadway production of the year. I was on a roll.

My upstairs neighbor, the writer Muriel Spark, added further spice. She and I moved into the building within days of each other and, as New York novices and partly for each other's amusement, feigned helplessness, shared alarums, offered constant mutual reassurances. Even though she nodded off during the second act of *In White America*, I found her jaunty company, an amusingly fey woman far less tame than her kewpie doll good looks suggested. But it soon turned out that Muriel had a professional gift for swooning melodrama way beyond my amateur skills.

Convinced one day that the workman she had let into her

apartment to wash the windows was in fact intent on rape, she screamed for my help. I rushed upstairs, found the man had fled at her first shriek, and tried to calm her down. But she had instantly made up her mind to move and put in an emergency call to the *New Yorker* (*that*, I recognized, was real clout). Down came two staff members in a flash, somehow managing to stop on the way for a picnic hamper to give Muriel sustenance while they packed the dear, limp thing's bags; and off went Muriel to take up residence in the midtown Beaux Arts Hotel. Next day she gleefully described it to me as "a high-class whorehouse," and I had no idea whether to chalk that up to fantasy, too.

Madcap exaggeration somehow seemed just the ticket, just the right antidote to years spent in the cramped quarters of academe. Having now gotten the taste, I wanted more amplitude still, but I was too career-oriented not to complete my books on the antislavery movement and on Lowell. I knew I couldn't let go of productivity without letting go of self-esteem. But now I decided to make time to work on some new plays as well.

In one of my more euphoric moments I made the mistake of telling an academic friend that I would rather be a fourth-rate playwright than a first-rate historian. He wrote me an alarmed letter saying the remark had impressed him "as evidence of fatigue." He suggested I take a rest for the long run and button my lip for the short. Wanting to write plays, I wrote back, was not a character defect; it felt like an authentic interest and I intended to pursue it—without abandoning the profession of history, since I saw no reason to make a choice between the two. Secretly, of course, I was hoping a choice would soon be forced upon me, as Hollywood begged me to take up residence.

While one friend was deploring my neglect of history, another and better friend, Nancy, was expressing concern over my neglect of therapy. "It seems," she wrote me from Toronto, "that you are giving up, opting out, burying everything beneath the surface. It seems to make the last seven years so meaningless if you give up now. Is the excitement and stimulation of New York and the theater world the same sort of 'escape' that you used to say burying yourself in your books was? It's wonderful that you are feeling so much happier now, it truly is; but what will happen in five, ten, fifteen years' time? Are you really opting out of the possibility of a wife and kids for then?"

Nancy, a trusted, well-intentioned friend, who I knew genuinely cared about my happiness, nonetheless was delivering
the same message as the culture. And it was a message, in the
wake of Bieber's 1962 book, that continued to be regularly
sounded everywhere. The 1957 Wolfenden Report in England
had recommended the elimination of criminal penalties for
homosexual acts between consenting adults, but when the report was published in the United States in 1963, Karl Menninger, the famed head of the clinic that bore his name, wrote an
introduction that applauded decriminalization but sternly
warned that "there is no question in the minds of psychiatrists
regarding the abnormality of such behavior." The following
year, the New York Academy of Medicine went further. Echoing
Bieber, it insisted that homosexuality was a disease and, going
beyond Bieber, warned that the disease was spreading, threatening the general welfare.[14]

According to a March 1963 article in *Harper's*, there were
fewer than two dozen gay bars in all of New York City—as
compared with many times that number today. Yet the police,
as if taking to heart the New York Academy of Medicine's warning, now clamped down. Even the previously sacrosanct Exotic
Ball & Carnival proved fair game. That yearly transvestite event
went back to the late nineteenth century, and at various times,
Vanderbilts, Astors, and *tout le monde* had eagerly attended the
festivities. I myself recall being taken by my friend Harry in the
late fifties to a spectacular transvestite ball at a Manhattan ar-
mory, where the police had themselves cordoned off the en-
tranceway to ensure orderly access for the begowned guests and
their tuxedoed escorts as they stepped from limousines into the
klieg lights. Now, in the early sixties, the police turned from
protectors to raiders. Forty-four men were arrested at the Exotic
Ball & Carnival for "masquerading as women."

But I was too content for the moment to heed the gloomy
portents, though they seemed everywhere. Part of that contentment came from getting more connected to public issues.
My involvement throughout the sixties would remain occasional
and even marginal, but getting off the dime of self to any degree
helped me see how small that dime was—even though for many
of us, the preoccupying vanity of the self was not so much
usurped by politics as differently refracted through it. Like many

others in the sixties, too, I got to find out more about myself from involvement in political work than I did through formal, obsessive analysis of who I was. I also got to like myself better. The analytic view of me, of all homosexuals, as "truncated" human beings felt stale and mistaken when measured against the competence I displayed in and the respect I earned from my work in the movement.

Even while still living in Princeton, I had shared *In White America* royalties with SNCC and had served as informal faculty advisor to the Students for a Democratic Society (SDS) chapter which had begun to emerge on campus (at national rallies, its banner EVEN PRINCETON raised cheers). After I moved to New York, my political commitment increased, but I remained a writer-supporter of the movement, far removed from frontline activism. I published a variety of reviews and articles on New Left books, topics and leaders and, as a spin-off of those writerly functions, served on an occasional panel, sat in on assorted organizational meetings, and signed the regular flow of protest petitions that crossed my desk.

My major writing effort was a series of newspaper articles on "Black Power and the American Radical Tradition," in which I argued that the new direction within SNCC was "based on the truism that minorities must argue from positions of strength rather than weakness, that the majority is far more likely to make concessions to power than to justice." To insist otherwise, I wrote, "to insist that Negro-Americans seek their goals as individuals and solely by appeals to conscience and 'love,' when white Americans have always relied on group association and organized power to achieve theirs, would be yet one more form of discrimination."

Twice I emceed television programs for PBS, celebrating the lives of Old Left heroes. Norman Thomas and A. Phillip Randolph. Both men, courtly in manner but militant in voice, amply lived up to their long-standing billing as *gentlemen* of the left. When Thomas and I were taking leaks in side-by-side urinals during a break in the taping and I complimented him on his energy—he was then in his eighties—he leaned sadly toward me and said, "No, no, you have it all wrong. I only feel animated when I speak in public—it gets the adrenalin going. That's why I agree to do these shows."

When PBS next asked me to take part in a television "dialogue" with New Left guru Paul Goodman, the results were a good deal more strained. Dialogue, it turned out, was not Goodman's forte—or perhaps he simply didn't want to have one with me. Throughout the live, hour long show he blew smoke in my face, embarked on opaque, self-generating monologues, and, when I did get up the courage to offer an opinion of my own, quickly squelched me, at one point saying, "Surely as a historian, Mr. Duberman, you ought to know *that!*" I had arrived at the studio an admirer of Goodman's. I left it feeling humiliated and repelled.

That residual anger undoubtedly contributed to the negative review I wrote in the *New York Times* a few years later of Goodman's excerpted diary, *Five Years*. But what contributed still more was my homophobia. Goodman's diary put explicitly into print a sexual interest in men that he had never taken much trouble to conceal. It was only later, when I came to write the history of the experimental community Black Mountain, that I learned more about Goodman's historic openness; back in 1950 he had been denied a regular faculty appointment there not so much because of his bisexuality but because he refused to be reticent or evasive about it.

There was much to dislike about *Five Years* that had nothing to do with its sexual revelations—its pontifications, its aura of moral superiority, its theoretical self-importance. But what was telling about my own response to the book was the insistent way I focused on its sexual aspects and, like some sanctimonious schoolmarm, pronounced them distasteful. I had recently shown a similar strain of fastidiousness when reviewing Sammy Davis, Jr.'s *Yes I Can* for the *Times*, offering up his book (for which I had considerable praise) as a prime example of what I called the contemporary confusion of confession with autobiography. There is a common assumption, I wrote, "that if we divulge our behavior in certain 'taboo' areas such as sex, we have thereby revealed the whole of ourselves—as if our identity consisted of the sum of our socially disapproved acts." What I was up to here, I now think, was to deny all at once that *my* sexuality was central to my identity and, more generally, to express disapproval of any public revelation of sexual secrets.

When reviewing *Five Years*, I specifically accused Goodman

of "glamorizing" his homosexuality, of being overly indulgent of his "frailties," and of falsely claiming that his homosexuality was intrinsically connected to his general stance as a rebel, experimenter, and nonconformist—a connection, in Goodman and in others, that now seems stupefyingly obvious. And I closed the review with a peroration that was not without insight into Goodman's temperament but which told far more about my own at the time:

> By insisting that we accompany him on his round of the docks, on his endless pursuit of erections and orgasms, he has forced his private life on public attention. There is immense grandiosity in this—it is assumed we *must* be interested in all that relates to him—and also, finally, immense sadness— the kind we feel when an unloved child jumps through every hoop, employs every device of shock, to hold attention and to affirm its own existence.

Not surprisingly, I got a number of letters congratulating me on my "brave" review—when in fact it had been a form of self-sabotage, a public condemnation of who I myself (and Goodman) was. One well-known literary critic who had recently "taken me up" (apparently not knowing that I, too, was of the "unhappy persuasion") sent me particularly fulsome praise for having exposed "a would-be Socrates who falls into the trap of narcissism." I read that now and cringe. I had given the homophobes fuel for another auto-da-fé. It's perhaps ironic—and may yet bring fitting retribution down on my head—that here I am, twenty-five years later, writing a comparably explicit, personal book and doing so in the absolute conviction, which I could never have entertained back then, that we all *must* tell our secrets, must come out of our "shameful" closets if a more humane, genuinely diverse culture is ever to emerge. Saying that now is not meant merely as belated exculpation for the way I once reviewed Goodman's revelations.

Goodman was not entirely alone in the mid-sixties in describing homosexuality unapologetically. A small group of perhaps two dozen outspoken homosexuals had formed the Washington, D.C., branch of the Mattachine Society and was sounding a note of self-affirmation akin to Goodman's own. This group I did not condemn—I simply didn't know it existed, my own involvement in gay politics still half a dozen years away.

Franklin Kameny was the guiding spirit of Washington Mattachine. A Harvard graduate who had taught at Georgetown, he had been fired from his job with the U.S. Army map service after a government undercover investigation found he had once been arrested for "lewd conduct" (then a standard charge used against anyone caught in a police raid on a gay bar). Kameny went to court to fight his dismissal, but to no avail. Refusing to give up, he helped found Washington Mattachine, bringing to it a militant spirit that sharply contrasted with the cautious, hat-in-hand accommodationist attitude characteristic of most of the fledgling homophile movement. Kameny described homosexuality as "right, good and desirable," argued for a homophile movement based on the direct action strategy of the black civil rights struggle, and through Washington Mattachine, won a landmark ruling from the U.S. Court of Appeals in 1965 that enjoined the federal government from dismissing employees on vague charges of "immorality" or "incompetence."[15]

I was in Washington during that year doing some final research for my Lowell book, but heard nothing of Mattachine and its liberating efforts. The fault was not entirely mine: the Washington press carried only limited coverage of the landmark court case and the *New York Times* carried nothing. All I recall of my stay in Washington that spring was that I took a room at the inexpensive "gay" YMCA, but made a careful point of not lingering long in its notorious corridors and bathrooms. I also remember a disspiriting visit one evening to a gay club, where I discovered that patrons, denied the right to congregate at the bar itself, had to sit at separate tables, with contact confined to furtive glances and an occasional note.

Washington Mattachine's militant spirit was surfacing in a few other places as well. San Francisco, like every other urban center that could boast a public gay/lesbian presence (and not every city could), continued in the mid-sixties to be plagued by police raids and scandal-mongering press assaults. But those same years saw the convergence of a gay subculture with the beat scene in nearby North Beach, and together these nonconforming, outcast groups were shaping a distinctive, unapologetic consciousness that would, by the seventies, prove a beacon for gays around the country.

Militancy also characterized the activities of ECHO (East Coast Homophile Organizations), a coalition of four local organizations whose efforts at intergroup cooperation, though loose and occasional, helped to establish the skeleton of a regional network. In May 1965, ten brave men and women with ECHO affiliations actually dared to parade in front of the White House carrying signs that demanded civil rights for gay people—the very same day an antiwar demonstration sponsored by SDS drew twenty thousand to the Washington Monument.

One of the three women marching in front of the White House was Barbara Gittings, editor of the pioneering lesbian publication *The Ladder*. She had already served as president of the New York chapter of Daughters of Bilitis and, along with Kay Tobin and other outspoken women, worked during the mid-sixties to give DOB (which in 1965 had only about two dozen members) a more activist cast. The old guard conservatives in DOB managed to retain control over its organizational reins, but individual women like Gittings, instead of giving up, transferred their energies and allegiance to more militant groups like ECHO.

In New York City, too, a new spirit was flickering into life. In the early sixties Randy Wicker's one-man crusade to win more extensive and favorable coverage of gay life from the mainstream media had had some success, and by 1965 the new militants, spearheaded by Craig Rodwell and Dick Leitsch, had won contested control over New York Mattachine. In the wake of that victory, the membership rolls went up from about 100 in 1963 to about 450 two years later.[16]

The numbers were still tiny, but they did represent a defiant new attitude discernably different from what had preceded. Gone was the obsequious kowtowing to the "experts," and especially the medical experts, the decorous (and soul-destroying) begging for crumbs, the self-disfiguring deference to mainstream values. This new assertiveness, however, this new insistence on the value and viability of gay life and its entitlement to minority protections of all kinds, was confined to a limited segment of the gay and lesbian population. The vast majority of gay people continued to lead lives of secrecy and self-deprecation, the workings of a positive new spirit far distant from their consciousness.

I was among the majority, though perhaps in advance of many—not from any special enlightenment but from the simple fact of living in a large city. In New York it was possible at least to lead an active *underground* gay life, to have a terrain to explore, to enjoy the possibility of comfort from friendships with others similarly oriented, and maybe even to entertain the hope of finding a lover. Given the endemic denial and concealment of gay life in these years, to be able to find gay friends and sexual contacts was automatically to be in the fortunate vanguard.

A friend who had left New York to live in Los Angeles sent me his scornful comparison of gay life on the East Coast with the abundance he had found out west: "gay beaches, about 100 bars (really quite wild), 'health clubs'—if one must be, this seems the spot to be one. The whole situation is far more intense and open than in New York. All those NYC police horror stories apply here only to parks and johns. The bars they let be—and let flourish." But having lived in guilty celibacy in the confining small-town culture of Princeton, I was more than grateful for the manifold blessings of New York. And I began to explore some of the dimmer byways of big city life.

For someone who for years had uneasily pondered the pros and cons of a trip to a gay bar as if life itself hung in the balance, I now let myself, with surprising nonchalance, enter two Times Square hustler hangouts that most patrons of the gay bars would have shunned as seedy and dangerous. It would be several more years before I would go to hustler bars with any frequency, and it would take me a long time to feel even partially comfortable in them. Yet in several senses, my arrival at their door, rather than having been a surprise, may well have been over-determined.

Having lived tightly bound by society's conventions, it made a kind of irrational sense for me to rebound to an opposite point—to thumb my nose at all convention—as a device for loosening their hold on me. Besides, a hustler bar had far more drama and danger than the ordinary gay bar and, by exposing myself to both, I could all at once sate my new appetite for amplitude, act out my designated social label as disreputable and disordered ("Unfit for intimacy? Okay, let's go for fireworks instead"), *and*, contrarily, act out my designated family role as someone willfully entitled to have what he wants when he wants it ("Let's get that excitement *now*, and on my terms"). I could even guarantee, as I could not in a gay bar, that I would be a star attraction; my youthful good looks in startling contrast to the other patrons, the odds were high that I would be noticed and courted. For someone who liked controlling attention and writing the script, who lusted after straight-seeming, butch young men but hated wasting time wooing them, the cash-and-carry ethic of a hustler bar had a persuasive appeal.

All of this was far, far from my conscious mind when I made my first timid foray into the two Times Square bars called Kelly's and the Wagon Wheel. They were on the same block, nearly across the street from each other in the west Forties. Kelly's was indistinguishable from twenty other friendly Irish bars in the area, except for being better swept and lighted. Frank, the nervously agitated owner who presided over Kelly's, looked for all the world like a Mafia third-stringer out of Central Casting. Above all, Frank wanted *no trouble*, and his permanently furrowed brow was at least partly due to real concern for his customers—especially for the Johns. If he saw a regular customer talking to a hustler he either didn't know or didn't trust, he'd take the regular aside for a cautionary conversation.

Not that Frank's concern could guarantee risk-free sexual shopping. But danger centered more on harassment from the police than from the hustlers. I remember one incident when a member of a foreign delegation to the U.N. was arrested by a plainclothesman posing as a hustler. The U.N. delegate had casually chatted with the man at the bar, had decided that he was not interested in him sexually, had politely said good night, and had headed out the front door. The plainclothesman was off his stool in a flash, raced outside after the man, and placed the startled U.N. delegate under arrest on charges of "solicitation." Frank fumed over the "injustice of it all" for weeks.

The Wagon Wheel, on the other hand, seemed to court trouble. Only the front bar was considered hustler territory, and even there the mix was uncertain and volatile; the tough young hood sweet-talking an older man one minute might the next disappear with some stringy-haired blonde woman into the straight dancing area at the back of the bar and spoon away the night. If the unlucky older man experienced disappointment, he could console himself by remembering the beatings and robbery rumored to befall "lucky" patrons who succeeded in bringing one of the young toughs home.

My friend Harry accompanied me on my first trip to the Wagon Wheel and seemed, for all his worldly experience, nearly as timid about being there as I; we had gotten through the front door by calling each other's bluff. Determined to observe only—and from a safe distance—we sat in a booth facing the bar and tried to look nonchalant. Not that anyone initially tried to get our attention: we seemed too old to be selling and too young to be buying—an estimate we would have agreed to with relief.

But quick double scotches soon dissolved our circumspection. Harry became intrigued by an intricate gavotte in process at the bar, in which four or five aging men danced attention on, and elbowed each other for proximity to, a square-jawed young man built along the lines of a prototypical college football player (which is precisely what he turned out to be). The young man feigned indifference but avoided the sort of curt dismissal that might actually have frightened his admirers off.

After another scotch, Harry suggested I try my luck with the footballer: "I'll bet you could win him away easily from those old aunties." Now it was my turn to feign indifference—slightly compromised by indignation. I reminded Harry that I had never paid for sex and had no intention, at the tender age of thirty-five, of starting now; I found the whole scene "bizarre." Harry, knowing synthetic moralism when he heard it, glanced back toward the footballer: "Bizarre? Even his gorgeous buns, dear?"

Relieved laughter, another round of drinks, more egging on by Harry, some raucous speculation about how butch numbers were always the best fucks—and there I was, suddenly at the footballer's side. He looked up in surprise at my open approach, and maybe at my boyish looks, and his guard dropped. I said something about what a "wonderful looking guy" he was and how much I'd like to go home with him. "What's in it for me?" he asked, clearly interested. "Dunno," said I, having no idea of the going price range, and unsure if I wanted to pay it no matter what it was. He supplied the answer: "How about fifteen dollars?" "Sounds okay," I said, to my own astonishment. "Where can we go?" "I'm staying at a friend's—c'mon." As I followed him out of the bar to the audible growling of my rivals, Harry gave me the high sign. I looked stonily ahead.

When we got to his friend's apartment, my nervousness was palpable, but he did his best to put me at ease. He told me about his life growing up in Ohio, his football scholarship to the state university, his loss of the scholarship six months earlier because of an injury during scrimmage. I believed every word, made sympathetic noises about his bad luck in losing the scholarship, encouraging ones about the likelihood he could get it back again. New York had been good to him, he said, and he opened up his mouth to show me the full set of new teeth a "dentist client" had provided free of charge.

As I dutifully stared at the row of enamels, he affectionately put his hand on my leg. I jumped, involuntarily. By now I knew I couldn't go through with it. Ancient moralisms about the sin of prostitution had thoroughly clogged my gonadal secretions. "Whatsamatter?" he said, "dontcha like me?" He seemed genuinely hurt and offered to take his clothes off to prove that his body was just as good as it looked. I assured him that wasn't necessary, told him again what a "wonderful-looking guy" he was, and then confessed that I had never paid anyone for sex. He told me in a conspiratorial voice that he was worth it and that he needed the money. I explained that I couldn't handle the self-image of somebody who paid for sex and offered to give him the fifteen dollars anyway. To my surprise, he accepted it and we called it a night. He gave me his number should I ever feel "in the mood."

I never called him, and it was months before I ventured back into the Wagon Wheel. But when I did, after my nerves had steadied, I learned about yet another aspect of the scene. A curly-haired young Italian guy started talking to me with a casual friendliness that suggested he was not in the bar to hustle— at least not to hustle himself. It turned out he got his kicks in life, and part of his income, from fixing people up. He combined the tastes of a madame and an entrepreneur and, not incidentally, got the side pleasure of enticing some of the more reluctant studs into his own bed, free of charge, by promising to fix them up with prosperous older men.

"Clearly," he said, with a winsome grin, "you aren't an older man—at least not old enough to be prosperous enough. Unless you got some inherited money. Do you?" I explained my limited means, gave him an ingratiating Tom Sawyer account of my life as a struggling writer, and kept mum about my academic credentials. He excused himself for a few minutes and then reappeared with "Ned" in tow. He wanted me to meet Ned, he explained, because Ned, too, was a "struggling artist." Now that, I thought, really is charm. Ned, at first glance, was no more than eighteen, and since physical culture was not in the sixties an established art form, I couldn't imagine at which temple of the imagination this astonishing-looking young man burned his devotional candles. Whichever it was, I knew instantly that I would soon be hand-laying some of the bricks.

I can't remember when or under what particular circumstances Ned and I finally went to bed, but once it happened addiction became inevitable. He had, quite simply, the most perfectly proportioned body I had ever seen, and he used it with an uninhibited passion rare in someone so beautiful. As if that wasn't devastating enough, Ned proved about as smart as anyone I had ever met. Not smart as in book-learning, but in his ability to size people up instantly, to get to the emotional truth beneath the words. That's sometimes called "street smarts," but Ned's sassy tenderness raised it to—well yes, an art form.

When I met him, Ned had been hanging out in the Port Authority men's room turning five-dollar tricks; after we met, Ned went right on turning tricks, in bathrooms and out of them. Fond though we grew of each other, we never talked the language of love or entertained anything like the notion of a commitment. Even I, a born romantic, knew truly terrible odds when I saw them, and I was able to resist Ned's periodic urging that I let him move in with me. But we did see each other fairly often, and over time Ned began to confide in me.

A school dropout, he lived in New Jersey with a father who, as Ned would tell it (his eyes bright with admiration, and even lust), was still more sexual than he. It was to his father that Ned turned for advice (with occasional career counseling from me) when he started to get romanced by the Warhol crowd. He had stumbled into the Factory one night, stoned on drugs and desperate for more, steered there by somebody who realized that on all counts the match would be electrifying. A home movie was in process, and Ned was invited to remove his clothes and help himself to drugs. A release form was put in front of him to sign.

The next thing Ned heard several months later was that the home movie was being shown in a commercial theater on Bleecker Street. His father angrily threatened to kick him out of the house unless he stopped hanging around with such "no-goods" ("Imagine not even *paying* a kid for his time"). Ned shrugged agreement and forgot all about the Factory. Some six months after that, the phone rang one day in the Jersey house and it was Andy Warhol himself inviting Ned to come out West and make another movie. Ned's father hung tough: "Absolutely not—unless he gives you a return plane ticket in advance." Warhol sent the ticket, Ned went out West—and the resulting movie, widely reviewed in the mainstream press, brought him considerable attention.

He came over to my apartment to show off the reviews. They were neatly pasted in a scrapbook, my first clue to Ned's new seriousness. His instincts had always been good, and now his ambition, which he had never dared acknowledge before, came surging forward too. "This is it," he told me. "This is my big chance; and I know how to play it." Paul Morrissey, Warhol's right-hand, had, according to Ned, fallen madly in love with him, and Ned knew "just how to play him"—not to let Morrissey touch him. That way, Ned reasoned, Morrissey would star him in the next Warhol film and teach him the trade. And that, indeed, is precisely what happened. Ned's next two films were huge hits—in the mainstream as well as on Bleecker Street—and Ned was off and running. We lost touch almost immediately afterward, as Ned moved up to Mick and Bianca, and himself became a *Rolling Stone* item. He was soon established as a gay icon, and for years thereafter, when his name came up, I could count on making everyone instantly hate me by casually saying, "Oh yeah Ned—he and I used to make it together."

So Ned was gone, but the underground scene was still there. Surely, I reasoned—the paternal and predatory coinciding—it would turn up other bewitching diamonds in the rough needing my sympathetic ministrations. The next "Ned" did step quickly into view, but this time much deeper fantasies of eternal bonding were released, and with much more traumatic repercussions.

"Jim" was twenty-three when we first met, married with a baby, living and working as a carpenter in a small town in New Jersey. The electricity on both sides was instantaneous: mine, as always, impatiently obvious; his, muted and controlled. Jim fit all of my stereotypic fantasies: the working-class high-school football star, the volcanic good old boy, the buried and bereft American male desperate to have his distant dad hold him in his arms at night. Oh, I knew those men, partly because, beneath the middle-class academic veneer, I was one of them, American and bereft, and therefore if given the chance could cuddle us both, could give us both, at last, the good father. Still, the sum of the fantasies didn't account for the fullness of the attraction. I suppose nothing ever does; the French have an expression for it: "hooked atoms."

Jim was full of self-protective lies. Even, at first, down to his name. "Bill Steadman," he told me in the beginning, "on an athletic scholarship at Trenton State, though I'm in trouble with my coach." An emblematic statement if ever there was one, but for a long time we dealt with his "coach" as if he was a tangible rather than symbolic figure. One week the story was all about losing his scholarship through an injury (where had I heard that before? Did the Wagon Wheel, for a fee, hand out little brochures to the novice hustler—"Ten Fantasies Most Likely To Turn On Your Clients"?). That soon transmogrified into losing the scholarship because the coach was angry at his unreliability ("Yeah," Jim confessed with a boyish grin, sounding like "Brick" in the current *Cat on a Hot Tin Roof*, "I got this little drinking problem"). But then the problem—all the problems— was suddenly resolved, without explanation, and I would hear buoyant stories about rough-and-ready scrimmages, putting on weight at the training table, taking extra classes at night—until all would once more reverse, the coach wrathful, Jim unable to pay his bills (that was my cue), and with a sick baby at home no less.

None of this was as transparent as it appears in the retelling, or perhaps I refused to see it as such at the time. I was enchanted by this wounded, tender man, his poignant need to matter, to spin out tales of derring-do, his sweet smile, his unpredictability.

Jim's troubles changed focus but never lifted. When he tired of recounting tales of athletic heroism, he would shift to muted complaints about his worrisome physical symptoms (the suddenly felled warrior, carried on a stretcher from the hushed stadium, stoically fighting back pain). First it was his stomach. Plagued with severe cramping, he would wave away my concerned questions, dismiss my suggestion that he see a doctor. When the attacks got more frequent and I said I would foot the bill for a New York specialist, he finally agreed to go—and then didn't show up for his appointment.

Next it was a heart attack, induced, he reported, when he plugged some tool into the wrong electrical socket and went into cardiac spasm. Rebounding from that, he promptly sliced off part of a finger on a lathe; it then became gangrenous, and for a time his whole hand was threatened. His boss got fed up with the string of sick days and laid him off. At which point his baby got sick again, his car broke down, his well got polluted (his well? that homey rural detail struck a special cord in my hardened city heart), his wife started making noises about leaving.

Everyone lost patience—everyone but me. Passionately obsessed with this wild, tormented, beautiful young man who seemed to need me so desperately, I swallowed every tall tale, ran (with checkbook in hand) to rescue him from every threat of disaster. But even I had my limits, which were not just financial. When Jim said he wanted to leave his wife and move in with me, I balked. By now, a year into the relationship, I had finally let some facts register: Jim wasn't remotely capable of sustaining a consistent and mutual relationship with anybody (which is perhaps why I'd chosen him), would reappear when in need and disappear when not, sometimes making me feel lonelier for him when we were together than when we were apart.

I finally, slowly, distanced myself. But it took years to exorcise him. To help the healing along, I found myself in 1968 writing a play about him, about us, called *Payments*. Much of the play's details and events are invented, but the portrait of Jim is essentially as I saw him: the all-American macho man, lost in constricted reverie, on the outside a beautiful animal, but complex to a degree he didn't himself understand, being neither introspective nor articulate. He yearned for options he hadn't defined, seethed with resentments he couldn't clarify, longed for someone to "save" him but could envision neither the person nor the process.

The character in *Payments* based on myself is largely unattractive. I made "Paul" intelligent, superficially charming, and basically decent in his instincts, but what I most emphasized was his manipulative greediness. Though I still consider *Payments* among the best two or three plays I've written (when it was produced at New Dramatists in 1971, someone called it "an icepick in the heart of America"), it was in part an exercise in homophobia: nobody gay ends up well, all are lost to varying forms of self-destruction and self-pity.

In this, *Payments* was similar to Mart Crowley's *Boys in the Band*, which, that same year of 1968, I reviewed negatively in *Partisan Review*—*not* because I objected to Crowley's play as self-hating but, to the contrary, because I thought it romanticized the bravery and wit shown by the Boys in coping with "the unlucky hand" fate had dealt them, and would thereby "help to confirm homosexuals in the belief that theirs is merely a different not a lesser way."

To write that—and *publish* it!—amounted to nothing less than a ferocious attack on my own humanity, and I would later shamefacedly repudiate the review. Indeed, within a few years of writing it, after *Boys* had become the object of general assault in the gay community, I defended the play as truthful to its time—as an accurate reflection of the self-sabotage then endemic to gay life. I knew whereof I spoke (though I sometimes think I retrospectively exaggerate my unhappiness in the pre-Stonewall years—perhaps in order to exaggerate, to the same degree, the liberating aspects of post-Stonewall.)

But I've jumped ahead. The turmoil of my relationship with Jim succeeded in destroying my newfound contentment and in raising again the specter of a lifetime of repetitive miseries, as I sought comfort and connection, again and again, with people who were unable to provide it. Some of the old refrains came back into my head: homosexuality, by its very nature, meant a lifetime of wrong connections, the impossibility of nurturing commitment. From there it was only a step to thinking once more about conversions, cures—the whole nine yards of incantatory psychoanalytic rhetoric I had thought my ears permanently closed to.

And so, before I knew it, at age thirty-five in the year 1965, I was sitting once more in a therapist's office, asking yet again to be "fixed." This time—the last time—would prove far and away the most traumatic. It would involve five years of treatment that would take me to the brink not of reconstruction but of near-negation. It would so thoroughly undermine my ability to accept my own nature that—as the 1968 *Boys in the Band* review would demonstrate—I would become nearly as homophobic as the culture itself. Nor was my subsequent emergence foreordained.

# 7

# THERAPY

"K ARL," THE NEW THERAPIST, had come highly recommended. A diplomate of the American Board of Psychiatry, past president of the Association for Group Psychoanalysis, he was also the author of several articles and one book. He was a vivid, electric, physical presence—a short, wiry, energetic man in his late forties, exuding confidence and certitude, with piercing eyes and a trim Van Dyke beard that gave him a Mephistophelian look. His clipped speech was unaccented, but nonetheless sounded vaguely foreign—as did the way he would sometimes struggle for the apt word, impatient that absolute precision in expression should prevent him from proving the absolute correctness of his insight.

At our initial meeting, he asked me the traditional first question: What goals did I have for myself in therapy? I said that I was confused and unhappy at my inability to form a lasting relationship with another person, but that I distrusted my own perception of what was at stake. I did, after all, have several close friendships that had endured (and here I talked particularly about Ray, and somewhat about Nancy—recognizing that she might be a more clouded example), and I had gotten considerable sustenance from them. What more did I need? Besides, I said, I sometimes thought that my wish for a "mate" wasn't really intrinsic to my temperament. Essentially I was a self-absorbed loner, a hermit-scholar, and perhaps I had artificially adopted somebody else's—the society's—specifications for a good life. But beyond all that, I added, perhaps homosexuality was itself incompatible with lasting attachments. My own search, at any rate, had come up empty. Yet the notion of settling down with a woman struck me as fanciful. I found women *humanly* more attractive by far than men, and, yes, some were my best friends; but having never felt any sexual interest in them, at age thirty-five I doubted that I ever would. Surely a leopard could not change its spots.

Karl greeted all this with a benign smile and an aphorism. It was clear to him, Karl said, that I was "starving to death," that I craved reciprocal intimacy, and had the capacity for it, but had been looking in all the wrong places. I gulped at that, fighting back tears. I was salvageable? My capacity for intimacy was intact? There could yet be a happy ending? The tears flowed. Karl looked moved, passed me some Kleenex and spoke gently of his *certainty* that my "heterosexual yearnings could be unblocked" so long as I was willing to commit myself to that goal. Was I? Was I willing to be happy, or was I determined to hold on to my neurotic lifestyle, to wallow in suffering?

I told him that I frankly didn't know. I had made other attempts in the past when I was younger and more hopeful of change, but no matter how strenuous the effort, I had always returned, defeated, to homosexuality. He said his own experience with homosexual patients had been quite different; of the half dozen such men he had recently treated, all, without exception, had succeeded in making heterosexual adjustments. What were their ages? I wanted to know. All ages, Karl said, then animatedly added, "In fact I might put you in a therapy group with one of them, Dick—he's about five years older than you, and living happily with a wife and two daughters. Have you ever had group therapy?"

When I said no, his eyes brightened: "Ah well, then, perhaps that's one reason you haven't gotten better results." He told me he had been one of the clinicians who had pioneered group therapy in New York, and while he still insisted on seeing each of his patients once a week in private session, he strongly believed in the greater efficacy of the group process. "You see," he explained, "in a group of ten people, you can't control the climate to nearly the same degree you can in individual therapy. Too much comes at you from too many different directions. Your defenses can't stand up to the barrage."

"It sounds like warfare," I said nervously.

He laughed. "Let's say it's the war of health against disease, with health on the winning side."

"Would you put me in a group right away?"

"Immediately. You've already lost too much time in traditional therapy, you're too tuned in now to its strategies. Traditional therapy could no longer work for you—if it ever could. I have the feeling that from the beginning your skill with words defeated your therapists. You were able to talk your way out of everything, including hope."

I was impressed. Karl seemed quickly to have understood me; he offered a whole new kind of therapy, and he seemed all but prepared to guarantee results. But I still had one major question: would I again have to take the veil, give up sex? "Of course not!" Karl thundered. "I'm here to help you, not punish you. Rome wasn't built in a day, and while we're putting up the new building, you have to live *somewhere*. In time you yourself will want to give up your stale homosexual routines, but that time isn't now."

I smiled with relief and repressed excitement: "Sounds too good to be true—like having my cake and eating it."

"You've picked up a lot of bad ideas from your earlier therapists. Maybe it's because I wasn't born in this country, but I don't believe you have to mortify the flesh in order to win the kingdom of heaven. You're in a wholly different ballgame now."

That won me over. It would have been nearly impossible for me to work up any enthusiasm or confidence in "more of the same," but this sounded like an entirely new, and hopeful, beginning.

We agreed that I would start therapy right away—an individual hour once a week with him, plus two evenings a week in group sessions that lasted an hour and a half each. Before leaving, Karl gave me the ground rules for the group meetings: when I arrived I was to sit in one of the chairs set up in a semi-circle in the room adjoining his inner office; no conversation was allowed until he emerged from his office and formally began the session with a "good evening"; last names were never known, and all social contact on the outside was strictly forbidden.

That Wednesday evening I met with the group for the first time. There were nine of us, including Karl and me, and he introduced me simply as Marty—no last name, no background data, no description of my problems. It made me uneasy. Shorn of my credentials, I wasn't sure what else to trade on, how else to win respect. *That*, Karl told me in our individual session later in the week, was the whole point: I would now have to relate on other grounds entirely.

It was a desultory session. My strange presence understandably inhibited the flow, as silent judgments and adjustments began on all sides. Such interaction as there was focused on "Kate," a conservatively dressed, rather prim-looking woman in her late thirties who, I quickly gathered, had been brought up to believe sex was dirty and literally had to go on vacation to Italy before she could feel entitled to get laid (and even then, would infallibly wake up the next morning with her eyes puffed out in an allergic reaction). The other members of the group kidded Kate good-naturedly, and "Dick"—whom Karl had earlier identified as a successfully converted homosexual—tried teasing her with a few sexy words of Italian ("Mangia mi, baby, mangia mi").

Two of the group members sat entirely silent during the kidding. One was a painfully thin woman, well over six feet tall, named "Frances." She seemed a genuinely strange creature—I kept getting the image of a heron, aloof and still, alone on her rock in the mid-Atlantic. The other, a man of about thirty named "Stan," was an altogether more threatening presence. He scowled often, made patronizing, disdainful sucking noises, and, when he did talk, tended to lecture the others on their "immaturity" or "irresponsibility."

The two people I felt most drawn to were Dick, whose campy wit felt like a touch of home—even if he *had* entered the exalted ranks of the convertees—and the group's oldest member, "Helen," a warm, serene-looking woman of about fifty, to whom the others seemed to defer as something like Karl's unofficial co-leader. I felt mostly indifference toward the two remaining members of the group: "Nelson," a self-deprecating forty-five-year-old, talked in an insight-free monotone that careened

alarmingly into rapid-fire monologues; and "Judy," an extremely attractive woman in her mid-twenties, seemed a seductive, stereotypic swinger way out of my league.

Most of these initial impressions held, though I was continually surprised at how people would break free from the categories in which I tried to confine them. That became one of
the durable lessons of the group experience. Assured Judy
would turn into a shy, insecure teenager. Hysterical Nelson
would settle down into almost statesmanlike serenity. Stan, sullen and uncommunicative, would reach out unexpectedly for
confirmation.

Karl's personality was the most unvarying. He was more charismatic than warm, often radiating a fiery conviction that proved
difficult to resist. Even when he reached for humor, the essential
iron came through. In the early months of therapy, I tended
to think of that as a function of how "well-integrated" he was,
and envied his strength of character.

Within six months I felt very much a part of the group. By
then, I had made some allusions to my homosexuality but not
dwelt on it (Karl had coached me to present it as one aspect of
my life rather than the whole of it). I had let it be known that
I wrote and taught, but had withheld all details. ("If you insist
on listing your credits," Karl had warned, "you will intimidate
and alienate the others. That's what you've always done. Let's
make it different this time around.") I had begun to form attachments and preferences within the group, had begun (as
Karl enthusiastically put it) to "recapitulate—and thereby resolve—primal relationships from my *original* family."

My initial fondness for Dick and Helen held and deepened.
When I began to talk about my homosexuality, I watched carefully for Dick's reactions, hoping for an over-reaction, some
unwitting confirmation that his touted "cure" was only skindeep. But he seemed unsurprised by my revelations and im-
pressively detached; among his few direct comments was a
gentle, not hectoring, "I hope you'll get on the side of your own
health." A *mensch*, I mumbled tearfully to myself, a *mensch* who
cares about you and can serve as a model for you.

Helen was my special favorite; a tiny woman, she was alive
with energy—and compassion. I was puzzled at first that she
seemed above the fray, more a mediator than a participant in

group tangles. But I soon learned that Helen had begun closure, had resolved the horrendous set of issues centering around an abusive husband that she had brought to therapy some half dozen years earlier, and would soon be ready to terminate. What neither I nor anyone else in the group knew, and wouldn't learn for several more years, was that Helen and Karl were already lovers and living together.

Frances and Stan, on the other hand, continued to make me uneasy. One of the central dramas during that first six months in therapy centered on whether or not Frances should get rid of her pet raccoon. The mere news that she had one startled me. Those adorable, funny-faced creatures, I had somewhere learned, were in fact among the most unpredictably vicious in the animal kingdom, and the notion of trying to keep one as a domestic pet in a New York City apartment struck me as bizarre. But it was calmly explained to me that "Jill" had been an invaluable "bridge relationship" for Frances, teaching her nurturing skills of which she had been nearly bereft. That surprised me, since Frances earned her living as a nurse, but I bit my tongue and nodded with appropriate sympathy.

Jill, it seemed, had outgrown a New York apartment and had taken to demolishing it. When, session after session, Frances reported some new outrage—like Jill eating her way through the bathroom wall—the group began gently to suggest that it might be time for Frances to "move on" (Yeah, thought I, to the loony bin). She resisted the suggestion for months, but then tearfully agreed that with the coming of warm weather in the spring, she would take Jill in the car to Bear Mountain and leave her there.

Even I was moved when Frances later described her final leavetaking at Bear Mountain—how Jill had "scampered right out of the car up to a large rock and sat there silhouetted against the sky. She looked, well [here Frances began to cry], majestic. That was the last glimpse I had of her. I hope hikers start to go through soon. After all, it's people she knows best . . ."

Throughout the long saga Stan had sat impassive, but now at its climax, he turned to Frances and said laconically, "The trouble from the beginning is that you treated Jill like a person rather than an animal." Pleased with his own summary, Stan then broadened the indictment to include the entire group, said that under the guise of being "nice" to Frances we had bought into her foolishness, had encouraged her incompetence in *human* relations.

That kindled some rare anger in Helen. She suggested to Stan that discovering "incompetence" in another person was his chief aim in life; God forbid he should ever find a quality to admire and praise! Stan sneered back that he had no intention of joining the group's contemptible "mutual admiration society," preferring to remain isolated if that was the price of integrity. "You know you're alive only when you're mobilized for war," Helen snapped, and there the exchange ended. Jill was back home in the wilderness, and Stan, our resident wild animal, had temporarily drawn in his claws. But I had marked him carefully: a man of considerable intellectual power (his point about a mutual admiration society had some validity, I felt) and even more suppressed violence. And though I would not know it for a while longer—Stan kept his own counsel until ready to pounce—nothing brought out that violence more than homosexuality.

My six-month balance sheet was decidedly positive. I had developed some limited antipathy to Frances and Kate and downright aversion to Stan, but the real trust developing with Helen and Dick easily outweighed that. And all the interplay had been appealingly dramatic; "I've heard more good theater these last few months in group," I reported to Ray, "than in a year of attending Broadway." Initially I had been afraid of getting bored, of finding myself trapped in a kaffeeklatsch of interminable length and whiney triviality. What I discovered instead was that nobody's life was boring when the premium was on describing it truthfully.

I was giving the group high marks for its entertainment value, for the moment entirely unconcerned about whether and how this engaging process could possibly effect any change in my sexual orientation. That issue was happily on hold. No one had made any judgments about my life, or any demands that I remodel it. I had been welcomed into a surrogate family that seemed uniquely uninterested in imposing its special values.

These initial months in therapy coincided with—and I was therefore tempted to give them credit for causing—an upsurge in spirits and in good fortune. Nineteen sixty-six was shaping up in every way as a banner year for me. A second national tour of *In White America* was making its way into seventeen states (though banned by the local school board in Massapequa, Long Island, because, as the *New York Times* reported, it "might create a controversial situation"). In January an offer arrived to turn the play into a movie, with me co-authoring the screenplay. The Paris production had also proved a hit (Janet Flanner reported in the *New Yorker* that it had been viewed as "one of the few valuable national productions so far given here"). And John Gassner had chosen the play for inclusion in his Best American Play series.

Princeton upped my salary to twelve thousand dollars and then nominated me for a Junior Chamber of Commerce Award as one of the Ten Outstanding Young Men in America. I tried to treat it as a joke. (Was I *that* white? Didn't they know I was a rabid queer?) But in fact I was willing to stand for any award that might help further certify me as an acceptable human being, and I let Princeton submit my name. But I did add one condition: that no government sponsorship be involved; one reputation I was *not* willing to jeopardize was for opposition to Washington's policies in Vietnam. When it turned out that the Chamber of Commerce was unaffiliated with the federal government in any way, I let the nomination go through, but with a gulp (what *would* I tell my friends at the Wagon Wheel?). I gulped even harder when I didn't win (perhaps one of my friends at the Wagon Wheel had told *them*).

In returning to therapy, I had to give myself a pep talk about the ability of people—or countries—to change course. I had no trouble arguing it in terms of countries. National habits, I wrote in one of my antiwar, pro-SDS articles, "can be radically and drastically changed, even when deeply rooted. No determinant, be it instinctual or traditional, need preclude the alteration of behavior." By nature I was an optimist—it's the only possible temperament for a progressive: in order to protest injustice, one must always assume that only *will* (and never biology or the divinity or the power of history) prevents us from remaking society in the more egalitarian image we wish. In those years I made the case for optimism more in political than in personal terms. It was easier for me (which in no way impugns my sincerity in the matter) to harangue the country about changing its ways than to change my own; perhaps because—a notion I can entertain only in retrospect—the country really *did* need to remake itself, whereas I did not.

Yet my hopes for "conversion" were higher in the first year or so after I returned to therapy than they had been in a long time. Without any special nudging from the group, I had begun seeing a woman named "Cynthia" and was enjoying her company. I had first met her at Houghton Mifflin, the publisher of my forthcoming biography of James Russell Lowell; an editorial assistant, she had sat in on several prepublication meetings. We had a business lunch, progressed to a social dinner, and moved from there to seeing each other regularly.

Cynthia was very Boston—reserved and cool—and when, after a few months, I had still made no sexual move toward her, she did or said nothing to suggest that she found that out of the ordinary. Recently divorced, and suffering the usual loneliness of a single woman in male-scarce Manhattan, she was apparently glad to settle (for a while) for a congenial dinner and theater companion. When my Canadian friend Nancy and her husband arrived in New York for a visit, I enthusiastically introduced Cynthia to them, as if to say, "You see, you see—the new cure is *taking!*" Nancy, who had encouraged me to go back into therapy, was apparently as eager to believe in its magical power as I. She pronounced Cynthia "smashing," and her staid husband added, "I very much admire your taste in women."

But as the months lengthened and I still showed no sexual interest in her, Cynthia's resentment grew. Her instincts were too decent and her style too contained to let her express anger openly, and she usually settled, when annoyed, for snappish indirection. Once, when her rancor came close to being naked, I called her on it, asked what I had done to warrant it. "Nothing specific," she answered between clenched teeth. "It's just that I'm feeling hostile these days toward everyone who has failed me."

That, in turn, got me angry, but smarting as I was from *self*-contempt at my lack of "manly" interest in her, my ire came out as a quiet reminder that none of us existed to meet the needs of others. I also reminded her that she had known my "limitations" for a long time (I had obliquely hinted that I was sexually "slow"), that we had both hoped I would "outgrow" them, but that since I hadn't and since we seemed, most of the time anyway, still to value and enjoy each other, it would be helpful if she would stop wishing for and demanding what was not there. She apologized, and I in turn sensibly assured her that no apology was necessary. It was all very sensitive and statesmanlike on both sides, and all quite unreal. We were in fact furious with each other—she at my "inadequacy," me at her daring to bring it up.

And the fury soon boiled over again. Late one night she called in a self-described "panic" to say that she thought she was pregnant and didn't know what to do about it. Whoa, I thought, how come you're turning to me instead of to a girlfriend—or is that precisely the category you're trying to reduce me to, you contemptuous bitch? What I *said* was something a great deal milder and more composed, something about my "lack of expertise" in these matters, and about how a girlfriend might be more helpful though I was of course available to support her in any way that seemed *appropriate*. Composed by now herself, she thanked me, with just a trace of sarcasm, for my "concern" and said she would indeed phone several women she felt close to. After we hung up, my rage returned. "I know what you were saying," I yelled into my empty living room. "You couldn't make me pregnant, Marty, but I managed to find a real man who could. So fine, so you found a real man—so have a nice life."

When I talked all this over with Karl, his view was that I had once more chosen the wrong person, though this time of the correct gender. Cynthia, he scoffed, was clearly a "ballbreaker," and he advised me to "get her out of your life." She apparently came rapidly to the same decision, and our relationship abruptly ended. Karl assured me that these "mistaken first steps" were an inevitable part of the process of reorientation and suggested that in the future a more appropriate place to take such steps was within the group itself, where the transaction could be monitored and commented on and its dynamics thereby revealed. Judy, he thought, might be just such a person for me to experiment with. "Judy!" I reacted with astonishment. "But she and I have nothing in common—she's practically a sexual professional, and I'm a sexual novice."

"We'll see," said Karl enigmatically, and there the subject was dropped for the moment.

Karl had something else at the top of his agenda. Several years before, while I was still living in Princeton, my father had died from a heart attack. It had affected me very little. I had thought about my limited grief long and hard, afraid that I might be blocking subterranean feelings, but had concluded that I was not in deep mourning because my father and I had not had a deep connection. Though I wished it had been otherwise, he had essentially been a stranger to me. What sense of loss I did feel clustered around the fact that there was now no chance I would ever get to know him better.

My mother was convinced that my father's death had been avoidable. She blamed the blunders of his doctors and her own failure to heed his symptoms in time, and grew obsessive over her "responsibility" for his death. To me, this was a displacement of her feelings about the inadequacies of their marriage, but her suffering was certainly real, and after my father's death I had tried to be more attentive to her. And that was what Karl now wanted to talk to me about.

Enough time had passed since my father's death, he said, to relieve me of any responsibility to stay close to my mother. Indeed, he added, with shocking abruptness, it was now high time to get her out of my life entirely, to cut all ties with her. He had become convinced, he said, that until I severed that "unhealthily symbiotic" relationship, I would be unable to form any other bond with a woman. I protested that I now saw my mother but little, that our relationship had been reduced to a weekly phone call during which she would detail the miseries of her life and I would offer distant, impersonal advice—which she of course would ignore. What possible harm was there in all that?

"Your mother has shifted strategies since your childhood, but her intent remains the same: to keep you closely bound to her. Now she does it through complaining, hoping to manipulate your guilt so that you will rush to her aid."

"I don't think so. Whenever my mother and I do get together, for lunch or whatever, she seems as uncomfortable as I am and nearly as eager to keep the contact brief. She's really a very good woman, you know—energetic, generous, funny—and I owe her a lot. It would be cruel to cut off all contact with her, especially now that she's a widow."

Karl smiled like a Cheshire cat. "Your little speech, if you care to look at it, confirms everything I was trying to say. What would cause you to defend your mother so vigorously as 'a good woman' other than guilt?—which in turn, of course, is a mask for incestuous wishes you never worked through as a child. You and your mother are not separate people, and that is why your gender identity remains faulty. Until you pass through a separation phase, you will never be your own person—and none of your relationships can become adult ones, which is to say, post-familial."

I felt extremely uncomfortable. I had thought of Karl as being on the therapeutic cutting edge—yet his words now seemed direct echos of Irving Bieber's mainstream views. I thought he didn't believe in punition—yet here he was asking me to inflict profound pain on my mother. And the rationale for such cruelty seemed far from clear.

"Even if you're right," I said, "about needing to separate more from my mother, surely that should be a gradual, inner process. To do something as abrupt and mechanical as refusing ever to see her again would do nothing but increase my guilt about her."

"As always, you're a clever talker. And as always, it's at your own expense. Look, I'm not here to force you to do anything. My job is to tell you what I feel is therapeutically advisable. The rest is strictly up to you."

"Let me try to get this straight. Are you suggesting I should stop seeing my mother, stop talking to her completely?"

"Yes. Precisely. And that you should also return her money."

In an effort to circumvent future inheritance taxes, my mother had recently given my sister and me each ten thousand dollars as a gift, with the stipulation that we put the principal in the bank and pay her the yearly interest on it.

"Can't you see," Karl went on, "how manipulative her terms are?"

"Actually my sister and I suggested them. We wanted to protect our future inheritance and at the same time not strip my mother of her limited income."

"Have it your way," Karl sighed wearily, as if tired of dealing with a stubborn child.

My way was to straddle the issue. Living in a culture in which mother-blaming (as an offshoot of woman-hating) was commonplace—and her "responsibility" for a homosexual son "authoritatively" established—I was prone to join in the chorus of denunciation. But I was held back by the certain conviction that my mother had loved me and still did. It was one thing to say that her influence as a parent had been baneful—that much I might be prepared to accept—but quite another to suggest that she had deliberately done me damage; knowing her affectionate nature, I could never accept that superficial judgment. And without intentionality how could there be criminality? By what system of ethics could I justify punishing her for acts over which she had no control? *If* my mother had done poorly, she had meant well.

On that rock I held my ground. I was prepared, I told Karl, gradually to start detaching further from her—to keep our phone calls briefer, our meetings less frequent. I would even return her ten thousand dollars. But I would not act in a way I thought needlessly brutal, would not, as Karl had suggested when I pressed him for specifics, hang up on her without a word whenever she phoned ("She'll soon get the message," he had chortled, with a coldness that struck me as sadistic). "I have only your interest in mind," Karl added (sounding remarkably like my mother), "but you are not yet ready to act on behalf of your own interest. So be it. I can wait."

What I *really* wasn't ready to acknowledge was that seeds of doubt about Karl's judgment had been planted, the spell of his omniscience weakened. Yet I couldn't afford to explore those doubts, given my continuing goal of a "heterosexual adjustment" and my continuing assumption that therapy was the sole instrumentality for achieving it. (Many gay men entered into heterosexual marriages in these years, but few apparently shared my view that therapy was a necessary precursor.) For now, I was still into placation, still wanted desperately to bury my own distrust of Karl's competence. And so when it came time, in the fall of 1966, to correct proofs on my biography of James Russell Lowell, I made a peace offering: I removed from my name the middle initial I had previously used (B., standing for Bauml, my mother's birth name), as if to imply that I was removing her from my life. On the surface at least, my capitulation was complete.

Yet by temperament I had always felt uneasy with authority. Even as I yielded to a purported expert in one area of my life, I was moving into a public stance of opposition to several other kinds of authority. Never attracted to ideology of any sort, I was nonetheless, by the mid-sixties, coming to think of myself as an anarchist, as philosophically in opposition to all received truths, whether legislated by state, church, the family, or the law. However much this stood in contrast to the obedient spirit I had shown in therapy, no necessary hypocrisy was involved. In being submissive to Karl, while elsewhere decrying submissiveness, I was yielding control in the *one* area of my life— sexuality—about which I had been taught to feel incompetent.

Perhaps too, I was subliminally trying to find some balance for a life that I instinctively sensed was too heavily tipped toward control. The prime lesson of male gender training, of course, is to repress any impulse toward submissiveness. We are taught never to bend the neck or will, to stay on one side of a human pendulum that would otherwise swing naturally back and forth between assertiveness and compliance. Gay men, valuably, have often escaped full socialization into that male gender role. For many of us, varied impulses have never been successfully submerged into one; multiformities persist into adulthood, making for rich discordancies that *others*, more tightly bound, need to deplore as "contradictions."

The anarchist impulse to defy authority did authentically exist in me, side by side, with a long history of trying to live by the book. That impulse worked itself out in these years not by defying the authority of therapy, but in my political allegiances and, above all, in my teaching.

I contended early on, and argued in several essays that I published in the mid-sixties, that the New Left had close affinities with philosophical anarchism and that a greater awareness of those affinities could provide the movement with a useful perspective on its own values and strategies (an awareness that subsequently developed). I had in mind especially the affinity of the New Left with anarchism's historic denial that human nature was (as conservatives would have it) intrinsically "evil" and therefore had to be put under coercive restraint.

Anarchists, to the contrary, had always stressed (as I argued in an article for *Partisan Review* entitled "The Relevance of Anarchy") that human aggression and cruelty were the products of imposed constraints, of authoritarian family structures, social curbs on nonconformity and a capitalist ethic that encouraged competitive zeal and greed, institutionalizing the warfare of each against all. According to the anarchist creed, I wrote, if people could be "economically freed from the struggle for existence, intellectually freed from the tyranny of custom, emotionally freed from the need to revenge their own mutilation by harming others," then quite different, no less "natural" human feelings of cooperation, fraternity, and mutual assistance would have a chance to emerge.

The New Left, moreover, like its anarchist predecessors, located virtue not in current institutional arrangements, but in "the people." It tended to hold to the "romantic" notion that (as I wrote in another article) "the poor, the downtrodden, the alienated were a special repository of virtue: having long been kept outside the system, they had been uncorrupted by its values. . . . Even while demanding that the lot of the underclasses be improved, the New Left implicitly venerates that lot; the desire to cure poverty cohabits with the wish to emulate it."

The movement's distrust of a bureaucratic federal government and its investment of faith instead in decentralized decision-making and "participatory democracy" were other direct links to anarchism's historic view that the State was an instrument of oppression, the tool by which the privileged and powerful maintained themselves. In terms of personal style, too, I argued, the members of SDS and SNCC, like the anarchists before them, stressed the values of spontaneity and experimentation, were conscious rebels against "established pieties in dress, speech patterns, musical forms, social and sexual behavior, and even in stimulants (pot not booze)."

That bare mention of "sexual behavior" was about as far as I (or the New Left) ever got in carrying the message of unorthodoxy into the sexual realm. Homosexuality went wholly uncommented on in movement publications in the mid-sixties. Repressive silence was the order of the day—an order long familiar to gay people, who had learned how to read a father's silent disapproval of a son's voice pitched too high, a mother's silent disdain for a daughter not smitten with shopping. But it was okay with me. I was eager to be liberated *from* an unorthodox sexual life. I saw therapy, not fringe politics, as the instrument of that liberation and would have rejected, even if I had understood, any gesture made to include homosexuals as part of a virtuous, oppressed underclass.

In its treatment of women, the movement was equally blinded by traditional values. New Left males questioned power relations throughout society, but rarely questioned them within their own organizations or lives. Male chauvinism reigned supreme. Men did the talking and made the decisions. Women answered the phone, worked the mimeo machine, made the coffee.

Yet that is not the whole story. If the New Left was uninterested in liberating some categories of people, it nonetheless released impulses that ultimately allowed those people to liberate themselves. If the movement failed to apply its powerful notion of "struggling around one's own oppression" to gay people or to women, both ultimately got the message. Connecting it to their own lives, they stopped being timid about their resentments, stopped submerging their needs to what they had constantly been told was the "larger" struggle of freedom for Vietnamese, Cubans, farmworkers, and blacks and, by the late sixties, started to organize political movements that directly addressed their own issues.

Perhaps I had some slight inkling of what was to come—though I certainly wouldn't want to exaggerate the prescience of someone as stone-blind to issues of sexual politics as I was in those years—when, in a symposium called "What's Happening to America?" I publicly drew attention to the lack of *emotional* (as opposed to theoretical) identification with the disinherited among the adherents of SDS. I didn't specify *which* disinherited groups I had in mind and doubt very much if I would have consciously included my own, but some rebuke, however subterranean, was nonetheless implied.

I even went on to predict that because so few white under-graduates had "known enough private pain to identify on a gut level with the sufferings of the underprivileged," and because only such a gut-level identification could *sustain* a protest com-mitment, SDS would be unlikely to grow. The future, in my view, held out little promise for protest politics: "By the time, as adults most Americans *do* meet with their natural portion of affliction, they will spend their energies trying to deny and con-ceal it, for in America calamity is not considered part of the human condition but rather the result of personal inadequacy."

I channeled a lot of my energy during these years into trying to restructure the way I taught. I wanted to bring an anarchist perspective into the classroom, supplanting staid paternalism with a little lively democracy. In the fall of 1966, I dispensed with all grades in my undergraduate seminar at Princeton on "The History of Radical Protest in America." My rationale (as I later wrote in an article about the experiment) was that "only when the necessity to please others is removed, can the main job of *self*-evaluation begin. Most young teachers, like most stu-dents, are afraid much of the time they are in class, and fear guarantees that energy will go into defensive strategies rather than creative explorations." I did not see at the time that my advice to others to forswear people-pleasing as a form of self-sabotage applied in full measure to my own attitude toward therapy.

All I saw was that I wanted to reverse the traditional emphases in the classroom whereby the teacher's agenda dominated and the students' efforts were directed toward fulfilling that agenda, with their worth evaluated in terms of how well they succeeded in meeting goals and needs essentially set by others. That train-ing, I argued, carried high costs: "The acceptance of disguise as a necessity of life; the unconscious determination to manip-ulate others in the way one has been manipulated; the convic-tion that productivity is more important than character and 'success' superior to satisfaction; the loss of curiosity, of a will-ingness to ask questions, of the capacity to take risks." How, I asked, can we "expect aliveness and involvement when we are busy inculcating docility and compliance?"

Though I did away with grades, I realized that was not sufficient in and of itself to reverse the passivity that traditional schooling engendered. What also needed to be broken down was what I then called the "false separations" between students and teachers. A crucial distinction needed to be made, I argued, "between authority and authoritarianism. The former represents accumulated experience, knowledge, and insight. The latter represents their counterfeits: age masquerading as maturity, information as understanding, technique as originality. Authoritarianism is forced to demand the respect that authority draws naturally to itself. The former, like all demands, is likely to meet with hostility; the latter, like all authenticity, with emulation. Our universities—our schools at every level—are rife with authoritarianism, all but devoid of authority."

My experiments in the classroom were varied over the next few years—as were the results. Those assorted trials and errors are irrelevant to this memoir, but what is not is the way I avoided applying my insights about authority to psychotherapy, and in fact went in the opposite direction, *crediting* my experiences in group therapy for some of the perceptions that propelled my classroom experiments. It was a measure of my thralldom to psychotherapy that I could write in 1966 that group therapy had made me aware "of how many levels of the person can be 'educated' simultaneously when a group is functioning well— that is, when an atmosphere of mutual trust and forbearance prevails. . . . My experience in therapy made me impatient with other group enterprises that were narrowly functional—like a university seminar that *merely* engaged in the transmission of factual information."

When some of my colleagues objected that I had confused the purpose of a university seminar with that of a group therapy session, I in part denied and in part embraced the accusation. Agreeing that my professorial function was not to treat personalities but to develop minds, I denied that my seminars were chiefly designed to encourage members to reveal pathology or that our purpose in coming together was "curative." And yet, I argued, neuroses *were* revealed and something that could be called "therapy" did take place; in the process of actively engaging each other, and on more than a drily intellectual level, personality traits of all kinds were exposed—and it was then up to the individual student (and not the group, as in a formal therapy setting) to take home and ponder whatever had been revealed about him- or herself. The result of that, in turn, could indeed lead to the kind of awareness and personality shift in which psychotherapy officially specialized. I embraced the view that any humanizing experience could validly be seen as psychotherapeutic and therefore *welcomed* the accusation that my courses partook of psychotherapy—"for I do not know what 'education' is," I wrote, "if not self-examination and change."

I was careful to retain some distinctions. Rather than advocating that education and therapy should henceforth become interchangeable processes, I was working instead to undermine the simplistic dualism which pretended that education is concerned solely with informing the mind, and therapy with understanding the emotions. Such neat categories falsify our everyday experience, for our emotions, I argued, always color our intellectual views and our minds are continually "ordering" our emotional responses. Even in a university seminar, purportedly devoted to a high-level exchange of ideas, passion and irrationality inevitably color that exchange (and are in turn influenced by it)—and it was precisely that fact which traditional education, to its detriment, ignored or evaded.

Karl complimented me on my educational experiments and said he agreed with my estimate that he had—"unconsciously at first"—taken on a kind of "training analysis" with me in the proper functioning of groups, whether nominally therapeutic or educational. He was so pleased with the links I had established between the two that he suggested we might some day pursue the inquiry together, outside of therapy. It would be several more years before such a collaboration would take place, but from the time Karl first alluded to the possibility, it made me uneasy. I sensed from the outset that he was being a little too quick to accept credit that I knew I had over-elaborated in order to please him.

But I was still into burying my doubts about him, in no small measure because the culture was still assuring me that my only hope for happiness lay in shifting my sexual orientation—and Karl still seemed the key to that shift. *Time* magazine, in 1966, summed up the general view of homosexuality, which to some significant extent I had made my own: "It is a pathetic little second-rate substitute for reality, a pitiable flight from life . . . It deserves no encouragement, no glamorization, no rationalization, no fake status as minority martyrdom, no sophistry about simple differences in taste—and, above all, no pretense that it is anything but a pernicious sickness."[17]

Both Hollywood and the police, those twin cultural enforcers, continued to compel allegiance to the majority view. Hollywood now allowed a few nonstereotypical gay characters to appear in films, but made sure that they were properly tortured and sinister—the lesbian schoolteacher who commits suicide in *The Children's Hour* provided the appropriate image. When the British-made *Victim*, a sympathetic portrayal of gay men hounded by blackmailers and unjust laws, tried to get a seal of approval from Hollywood's censorship board (the Production Code Administration), the movie was turned down because of its "overtly-expressed plea for social acceptance of the homosexual."[18]

In a similar vein, the New York State legislature, responding to pressure from the Roman Catholic hierarchy, declined by an overwhelming vote to rescind the sodomy law on its books that criminalized homosexual behavior. And the police, through bar raids and entrapment, continued their policies of harassment. When John Lindsay, a Republican liberal, assumed the mayoral office in New York City in 1966, there was some hope that the cloud of fear might lift. But Lindsay, like so many other "liberals" before and since, did not extend his professed compassion to homosexuals. He was no sooner in office than he sanctioned a police crackdown on Times Square aimed at "promenading perverts," and then, fresh from that triumph, moved on to a "cleanup" campaign to rid Washington Square Park in Greenwich Village of its "undesirables." In that, he overreached himself.[19]

To the surprise of city officials, the effort to clean up the Village led to sizable opposition. Aryeh Neier, director of the New York Civil Liberties Union (which had previously been indifferent to the fate of homosexuals) memorably warned Lindsay against "confusing deviant social behavior with criminal activity"; and Judson Memorial Church in the Village hosted a packed meeting protesting police entrapment. Within a few weeks, police commissioner Leary had instructed his officers to throw away their tight pants, sneakers, and polo shirts—the current entrapment costume—though bar raids and street harassment continued for a good while longer to be staples of the law enforcement trade.

Modest gains were also posted in the growth of the tiny homophile movement. In 1966 fifteen organizations, though their membership rolls were small and confined largely to the two coasts, were able to form a loose confederation designed to fund a few legal challenges and to organize a few demonstrations against the exclusion of gays and lesbians from military service and government employment. These activities, in turn, gained some press attention and helped to mobilize additional, if limited support from church, legal, and health care professionals for the decriminalization (though rarely for the moral acceptance) of homosexual acts. The organized gay movement had begun to make its presence known, but it remained largely invisible to most gays, distant from their consuming issues of survival and secrecy.[20]

And I, in turn, was consumed with issues of career and cure, with the former going notably better than the latter. The publication of my Lowell biography late in 1966 produced a spate of good reviews as well as nomination for the National Book Award. I published reviews that year in the *New York Times*, the *Village Voice*, and the *New Republic*, spoke widely on the theme of "Black Power and the American Radical Tradition" (arguing that the concept was a realistic adaptation to the depressing reality of white racism), and turned down an invitation from Oxford to accept the Harmsworth Chair in American History. Early in 1967 Princeton notified me that I was being promoted to full professor—at age thirty-six one of the youngest the university had ever named in the social sciences. But *the* sign of election, perhaps, was Jimmy Breslin's listing me in his New Year's Day column for 1967 as one of the people he "wasn't talking to this year." I hadn't the foggiest notion what I had done to offend Breslin, other than harboring the private feeling when introduced to him that he was an egotistical bully. Perhaps, as Breslin often claimed, he could read minds.

Near epiphany came at a party I gave in my apartment to

celebrate the publication of a friend's book. The friend, an up-and-coming literary critic, provided most of the guest list, and the event loomed as star-studded (at least as academics read the firmament), with the Trillings, Harold Bloom, Susan Sontag, William Styron, and other assorted literary luminaries sending acceptances. I hired the then-trendy Arthur Treacher catering service to do the hors d'oeuvres, bought a huge bouquet of white mums to decorate the apartment, and sat back to await anointment.

But the gods had other plans, deciding to deflate the sin of hubris through the unlikely medium of a bartender. Sent by the catering service, he showed up an hour after the party had begun (the hors d'oeuvres already having been burnt by their ancient, dotty waitress), and well into his cups. The early guests had been warned on arriving that "nothing was going according to plan" and were told to pitch in and get their own drinks. That created a sense of unexpected adventure, and for a while conversation was appealingly giddy.

But the bartender proved determined to get as drunk as possible, and he soon had the bar awash in spilled drinks as he kept missing his aim. His frustrated curses rose proportionately, while on the sly he stashed an occasional unopened bottle into his overnight bag. The guests affected embarrassed high spirits—that is, until the curses started moving away from the spilled drinks and directly toward them. The climax came when an alarmed woman whispered in my ear that the bartender had groped one of the men. She thought it had been Lionel Trilling, but perhaps the literary imagination fathered that wish.

I told the bartender he would have to leave. He refused, yelling that I was "a dirty Jew." (How bizarre, I thought with relief, he's attacking me where I *don't* feel vulnerable.) Just in case he should proceed to the next epithet, I grabbed him by the back of his coat and, in a brusque macho gesture calculated to separate me from unseemly gay gropings, threw him out. He then stood outside the building hurling abuse at the departing guests until he finally veered off to direct traffic in the middle of Fourteenth Street. Next day the Arthur Treacher people offered abject apologies, cancelled the costs of the party, and humanely sent the bartender off for therapy. The phone rang constantly with thanks for "a *most* lively party," but I was left with the uneasy feeling that some sort of cosmic psychodrama had unfolded in which closeted gay man giving gala for straight literati is undone by uncloseted gay man. The feeling didn't entirely fit the facts, yet the uneasiness lingered for days.

# 8

---

# POLITICS

W ITH THE LOWELL BIOGRAPHY behind me, I settled on a
new project, a history of Black Mountain College, the
experimental community in the foothills of North Carolina that
for over two decades (1933–56) had been a breeding ground
for the alternate culture that emerged in the sixties. I hoped
my research would carry me further into several matters that
had become of absorbing interest to me: educational innovation,
communitarian anarchism, and "group process"; and I hoped
as well to clarify the growing distrust I felt for traditional academic historical writing, with its safe subjects and its evasive
pretense of objectivity. Historians, I had come to believe, were
inescapably present in their books (though they preferred denying it), their values and assumptions shaping the selection
and highlighting of evidence on every page.

Influenced by the counterculture myself, I wanted to write
what I viewed as a more honestly subjective kind of history,
wanted to let the reader see the process whereby a particular
person grappled with a particular subject and body of evidence.
As I was later to write in my introduction to the book, "My
conviction is that when a historian allows more of himself to
show—his feelings, fantasies and needs, not merely his skills at
information-retrieval, organization and analysis—he is *less* likely

to contaminate the data, simply because there is less pretense that he and it are one."

That was the ideal, but realizing it proved more difficult than I at first imagined. Though I had been protesting traditional ways of writing and teaching history for some time, and particularly their defended, deadly impersonality, I was more tightly bound to those traditions, both by training and by temperament, than I liked to admit. I discovered just how tightly when I tried to break loose and become participant as well as observer in the lives of the people I was writing about, tried to let my feelings as well as my mind engage the documentary record. In this, as in all things, I was very much a product (and a prisoner) of a particular generational style, "wandering between two worlds"—in those favorite words from Matthew Arnold that have always haunted me—"one dead, the other powerless to be born."

The new book once more had me criss-crossing the country to read manuscript collections and to talk to people who had been at Black Mountain. Though I hated travel, I loved getting lost in work, loved the self-image of a heroic Stakanovite of research, driving myself to do more in a given day than most people would have thought possible or reasonable. I remember the kick I got from the dazed look on the faces of the staff at the state archives in Raleigh, North Carolina (where the bulk of the BMC papers were housed), when I arrived there in the summer of 1967 with my own portable xerox machine and a research assistant to boot, and proceeded, barely pausing for food and sleep, to gut the archive in two weeks' record time, carting home some ten thousand photocopies. My razzle-dazzle "New York" operation jarred the staff's well-bred notions of proper scholarly pacing, but what those genteel folk failed to realize was that I was doing more than writing a history—I was justifying my life.

Preoccupied as I was with the new book, I didn't expect (or even want) another romantic seizure. But "do not seek and ye shall find" once more held true. This time the lightning struck at a fancy theatrical party back in New York at which nobody was openly gay but everybody's eyes wandered only toward their own gender. Mine fixed on a husky thirty-five-ish blond whose cornfed good looks and unpretentious manner had me guessing him as somebody's square relative from Iowa until I was told (I had quickly asked) that he was in fact "Ted S.," a once-promising actor who had given it all up to tend to his lover's (a famous playwright) real estate interests.

I maneuvered an introduction, settled for a brief conversation *and* a phone number, and next day inaugurated an intense campaign. Ted made it clear from the outset that he and "Sid" were lovers, and that he would never leave him. But he assured me that he *was* attracted to me and that he and Sid didn't believe in monogamy. As proof, Ted invited me over to their large brownstone, introduced me to Sid, who lit up some good pot for the three of us, chatted away pleasantly for an hour, gave Ted an affectionate good-night kiss, and vanished to his own bedroom after wishing us "a happy night." I was astounded. Consumed with passion for Ted, I couldn't fathom so casual an attitude toward so desirable an object.

But Ted meant what he said: ours was an affair, not a match, designed for pleasure and brevity. Within a few weeks of our meeting, he went off on a ski trip to Europe—and left me feeling bereft. I poured out my feelings in group, explained how Ted had broken through my mechanical routines, had opened up a chasm of yearning for closeness that I had persuaded myself work satisfactorily filled. Just as Helen and Dick began to cluck in sympathy (and Stan to glare in resentment), Karl interrupted to ask how I could have thought I had filled a chasm that in fact I hadn't even excavated.

That startled me, but Karl had still more to say.

"You've been skating on the surface ever since you entered therapy, chatting us up with stories about your social life and your love life, always quick to analyze everything and everybody but yourself."

The room became hushed. Helen and Dick took on pained looks of remorse, as if they had been caught overindulging a spoiled child. Stan smiled contentedly.

"Well, I'm tired of it," Karl went on. "I figured you'd take hold eventually, but you haven't. So now I'm going to draw the line *for* you, since you won't do it yourself. From now on, I don't want to hear another word in here about your homosexuality. Not another word, is that clear? You've wasted enough of the group's time, and your own time, on this 'as if' behavior. If you need to go on acting out, that's your business. But we don't need to hear about it any more. Maybe if we stop indulging you, you'll finally get around to exploring more important matters."

"Like what?" I said quietly, my heart in my mouth, knowing perfectly well what the answer would be.

"Like your feelings for Judy," Karl replied—which was *not* what I had expected.

"I don't know what you mean," I said and turned toward Judy. "I like you, Judy, I'm fond of you, but my feelings toward you just don't go very deep, one way or the other."

Karl snorted with derision. "You really won't take a chance, will you, you really won't move one inch out of your rut."

"Take what chance?" I said, genuinely mystified.

"Well for starters, how about taking a different seat?"

Helen began to titter appreciatively, so I assumed Karl had said *something* intelligible, even if not to me.

"What do you mean?" I repeated.

When Karl stayed silent, Helen jumped in with clarification. "Marty, you've sat in the same seat in here for months. Karl is suggesting you stop being so self-protective, get into a different space—literally."

"We all tend to sit in the same seats," I answered, suddenly feeling like the object of a conspiracy. "What's the big deal?"

Karl's eyes twinkled impishly. "If you changed seats with Helen, you'd be sitting next to Judy."

I was reassured to see Judy jump in surprise, looking as uncomfortable as I now felt. But she recovered rapidly.

"Sure Marty," she said cheerfully, "come on over here next to me."

The sexual innuendo was now unmistakable, and it made me angry. I felt as if I'd been sand-bagged.

"I wish I knew what the hell you were all talking about," I said peevishly.

Dick chimed in from left field, "The hell with understanding it, just do it."

Suddenly my allies had become my enemies, or so it felt. But as if reading my mind, Dick went on to say, "Marty, you know we're on your side, we want only the best for you. Why not just take a chance, it's no big deal. Maybe something unexpected will come out of it."

I pushed my chair back and crossed the room. Helen, smiling, immediately got up and exchanged seats with me. As I sat down there was a chorus of approving noises. Judy leaned over and patted my arm appreciately. I felt flushed with stupid exhilaration.

"Well done," said Karl gently. "We're not going to give up on you yet."

Uh-oh, I thought with alarm, *now* what's he got in mind?

Nothing more, it turned out, for that session. It ended soon after, and on my way home I mulled over whether Karl had literally meant that I was never again to bring up anything in group relating to homosexuality. Having already spilled my guts about Ted—who on returning from his ski trip, quickly distanced himself from my pestering intensity—I figured I would simply wait and see.

I went back to fourteen-hour days on Black Mountain. And I filled the occasional free minutes in between with politics. That still took mostly marginal, self-protective forms. I did volunteer to work with dropouts in a Harlem storefront school, but lacked the skills to teach the basic reading and writing courses most needed; I gave a few sessions on black history, but they were apparently pitched at too abstract a level to catch the students' attention, and interest in the classes quickly petered out.

That hands-on foray aside, my limited contributions consisted of signing assorted petitions (like the Writers and Editors War Tax Protest to "dissociate myself from my government's actions in Vietnam") and writing assorted articles supporting the antiwar movement and the continuing struggle for black rights. In several of those articles I tried to use a historian's perspective to modify what I thought were the too sanguine or too cynical positions sometimes adopted by movements I otherwise deeply sympathized with.

Thus I strongly supported SDS's general indictment of U.S. intervention in the internal affairs of other countries, but I took issue in the *Village Voice* with SDS leader Carl Oglesby's characterization of it from the earliest days of the Republic as having been always motivated by the wish to maximize profits for American business. This economic explanation, I argued, was too simplistic and, as related to the present day, even naively partial. For in my view Lyndon Johnson and Dean Rusk were dangerously misguided men not solely because they had become the willing tools of American business, but also because they were the unwilling prisoners of their own altruistic fantasies, *genuinely* believing that they were saving the world for democracy and from communism. To recognize the complexity of their motives in my view clarified rather than softened the indictment against them.

On the other hand, when John Gregory Dunne (in a book he wrote on the California grape strike) acidly dismissed the SDS radicals who showed up to support the strike as having no commitment other than to the latest action, the current "game in town," I defended the students in the *New Republic*, dismissing Dunne's "indictment by innuendo," challenging him, *if* he had a reasoned case to make against the student volunteers, to spell it out.

And when George Kennan published "Rebels Without a Program" in the *New York Times* Sunday magazine, denouncing campus radicals, in a tone of mandarin disdain, for their "massive certainties," their "screaming tantrums," and their consuming interest in "violence for violence's sake," I (and so many others that the controversy was subsequently published as a book, *Democracy and the Student Left*) wrote an angry rebuttal. Kennan's gross misrepresentations of the students could only mean, I argued, that he had never troubled to read the levelheaded, perceptive position papers that SDS regularly issued. The SDS members I knew at Princeton hardly fit Kennan's description of them as naive utopians. To the contrary, they seemed to me far more knowledgeable and far less imprisoned by preconceptions than the average undergraduate. That they believed there could and should be less suffering in the world hardly made them utopians. In 1968, in a long essay I wrote for the *Atlantic Monthly*, "On Misunderstanding Student Rebels," I bracketed Kennan with Jacques Barzun and Sidney Hook as starchy and sanctimonious men who were more interested in attacking campus radicals on mannerly points of personal hygiene than in responding to the genuinely important issues about American life to which they were trying to call attention.

Karl, in the privacy of an individual session, characterized the way I simultaneously reproached and defended SDS as "an over-developed sense of equity." He said he had been watching my efforts for some time, both in my writings and in group sessions, to be fair to every side of a given argument and had now concluded that that represented a form of psychic evasion. The sense of fairness that I had always believed to be one of my personality strengths, Karl now labeled a weakness. I was *using* the guise of fairness, he said, as a device for avoiding participation, for making anything like a full commitment (to a person or a movement). I was always in the process of weighing (is this person, this movement, good enough, pure enough, correct enough?), never willing to draw up any final balance.

This attitude, Karl suggested, was at bottom anti-life, for in real life one could never be *that* sure, and to await certainty was to provide oneself with a standing rationale for never acting in the present, never committing oneself. Yes, he acknowledged, my sense of fairness did make me a good historian—but at the expense of being an alive human being. In making this assessment, Karl was moving his indictment of me into the one area I had previously thought sacrosanct: my habits of mind. Karl dotted the *i*: it had been convenient for me, he said, to cordon off homosexuality as my "problem" while viewing the rest of my psychic structure as intact. The "problem," he was now suggesting, was in fact more encompassing—nothing less than the way I presented myself to the world.

Karl repeated what he had said a few weeks earlier during the group session: it was time for me to take hold. I had been in therapy nearly two years, he reminded me, and until now he had deliberately let the issue of my sexual orientation slide. But he had meant what he said in group: from now on homosexuality was a taboo topic. If I still needed to "act out," he couldn't stop me, but he could stop me from getting secondary excitement from my homosexual activities by talking about them in group. If I didn't like the new terms, he made clear, I was free to leave therapy. The choice was mine.

I told him I would think about it. Not trusting my own judgment, I turned to my old friend Ray. We had been mysteriously on the outs of late, and when we got together we spent the first few hours trying to figure out what had gone wrong in the relationship. The answer we came up with fed directly into a discussion of therapy. We had both, Ray and I decided, been trying to hold the other to an earlier image, dismissing evidence that now, in our late thirties, we were no longer the same people that we had been when we first met fifteen years before. Each of us resented the refusal of the other to respect the selves that had emerged, and at the root of that refusal, we concluded, was a lack of *self*-respect. How could we expect from others what we withheld from ourselves?

From there we quickly fell back on the familiar assumption that only in therapy could we learn to like ourselves better. We did not mean learning to accept who we were—that became part of the psychiatric agenda only in the seventies—but rather figuring out how to change ourselves into somebody else. We recited once again the psychiatric litany of what was wrong with us: we were narcissistically self-absorbed, we had proved incapable of sustaining a loving commitment to another person (thereby shockingly dismissing the significance of our own ongoing friendship), we were unable to enjoy what was enjoyable, feel the pain of what was not—in short, *experience* our own lives. And what, in turn, accounted for that litany of faults and failures? Homosexuality of course.

Ray confessed that he had all but made up his own mind to return to therapy, having taken a year's sabbatical on the assumption that "overanalysis" may have been feeding his unhappiness rather than helping to resolve it. But in the year he had been out of therapy, the unhappiness had deepened, and he now felt, approaching forty, that a renewed commitment to therapy was needed, a do-or-die effort to change his ways. He urged me to do the same. But what did a "do-or-die effort" *specifically* mean? I wanted to know. Were we supposed to "take the veil" again—even presuming we could? And *precisely* how was a strategy of celibacy supposed to create a personality transformation? Maybe, Ray suggested (sounding like a plant from Karl), my bottled-up libido would then spill out in group; maybe the work of transformation originated there. "More will be revealed," he added with a laugh; "hell, it's a leap of faith. What isn't? The alternative is to go on like *this*."

"Maybe 'this' isn't really so bad," I said. "Who are we comparing ourselves to, anyway? My life does work in lots of areas and lots of ways; more than most peoples' I suspect."

"You're toting up your prizes and publications," Ray retorted. "Surely by now, *dear one*, you've come to realize that none of that compares to a warm body in bed at night."

We were, with relief, heading toward camp. "But does it have to be the same body every night? Surely if I continue to win prizes, I can ensure steady companionship into old age."

"Enough, dear one. Continue with your therapy."

Nancy, long distance from Toronto, offered the same advice, though she was less sure about the necessity of therapy than she had once been. "I'm feeling really confused," she wrote me, "not knowing if I *want* you to go through miseries in order to fight the good fight [i.e., become heterosexual], or whether I wouldn't prefer you were just relaxed and happy—and resigned to being gay. But I know, really, that these aren't the alternatives. You can't *choose* to be completely happy the way things are." In referring to "the way things are" Nancy did not mean— as those same words, in the mouth of a comparably liberal and caring person would come to mean just a few years later, after the post-Stonewall liberation movement had burst on the scene—that the climate of the day discouraged gay self-acceptance. What she meant instead was that being happy wasn't in the nature of being gay.

And of course I agreed. And since I also believed, as a privileged white male, that it was in the nature of my birthright to be happy, I decided to persevere in the struggle to be entirely "okay." I told Karl I would stay in therapy and would abide by the injunction to stop talking about my homosexual experiences—but would not agree to stop having them. Karl accepted the package.

But something in my attitude had changed, something beyond simple weariness. Maybe too many doubts had by now accumulated about the therapeutic process, and about Karl as a practitioner. Maybe enough new voices were now being sounded in the culture at large so that they had begun to pierce, however dimly, my waxed-over eardrums. In the spring of 1967, a student homophile league—the first such group in the country—formed at Columbia University, and soon after, a group of Episcopal priests urged that homosexuality no longer be automatically regarded as sinful. The following year, the North American Conference of Homophile Organizations adopted the motto "Gay is Good." And at the American Medical Association's annual convention that same year, a group of homosexual activists protested the continuing emphasis on pathology.

These were as yet only straws in the wind. For it was also in 1967 that the Supreme Court sustained the constitutionality of an immigration law that barred aliens from entry or from citizenship if they were homosexual. And it was in 1968 that the psychiatrist Charles Socarides published his influential *The Overt Homosexual*, which reiterated the view that homosexuality represented a disruption in the normal developmental process and reiterated as well an optimistic assessment of the possibilities for psychoanalytical cure.

The older view of homosexuality as pathology still dominated, and by a large margin. Yet a measureable cultural shift had nonetheless begun, a shift that profoundly profited from the growing assertion by another despised minority that "black is beautiful," that being different was cause for celebration rather than apology. The young black militants who rallied under the Black Power banner carried a powerful message of liberation for all those who had previously attempted to define themselves by mainstream cultural standards and who had measured their "rightness" by the extent to which they had managed to conform to and won acceptance in that mainstream.

The young white idealists of SDS also made a powerful contribution to the spreading ethic of liberation. By challenging the corruption and inequity of a system that reserved power and privilege for the few, and by refusing any longer to defer to the "experts"—to the "best and brightest" who had landed us in the Vietnam quagmire—campus radicals helped to undermine all forms of traditional authority and to weaken the habit of automatic deference to it.

I sensed that my own liberation was being articulated, even though, for a while longer, I could not directly apply the message to my own cause. But it was a message I most assuredly heard, and I rallied strongly in support of those movements purveying it. Throughout 1967 and especially during 1968—that epochal year that saw the Tet offensive, Johnson's announcement that he would not run for the presidency again, the student uprising at Columbia University (and around the globe), the police riots at the Democratic convention in Chicago, and the assassinations of Martin Luther King, Jr. and Robert Kennedy—I wrote and wrote in defense of those who were challenging authority, celebrating diversity, insisting on a new social order.

And—despite Karl's having planted seeds of doubt about the "real" (i.e., negative) meaning of my penchant for seeing several sides to a question rather than wholly committing to one side— I continued to maintain a critical posture even toward those individuals or groups with which I felt most strongly identified. Karl had sapped my confidence in the psychic value of that posture, but not in its political value. Especially since I had the uneasy feeling that even as applied to the psychic realm, Karl might be doing a little special pleading of his own.

Did he want me to surrender my intellect to *him?* Was it to him that I was supposed to "wholly commit" myself, instead of reserving areas of doubt and disagreement? I had been ready from the beginning to surrender the direction of my affective life to him—ready because I had been taught to distrust it, to regard it as "disturbed." But my mind was another matter entirely. *That* I had never distrusted, and I would not yield its control to anyone. Fortunately. For it was my mind that kept me independent and insubordinate, kept me something of a disobedient outsider even in regard to a psychotherapeutic process to which I had outwardly committed myself, kept my rebellious spirit alive for the day when growing dissent within the culture at large about the meaning of homosexuality would finally free it up, finally give me the confidence and courage to employ it on behalf of my own liberation.

In the meantime, I honed my habits of defiance through the medium of political commentary, transgressed against the powers-that-be in the only way I then knew how. In a series of essays and reviews, I hammered away at the American majority for becoming ever more immunized against suffering, whether in Vietnam or in the ghettos.

It had been realistic in the mid-sixties, I argued, to hope that the country would mobilize its resources to assist the least fortunate. But in 1968 that comforting hope could no longer be sustained. Like the first reconstruction of the 1860s, the second one of the 1960s had stopped tragically short of its goals, the record of achievement depressingly slight. The civil rights bills passed in the mid-sixties had not been vigorously enforced; open-occupancy and equal-job opportunities were a mockery; and segregation remained the overwhelming pattern in the schools.

I challenged the common notion that the recent white backlash had largely resulted from urban riots like the one in Watts or from disgust at the nationalism and separatism represented by emergent Black Power sentiment in SNCC and the Congress of Racial Equality (CORE). In fact, I argued, those developments were the result, not cause, of white resistance to equality. In order to sustain hope within the black community, the militants of SNCC and CORE had turned to the concept of Black Power as a device for achieving political and economic solidarity and as a lever with which to exert maximum pressure on a recalcitrant white world. Whites would do well to remember, I suggested, that they had always considered self-defense acceptable behavior for themselves—and indeed had filled our textbooks with praise for those "heroic" Americans who in 1776 had taken up arms in response to the threat (more threat, it could be argued, than actuality) by British authorities to curtail colonial liberties.

White liberals had also taken to criticizing black militants for "deserting" the kind of coalition politics that had produced the civil rights legislation of the mid-sixties. But the call for further cooperation between whites and blacks was at base, I argued, a call to further futility. For the chief result of that earlier legislation had been to lull many white liberals into believing that the major battles had been won—whereas in fact little had changed in the daily lives of most blacks. Only a *radical* coalition devoted to scrutinizing the systemic inequalities of American life could produce the needed structural changes, and few whites were available for that kind of analysis and struggle. The likeliest candidates were either, like the campus activists of SDS, politically impotent or, like the organized labor movement, increasingly identified with the establishment.

When Martin Luther King, Jr. (in his 1967 book *Where Do We Go From Here?*) based his hope for a viable coalition on the fact that poor whites shared many class grievances with poor blacks, I questioned, in my review of the book, whether the reality of shared grievances was likely to get translated into political cooperation, arguing that with the limited exception of the Populist era, poor whites had always put race before all other considerations—including economic self-interest. My own feelings about the continuing prospect for social change wavered very much between doubt and hope, coming down by 1968 more often on the side of doubt. As I wrote in one essay, the national prognosis remained poor "until *something*—probably only an event of catastrophic proportions, such as a major war or a depression"—reduced us to a level of open-eyed despair that *might* force us to confront the tangled set of issues currently being dealt with through evasion.

Within a few years, after I had become active in the gay movement, I would apply many of these same arguments about separatism, group identity, and coalition politics to the condition of the gay minority in America. Now, in 1968, through the medium of writing plays, I began to approach the issues relating to my own oppression more directly. Inventing gay characters, and putting words in their mouths, allowed me to begin the slow process of coming out—a process that took place almost behind my own (and certainly Karl's) back—a process that would finally lead to my direct engagement with gay liberation itself.

# 9

# PLAYWRITING

I FIRST TRIED MY hand at some one-acters. The director Eddie Parone asked me late in 1967 to write a short play for inclusion in an evening devoted to brief works by some dozen playwrights (including Jules Feiffer, Lanford Wilson, and Terrence McNally). Delighted to be asked, I quickly turned out a two-character script that I called *Metaphors*.

It was essentially a homosexual seduction scene, set in the Yale admissions office. An atypical young man, more street hustler than preppie, is interviewed by a stodgy older man. The younger, through veiled homosexual allusions and vaguely threatening promises, ultimately pierces the interviewer's protective armor, forcing him to face some buried truths about himself—though at the end of the play he pulls back to his previous reality just as he is on the verge of succumbing to the younger man's blandishments.

It was a play about role reversals and unmaskings. And I used the persona of a young hustler—familiar from my forays to the Wagon Wheel—to present homosexuality as a somehow more profound form of honesty even though embedded in a possibly psychotic guise, all at once a lifestyle preferable to the hypocrisies of the mainstream and yet threatening, if embraced, to strip away the protective covering needed for survival. Nothing could have more perfectly represented my own conflicted feelings about homosexuality than did this first attempt to use the theme in a play. For me, expressing this ambivalence openly marked an advance, a step up from private negativity.

Somewhat to my surprise, the critics singled out my play for praise when the evening, entitled "Collision Course," opened Off-Broadway in May 1968. I'm not sure what I had expected, but suspect I was looking for a thoroughly hostile reaction, which might then—given my temperamental tendency to advance rather than retreat under criticism—have usefully propelled me still further out of the closet. I might even have thought I could *count* on a negative reaction, given how few plays on the American stage had ever mentioned homosexuality, let alone suggested something redeeming in it.

Oh, Richard Watts, Jr., the *New York Post* critic, did weigh in with a shocked negative ("We surely could have expected something better from Martin Duberman, who gave us the excellent 'In White America,' than an item about . . . the beauties of a homosexual relationship"). But Clive Barnes praised my "crisp and dry black humor," and the *Variety* critic not only wrote glowingly about the "snap and point" of my dialogue but actually called me on the phone to urge me to give up academia and devote the rest of my life to playwriting.

This was encouragement with a vengeance—and not only to a new career. I had risked publicly labeling myself as gay and instead of being drummed out of the human race had been hailed. Of course if I had presented homosexuality in a more positive light than I did in *Metaphors*, the reception would almost certainly have been quite different. The play—and the ones soon to follow—was still so riven with ambivalence and self-hatred as to prove acceptable to a critical fraternity that only a few years before had swooned with admiration over Lillian Hellman's suicidal lesbian in a revival of *The Children's Hour*.

Nonetheless, two things had irreducibly happened: I had put a toe in the water and not drowned; and I had gotten the message that a cultural shift was indeed in process, that a somewhat greater tolerance had emerged for discussing homosexuality in public.

I described all this excitedly to Ray, who was in Rome. I giddily demanded he leave off "gliding among the arches of the Coliseum nightly" (Ray had reported that all Italian men between the ages of sixteen and twenty-one were willing to sell themselves, but no Italian man older than twenty-one would acknowledge being gay), and return home to share in my triumph. Business was so good, I reported, that we had moved to a larger theater; and Lyn Austin, one of the show's producers, had taken me to lunch in order to say that she was putting her money on me as the "long-distance" runner of the twelve playwrights, and that Harold Clurman, the theater luminary, had told her he concurred with that opinion. They jointly urged me to turn full-time to playwriting.

For a while I did just that. Lyn Austin chose a new one-acter of mine—along with short plays by Terrence McNally and Bruce Jay Friedman—for presentation as "Three From Column A," all three to be directed by Elaine May. Thereafter followed a harrowing six months that somewhat dampened my ardor for the theater.

My new play, *The Recorder*, was again a two-character sketch and again had overtones of homosexual seduction in it. But my main concern this time out was in dramatizing—through the device of "a great man" ringing changes on his memory for the purported enlightenment of a young historian—the difficulties of recreating the "truth" about the past. I wrote a language play that minimized movement and narrative in favor of showing how personal interaction in the moment shifted the meaning of events from the past.

But Elaine May was not a language director. She professed to admire the play greatly and then proceeded in rehearsal to do everything she could to create a burlesque version of it better suited to her own comic vision. And in the process, she proved perfectly willing to reduce the play's homoerotic overtones to the stereotypic level of simpering silliness. Lines designed to be subtly seductive were dropped or flattened into belly laughs; a floor-length yellow scarf was draped around the neck of the actor playing the "great man," converting him into some sort of trashy vaudevillian; the "historian" was introduced by having him climb, madcap, over a scrim into the other man's apartment.

When I complained about the lack of consultation and the distortion of the play's tone, Lyn (who was getting to admire me less every minute) tartly replied that Elaine's style while rehearsing was always and necessarily improvisational and that "in due time" she would return to the script as actually written. One week before opening night, "due time" had not yet arrived—though by then Elaine had entirely dropped the Friedman play from the evening as "unworkable."

I appealed to the co-producer, Oliver Smith, who had largely been a silent partner up to that point. After sitting through a preview he announced that he liked my play as much as ever but thoroughly disliked Elaine's "fussy" direction of it. I was home free. Or so I thought—until Elaine huddled with herself and announced that her directorial touches were "of a piece" and to change *anything* would be tantamount to destroying her "concept."

That gave me two choices: let the play open in her version or withdraw it. Neither choice was clearcut. The preview audiences had been laughing loudly at Elaine's gimmickry, and all hands were predicting a hit. Besides, those same hands told me, I was a novice playwright who should be grateful that Elaine had taken my play on and through her comic genius made it work. But a compound of stubbornness and integrity led me to make the second choice—I told Lyn I wanted my play back.

Polite bickering instantly gave way to outrage, denunciation, and threats. I was told I could not have my play back for the simple reason that *I* no longer owned it—the producers did—and they had no intention, Lyn made clear, of cancelling the show three days before opening night. Okay, I said, in that case (Leos *hate* being crossed) I would issue a public statement of disavowal and on opening night either would leaflet the critics as they arrived at the theater or would stand up in the audience just before curtain and announce that the play they were about to see was *not* mine.

That did it. My play was returned and the opening canceled. But Elaine decidedly had the last laugh. She substituted a play of her own, *Adaptation*, combined it with McNally's play, *Next*, went back into rehearsals, and opened a few weeks later to critical acclaim. Worse still, she opened in a small Village theater *exactly opposite* my apartment, and day after day I had to restrain myself from jumping out of the window at the sight of ticket buyers lined up at the box office. I berated myself for months:

"Fame and fortune beckoned, you schmuck, and you threw it all away for a yellow scarf!"

But I was by now too drawn to the theater simply to renounce it. Within a few months, I had written another one-acter, *The Electric Map*, as a companion piece to *The Recorder*, and the two plays opened Off-Broadway in January 1970 under the combined title *The Memory Bank*. The critical reception—though no match for Elaine's—was good (Clive Barnes called the evening "exquisitely wrought," and *Variety* predicted that "it was unlikely anything this season will have more artistic quality"). But what was most noteworthy about the reviews was their treatment of homosexuality.

*The Electric Map*, unlike *The Recorder*, *was* centrally focused on a homosexual character—the sad, closeted, possibly alcoholic, decidedly self-destructive man who ran an electronic show re-creating in lights the Civil War battle of Gettysburg. "Ted" was *un*-ambiguously a negative stereotype. In the fits-and-starts nature of my coming out, he was an undiluted fit, almost a reflex reproduction of the pathetic, pathological gay I had been brought up believing was representative. If my channel for coming out was proving to be my writing, the gay characters I put in my plays in these years inevitably reflected the self-hating crowd I traveled with and saw represented in popular culture. More positive images would only evolve in tandem with a gay political movement that in these years had barely begun to surface.

The overt homosexual theme in *The Electric Map* brought the critics running. A fair number of them either treated the theme casually or, more suspect, entirely omitted reference to it (the most suspect was a closeted critic whom I had met socially and who not only avoided any mention of homosexuality in his review, but put down the whole evening as "dry academics"). But a fair number rang in with weighty—and in retrospect richly comic—protests.

Richard Watts, Jr., of the *Post*, once more professed himself scandalized, taking particular exception to my "references to sexual organs." Another critic adapted a tone of Olympian sadness at "witnessing a proven talent wasting itself on triviality." A third posited the existence of "two Martin Dubermans"—

"imagine restricting me to only *two*," I gleefully wrote Ray; "now *there's* a put-down!"—one who wrote "the stirring, luminous *In White America*," the other now "obsessed with homosexuality."

But it was left to Dan Isaac in the *New Leader*—perhaps conscious of his responsibility to present that journal's intellectual readership with a sufficiently dense argument—to elaborate a cosmology: what I was at base arguing in the plays, Isaac announced, was "a homosexual theory of American history, positing the Civil War as a convulsive sadomasochistic explosion of the kind that predictably accompanies exclusively masculine relationships." Hooray! I wrote Ray, "it seems, without my knowing it, that I am the possessor of a fullblown theory of American history—which qualifies me to embark at once on a magisterial work (to be preceded of course by some intense sadomasochistic field work)."

But two of the reviews amused me a great deal less. Harold Clurman, purportedly one of my admirers, wrote a sniffy piece in the *Nation* that included some praise but much more lofty disdain for my having mistakenly focused the evening on "sexual anomalies" and, in *The Electric Map*, on a homosexual man "pitifully in trouble on that account." Clurman's review bothered me: I didn't feel far enough in the clear, as an openly gay man or as a playwright, simply to shrug it off. But if I was troubled by Clurman's review, I was furious at John Simon's piece in *New York* magazine—not least because he and I were acquainted.

The headline on Simon's article read OUT OF THE CLOSET. I realized that one of the magazine's editors rather than Simon himself might have written it, but the sentiments in his review were in fact of a piece with the headline. The problem with my plays, Simon wrote, was that their "gifted author has not permitted himself to get immersed in the true theme of the evening: homosexuality." Simon did acknowledge that existing "legal and social pressures . . . militat[ed] against frankness and thoroughness," but I raged at the time about his cavalier attempt to push me further out of a closet from which I had still only barely peeped. But of course Simon had a point. I *was* still holding homosexuality at arm's length, I *was* still resisting its embrace. Indeed, recognizing that he had a point may have been precisely what accounted for my anger at him.

Karl was supportive of my playwriting. He viewed it as further evidence that I was breaking out of my old patterns. One of my new plays, after all, entitled *Groups* (it never got more than a workshop production), essentially presented a flattering portrait of the therapeutic process, and most of the other plays had gay characters in them who conformed to the dreariest stereotypes—suggesting to Karl that, despite all my surface resistance, therapy was "taking" and I was turning my back on gay life.

But several things did not please him. Since the break-up with Cynthia, I had not done much dating and when I had, reported only the most perfunctory, distant feelings. Nor had I reached out much toward the women in group, except for Helen, and certainly not toward Judy, who had been designated my "practice" mate. The likely reason, Karl suggested, was that I still had not broken with my mother, as he had long since advised, and as Helen had dutifully seconded. She told me that she, too, had been "the unhealthy homosexual love object" of her mother and that she was forever grateful to Karl for helping her to break from that "smothering grasp."

Karl suggested a new tactic to me: taping, without my mother's knowledge, all my phone conversations with her. Playing them back to myself later, Karl was persuaded, would give me a clear picture of how destructive the relationship was.

I agreed to try it. And a sad experiment it was. Oh yes, playing over the tapes did allow me to hear more clearly than ever before how querulous her voice was ("If you ever, ever, ever have a bit of good news to tell me, I would appreciate that . . ."), how repetitive her litany of complaints, how tireless her efforts to instill guilt ("What do you think I do every night, dear? I have very little to do"). But what I heard more clearly still was how a once warm-hearted and generous woman had been reduced through disappointment, loneliness, and lack of options to railing, in genuine bewilderment, against everybody's incomprehensible resistance to letting her run their lives, to recounting their inadequacies in bitter detail, to pushing people away even as she desperately needed them to stay close.

On one of those infrequent days when my mother and I did meet for lunch, she shyly drew a small newspaper clipping out of her wallet. "Well, Mart," she said as she handed me the clipping to read, "I've finally made it." She had started a tiny resale shop in Larchmont, named "Treasures and Trifles," in order to earn some extra money and to use up some of her free time, and the local paper had written up its opening in no more than five lines. "Yep," she said, with a shy glow as I quietly put down the clipping, "I finally made it. I finally got my name in the paper."

That summed it up—for her and for generations of women; after all the buried ambitions, all the unexpressed longings, she was going to leave behind some miniscule mark, some record of having been here. I had trouble fighting back my tears. Perhaps I was only where I was in life—able to leave behind several marks—because she had settled for having her name in the paper only once. No, I was not going to put this woman out of my life, as Karl insisted. I stopped making the tape recordings.

Karl told me I was indulging the most banal kind of sentimentality—elaborating fake emotions of sympathy toward my mother in order to evade deeper feelings of dependency and rage. Worse still, he went on, I was parroting some of the limpest rhetoric of the new crop of feminists who had recently been making their voices heard. "They are a destructive bunch," he had once said in group. "Competing with men is not the path to happiness for women. That lies where it always has—in the life of the emotions and relationships, in family." Having felt immediately sympathetic to the new feminist movement—as always, I was instantly alive to every protest movement but my own—I fought Karl to a standstill on that one. He finally cut the argument off with a disdainful, "You're a Jewish prince defending Jewish princesses."

That summer Ray and I decided to rent a house together for the month of August. Karl was away on vacation and the group was temporarily recessed. I needed a break from the high-pitched intensity under which I'd been working for months (for my whole life?), and someone I knew offered us a house in Quoque, Long Island, for an affordable rent. Quoque, we heard, was like dozens of other upper-class enclaves, beautiful and smug, but different in containing within it a separate enclave of wealthy, closeted gay men rumored to be at least as sedate as the surrounding community.

Most of them were theater luminaries of one sort or another.

Our landlord was himself a well-known playwright, and he took the new boys in town around for introductions and inspection. The general verdict was that we were "too serious." I had made the gaff during one poolside chat of explaining at length why I had shifted political allegiance in the presidential election from Eugene McCarthy to Robert Kennedy. Kennedy, I argued—the reverberating silence around the pool driving me on—had been far more of an instinctive radical than McCarthy, far more identified on a gut level with the world's outcasts.

"Precisely the trouble," the pool's owner, a successful Broadway producer, said in a quietly acid voice. "My vote goes to Nixon." That more or less ended the conversation, though I did manage to slip in the news that I had also signed public endorsements for the presidential runs of Dick Gregory and Eldridge Cleaver. That very nearly made us personae non grata, though surface politeness never cracked.

*I*, however, nearly did. My mounting unhappiness had little to do with the smugness of the surroundings, and I didn't pretend otherwise to myself. The issues, I knew, went far deeper than an inability to win acceptance with the gay aristocracy.

The trouble superficially focused on my inability to sleep. As far back as my teens—come to think of it, coterminous with the arrival of awareness about my sexuality—I had had trouble both in getting to sleep and in staying asleep. I had gradually resorted to an occasional sleeping pill, but beginning sometime in the sixties the occasional had become habitual and I was taking a pill, usually Doriden, every night.

Just before leaving for Quoque, I had resolved to kick the pills, with Karl strongly supporting the resolution. "You're numbing your feelings," he had kept telling me. "You've got to remember that the effects of sedation carry over into the daylight hours as well." I knew he was right, but had long fought a rearguard action, defending with lucid and wrongheaded stubbornness "the *need* to numb feelings if they threaten to be overwhelming." Finally, in the spring of 1968, I bit the bullet and went cold turkey.

For a few days it seemed easy, and Karl congratulated me on the discovery that what in advance seems "overwhelming" in practice often isn't (I nervously expected him to draw an analogy with having sex with women, but he mercifully refrained). But within two weeks I was back to waging a nightly struggle that, after hours of tossing, I usually lost. When it came time to go to Quoque, I announced that I was putting the struggle on hold; being away, like being idle, was always difficult for me and I decided that a vacation was no time for further self-torture.

But even *with* sleeping pills I had been unable to sleep in Quoque, rarely putting together more than a fitful three to four hours on a given night. On top of that, I began to develop symptoms of colitis, which had me trouping back and forth to the bathroom. All of which made me an anxious, moody housemate, and Ray, patient but put-out, socialized more and more without me. I tried making one-day trips into New York to break the negative spell of Quoque, but a trip to Everard's, the gay bathhouse, or a tour of the bars left me feeling still more woebegone. Suddenly *nothing* seemed to be working in my life. I toted up my blessings and accomplishments—all the items that presumably made for happiness—and remained just as unhappy. What *was* wrong?

Two weeks into August, with my mood failing to lift, I wrote to Karl "as a way of trying to understand what's going on with me. . . . I don't know if I'm physically ill and therefore emotionally upset, or whether it's the other way around. I can't . . . seem to find a way out of the maze." Was I simply, I asked, "too goddamn sick to let anything enjoyable and new happen to me?" Having grasped on to the familiar strategy of self-accusation, I launched into a full-scale denunciation of myself: I was willful and demanding, insistent on being the center of attention, fearful of being controlled, ambivalent about wanting to socialize, too restless and competitive to be a good companion, essentially unfit for ordinary life, and certainly unsuited for sharing it with one other person. In other words, good for nothing except work.

Having beaten myself up, I promptly felt better, and the Quoque vacation simmered down from anguish to boredom. When therapy started up again early in September, Karl and I took a closer look at what had gone wrong over the summer. He cautioned me not to overemploy self-denunciation—it was easier to blame myself than to change myself, and doing the one could serve as a substitute for not doing the other. He suggested another tack entirely:

"You're much more comfortable with being told you're a shit

than with being told you're lovable. Because your father was so distant, you cannot believe to this day that an adult male could care about you—and indeed that's the main reason you pursue males sexually, and especially unavailable males like hustlers: it's a way of belatedly trying to get your father's love while simultaneously confirming that you can't. In line with all this, I think the time is overdue for looking at your relationship with me. A lot has accumulated that needs discussion."

Karl said all this in so kindly a spirit that I felt genuinely moved and was quite prepared to draw the conclusion before the discussion: he, an older man, *did* care about me. But at his urging, we had the discussion anyway. He asked me why—if indeed I believed he cared for me—I so often treated him as if he were my enemy.

"I didn't realize that I did."

"You're constantly challenging me in group, nit-picking over this or that, holding me fiercely to point. You exaggerate my every imperfection—and God knows I have them—in order to discredit me, not only in your own eyes but within the group as a whole. You have a generous spirit, but toward me you show no generosity at all."

"I had no idea."

"Perhaps because you preferred not to. You'd rather go on sniping—and preventing us from connecting on any deeper level. Why do you resent me so much?"

"Because you have an agenda for me," I blurted out to my own surprise. "You want to turn me into somebody I'm not."

"No," he said quietly, "I have no agenda, other than to make you more comfortable in the world."

"Precisely. The only way to be comfortable in *this* world is to be straight."

"I believe that's so. Do you believe differently?"

That stopped me cold. No, I did not believe differently. I had seen very little comfort in the gay world and had not been able to draw the conclusion (as had the nascent homophile movement) that the endemic unhappiness reflected not on the inherent nature of homosexuality, but on the persecutions leveled against homosexuals by a hostile, intolerant heterosexual majority.

Seeing my silent capitulation, Karl shifted gears.

"As you know," he went on, "I have long believed that you needed to disentangle from your mother before you could form an attachment with another woman. You have chosen not to do that. Very well. I will now approach the issue from the opposite end. I also strongly believe that you must develop a trusting relationship with an older man if you are ever to heal the scars of having grown up with a detached father. The older man in your life right now is, inescapably, me. The opportunity exists for you right here in therapy to resolve the key issues in your past history and to move beyond them. But you have to decide to take advantage of the opportunity. A lot of hard work is involved, and I cannot do it for you."

I felt frozen with ambivalence. Everything Karl had said made sense—and didn't make sense; seemed to reflect the truth of my history *and* Karl's need to get me to submit to his prescription for my future.

"Do you have some specific suggestion for resolving the tension between us?" I finally managed to sputter, knowing that when in a tight corner, a question always bought more time than a statement.

"In fact I do," Karl replied with a contented smile, as if I had made precisely the chess move he had anticipated. "I think we need to work together in some cooperative setting, outside of therapy, which will serve to build up mutual dependence and respect. I have in mind that jointly taught university seminar we talked about some time ago."

I could feel myself stiffen with distrust. And then, two seconds later, with self-distrust, as I instantly questioned whether my suspicion about Karl's motives wasn't precisely the reflexive skepticism about an older man's kindly interest in me that we had just finished analyzing.

I must have looked nonplussed because Karl jumped in with a reinforcing argument. "Given the problems you've been having with the powers-that-be at Princeton, I think it would be particularly valuable if you and I were to join forces in a struggle against them. That way you would start to see me as your sympathetic ally rather than as the hostile authority you now do."

That did seem appealing. The problems at Princeton that Karl referred to had recently reached a boil, and it seemed as if my efforts at educational reform were about to be stymied.

The antagonism to me, especially among the starchier, senior members of my department, had been growing steadily. It was a murky mix of resentment over my preference for living in New York rather than in their midst ("We provincials flourish in our little town," one of them had once acidly written me), disapproval at my writing for the theater and participating in general in the tawdry life of Tinseltown (so antithetical to a properly bookish life), and discomfort with my outspoken New Left sympathies as well, perhaps, as my continuing state of bachelorhood.

But the only complaint against me ever openly voiced concerned my unavailability for departmental chores because of my living in New York. That was indeed true, but had been an explicit part of the package Princeton had offered me some years earlier when persuading me not to leave for a job at a New York university. Nobody, they had said, regardless of whether he or she lived in New York or Princeton, could find the energy to hold up equally well all three aspects of a professor's prescribed duties—scholarship, teaching, and administration. And since I was clearly a devoted researcher and teacher, it could hardly be a legitimate source of grievance if I went light on administrative functions.

But within a few years they had apparently changed their minds, perhaps in part because I had been applying a New Left perspective to an analysis of the American university itself, drawing, in a series of essays, an unflattering portrait and calling for major renovations in the system.

The contemporary university, I had been arguing, had placed ever-increasing emphasis on its function as a research center and ever-decreasing emphasis on its function as a teaching institution. Worse still, many academics were placing their research in the service of the government (one of my colleagues in the history department was a known consultant for the CIA and the campus Institute for Defense Analysis was directly complicitous in the war effort). Academics had been seduced away from their function as disinterested searchers for truth and coopted as defenders of the status quo—delighted to be on the Great Stage even if it meant carrying a spear in some modern dress *Götterdämmerung*.

Encouraging that attitude, the university was giving preference to promoting scholars who made names as researchers—including weapons research—and discarding faculty who were primarily devoted to teaching. As a result, very little teaching worthy of the name was getting done in our universities, and the young—well aware that nobody much cared about helping them discover their interests and talents—had become increasingly alienated; they regarded the university as a degree mill they had to trudge through in order to win the needed career credentials.

But the newest generation of students—or at least the vocal New Left minority within it—was not prepared to accept this situation passively. Disgusted with what they viewed as the desiccated rituals of mere information gathering, of technical proficiency in manipulating ideas and things, the student radicals were calling for the kind of education that would help them grow in ways they valued most—in emotional honesty, in openness to a range of experience and to a variety of people, in democratic sympathy.

It was a view of the educational process with which I strongly agreed, and I had been working hard in my classes to create a climate that would foster it. But after several years of experimentation, there had come a point by 1968 when I felt that something more was needed beyond dispensing, as I had been doing, with the traditional control mechanisms of assignments, tests, and grades. All that had turned out to be—so deeply was the habit of deference to authority ingrained in all of us—a mere palliative.

I wanted to go further, wanted to find a way to explore the emotional transactions that always take place in a university seminar, always color the exchange of ideas that are the purported subject of discourse—and are always either ignored or evaded. In my view, the seminar setting acknowledged only one kind of interaction, the intellectual, and yet even that transaction could not really be understood and, as it were, "purified," until we learned to deal more honestly with everything else that was going on in the room as well—with how we were presenting ourselves, how we were reacting to others, what we were trying to conceal or reveal, to what extent words and ideas were being used as mere pretexts for re-enacting some kind of buried psychic script not fully conscious in the individual. These non-

verbal transactions were always present, and if we could find a
way to explore them, I felt the process of real education—of
self-discovery—would be immeasurably advanced.

This is where Karl came in. I had thought of two ways to
heighten awareness of the hidden levels of exchange present in
a seminar setting, both informed by my own experiences in
therapy. The first was long-range: to see to it in the future that
all graduate students, regardless of their field of specialty, got
some training in group dynamics so that when their turn came
to lead discussions they would have more awareness of the many
kinds of interplay at work.

Pending that transformation—for nothing less would be required—of doctoral training, I proposed a pilot study to do some
initial explorations of the group dynamics at work in a single
seminar. As a professor of history, I made no claims to having
the insight and skills necessary to conduct that experiment and
therefore wanted to take on a therapist—a specialist, as it were,
in group dynamics—as co-leader of the group.

I had shared all this with Karl as I was working it out, and
now, in 1968, just as I was feeling ready to make a formal
proposal for such a seminar to the history department, Karl
was suggesting that *he* be the therapist to co-lead it. Accepting
his analysis that such an experiment would be good for me, for
us and for the future work of bridging the two worlds of psychotherapy and education, I agreed. Though I was willing to
donate my own time without getting teaching credit or salary,
Karl insisted on the importance of having official university
sanction for the undertaking, including an appointment, however temporary, and a salary, however minimal, for himself.

# 10

# EXPERIMENT IN EDUCATION

W HEN I PRESENTED MY proposal to the history department, there was immediate opposition. An issue had arisen that, controversial in itself, could also conveniently serve as a lightning rod for the assorted antagonisms that had developed toward me over the past few years. In an initial vote, the executive committee of the department turned the proposal down by two to one. But in doing so they cited such trivial, surface objections (mostly relating to scheduling issues) that I easily met them and was able quickly to re-submit the request with all their ostensible objections resolved.

The executive committee then decided that it could not sanction a course that might possibly infringe on the area of "mental health" without first consulting with the head of the Princeton Health Department. To their apparent surprise, he had an entirely favorable reaction to my proposal: "It's wonderful whenever members of the faculty recognize that education is more than the assimilation of information." When the department then pressed him for an opinion of Karl's credentials, his verdict was once again favorable. Well, then, what about the fact that he was Duberman's own therapist? I answered that one myself, arguing that that would in fact prove an asset: Karl and I would not—as would any other combination of professor and group specialist—have to waste a lot of time learning each other's verbal habits and nonverbal signals. Having run out of surface objections and being unwilling to state its underlying ones, the department on the second go-round voted its approval. It also recommended that Karl be appointed a senior research associate for a single term at the negligible (but to Karl symbolically satisfying) salary of fifteen hundred dollars.

But the battle was not over. R. R. Palmer, the noted historian, was then dean of the faculty, and he promptly announced to the undergraduate paper, the *Princetonian* (which had taken up the controversy with glee and at length), that he disagreed "radically with Duberman's own philosophy," calling my views on education "the ultimate flower of some form of Romanticism." I knew Palmer as a good guy with strong anti-authoritarian views of his own and, puzzled at his opposition, tried to tease him out of it. I sent him a flower with a note attached to it that read, "How right you were! I made a careful search today of the garden, and there it was—trying to hide beneath some ordinary ivy! The eyes seem to be particularly wild. I should add, though, that its ultimateness is not certain. Next to it was growing a monstrous bud, which I simply could not uproot. Rest assured that I shall keep it under constant surveillance."

Palmer was not amused. He thanked me for my "ingenious communication"—and promptly vetoed the proposal on what he called "financial and pedagogical grounds." Refusing to accept defeat, I asked President Goheen for the chance to explain the rationale behind the course directly to him, but he refused to see me, announcing that "he could not go against his dean." The *Princetonian* then joined the fray, interviewing all the parties concerned, and writing indignant editorials strongly championing my side of the dispute.

One of those interviewed stated openly that he had objected to the proposal because the therapist suggested for it had been Duberman's own—thereby publicly revealing that I was in therapy. That didn't much bother me, since the reason for my being in therapy was nowhere alluded to or, probably, known. But the revelation raised an indignant cry. Princeton prided itself on its good manners, and to reveal that a Faculty Member (no less!) had sought Professional Help seemed to many at the university beyond the pale. Even some of my antagonists offered apologies for so "unforgiveable a breach."

The thunderous *Princetonian* editorials on my behalf emphasized that the ostensible "financial and pedagogical" reasons cited for vetoing my proposal were transparent blinds for antagonism to me personally and to any experiment that might prove genuinely radical. After all, the editorialists argued, the total financial cost of fifteen hundred dollars was in fact a great bargain, and as for the pedagogical argument that the experiment would not be valuable because it couldn't be easily replicated, that objection in fact applied to any pilot study of a pioneering nature.

I myself burnt whatever bridges may have remained by telling the *Princetonian* that in my view a university administration claiming to be deeply concerned with education had reacted with almost knee-jerk orthodoxy to a proposal designed to finding out more about the actual processes of teaching and learning. The more radical the proposal, I suggested, the more likely it was to be vetoed. Princeton's unspoken motto, I said, "seems much like that of the society at large: 'we fully sanction experimentation (dissent) so long as it does not really threaten to change anything.'"

Since I was a tenured full professor, I could not be forced from the university, but the powers-that-be did their best to encourage my resignation over the next two years with a surfeit of bad mouths and cold shoulders and by giving me raises so miniscule that they could only be regarded as invitations to leave. By the end of 1969 I had the lowest salary one could have at the full professor level, a full five thousand dollars off the department's *average* for full professors—though I had published much more than the average. I began to put out feelers to other universities, but my actual resignation from Princeton, replete with one final, very public blowup, would not happen until 1972.

I had kept Karl posted on each turn of events, and he had responded with agitated absorption, phoning me at home to suggest strategy, exhorting me to continue the good fight. Neither of us ever considered giving up the idea of doing the course. After Princeton rejected it, I first tried offering it to Rutgers, hoping that their historic rivalry with Princeton would make them jump at the chance. But what counted for more, it turned out, was their historic fear of Princeton—fear of "jeopardizing good relations," as one member of the Rutgers history department confidentially told me. I sent R. R. Palmer my acid congratulations: "Big Brother's arm has a long reach. . . . We can now all go back to planting more ivy on the walls."

Blocked at Rutgers, I then offered the course to Bob Cross, the new president of Hunter College, whom I knew slightly. He sounded enthusiastic and said he would get back to me, which I suspected meant another brushoff. But to my surprise, an okay quickly followed, and our joint experimental course on "The History of Radical Protest in America" was slotted for the spring term of 1969.

In preparation, Karl suggested a series of phone conferences to hone our plans. We had decided early on what our general functions would be in the seminar: I would play the traditional professor's role of focusing the students on the subject matter, and Karl would be the "process man" interrupting discussion in order to clear up any problems that arose in communication. We both knew in advance—and had so warned Hunter—that less time than usual would be spent in the seminar on, say, socialism, but our hope was that with communication improved, discussion would be more concentrated and authentic than was ordinarily the case. Our aim was to create a promising hybrid: traditional academic exchange in an intimate setting that put a premium on openness and honesty rather than on the usual classroom staples of fear, concealment, and game playing.

Karl and I taped all our phone conversations about the seminar, and in the very first one he pressed me to acknowledge formally that "without design," we had "gotten into a state of supervision." I was puzzled at that but readily agreed to say for the record that we had inadvertently entered "a supervisory relationship, one that largely took place on a nonverbal level, because I identified with the way you led a group and wanted to lead my groups in a similar way." Karl needed such a statement from me, I presumed, for future protection should his psychoanalytic colleagues take him to task for our unorthodox collaboration or accuse him of exploiting a patient's academic credentials in order to augment his own.

That done, we got on to substance.

"You don't know it yet," Karl began, "but you and I are going to write a book together some day about educational theory that will transform how the classroom is viewed and structured."

I thought that a bit grandiose as a way to start, but chalked it up to overenthusiasm, which I certainly shared.

"A credo has struck me," Karl went on, "a credo that I feel is so important that I've written it out. I want to share it with you and get your feedback on it."

"Fine."

"A credo of the educative process: the objective of pioneer multidimensional, multiphasic . . ."

I felt myself instantly tuning out. Big words always embarrass me—I see them as an alarming symptom of lack of education and confidence. Karl, as someone foreign-born, had often confessed uneasiness when trying to express complicated thoughts in English. But pomposity seemed a poor solution for discomfort.

As he rambled on—something about "five interlayered states of being"—I felt impaled: annoyed at the pretentious gobbledygook, yet afraid to challenge it as such. (Would Karl angrily walk out on the experiment? on my therapy?) I tried to switch the conversation to something concrete, quite willing to indulge a little self-criticism in order to avoid criticizing him: "Am I right to think that my problem with authority might get us into trouble as we attempt to co-lead the seminar? Am I likely to resent not having all the controls in my own hand?"

Karl reacted peremptorily: "In bringing up your psychopathy you are trying to relate to me as your therapist rather than as your co-worker. That is not appropriate to this project. Let us stay loyal to the matter at hand."

Namely, his theories of education—of "multilayered, multiphasic human beings operating in a nonfragmented state." After enduring some twenty minutes of this, speaking only in order to interject some dutiful cue ("I'm not sure I fully understood that last bit. . . . Would you try explaining that another way . . ."), I suddenly heard Karl say, "It is appropriate for you to respond."

At which point I returned to the issue of my "authority problem." Karl confirmed that it had indeed been severe, requiring protracted clinical attention. But he felt the problem, thanks to therapy, was now much reduced, and he foresaw far more trouble in the seminar from what he called my "hypersensitivity" to his "failings," and particularly to his tendency toward verbosity. This sounded as close to a confession of weakness as I had ever heard from Karl, and feeling idiotically grateful (wow, gee, you mean all those run-ins we've had in the past weren't *entirely* my fault?!), I hastily reassured him that I would be on my guard on both counts. He in turn complimented me on my "acumen"—"you have learned much from being a patient."

We interviewed every student who expressed interest in the seminar before granting permission to sign up for it; Karl felt it was essential to increase the odds of the seminar's success by screening out those with "obvious" pathology. On his recommendation, we ultimately turned down two applicants. One was a young woman Karl decided was "overly aggressive and castrative." The other was a young man who had read most of my writings and during the interview "stared" at me and made deferential comments; Karl decided he was "definitely homosexual" and all too likely to "fall" for me.

The seminar began in February 1969, and the first two sessions went pretty much as we had planned. Karl had earlier urged the importance of establishing from the outset that the primary focus of the course was academic and that I was its primary leader, with Karl presented as an adjunct who was there only to help us handle the secondary matter of process. And in the beginning Karl did stay almost entirely in the background, waiting until the second session to say anything at all and then only making a few marginal comments on the order of "the seminar has gotten away from Martin's initial question" or "Joan has been asked a question but not been given the chance to answer it."

But during the third session, "a little personal pathology" (as Karl later labeled it) arose. Karl had taken a more active role in the discussion than previously, at one point drawing a helpful clinical distinction between "healthy aggression" and "hostility" (we had been talking about whether those who participated in protest movements shared common personality traits). One of the students said he was so impressed with Karl's definitions that he wanted to write them down. "Well then, why don't you?

Nobody's stopping you," I said benignly, though aware, as I acknowledged privately to Karl later, that I was feeling irritably jealous that he had gotten the first full compliment. When I confessed my envy, Karl nodded his head sadly: "Yes, I'm afraid your old authority problem *is* kicking up—along with your pathological competitiveness."

Duly chastised, I vowed to do better. But as I tightened up on my controls, Karl's own seemed to weaken. In the notes I wrote up following each session, I confessed my growing fear that Karl was failing to do the agreed-upon process work and was instead simply joining subject-matter discussions. When, for example, we debated whether the Constitution had been a betrayal or an extension of the American Revolution, Karl enthusiastically leaped in with his own opinion—and did nothing to help untangle communication on the subject among the students themselves.

I felt that our original objectives for the experiment were being forgotten, and finally, midway into the course, I talked to Karl directly about my misgivings. At first he hedged. True, he said, he had not done much process work *in the way* we had anticipated, but he had come to feel that a more honest climate could best be established by presenting his own person authentically—which meant "being who he was" in every sense, including being a thinking human being who had opinions on the matters under discussion.

When I countered that that was the function of any good teacher and that the role we had originally planned for *him* was that of a specialist in group communication, he acknowledged that by those lights he had been lax. By way of extenuation, he explained that he had simply gotten carried away by his own interest in the material, and that having always to maintain a neutral posture had proved a more difficult assignment than he had anticipated. He said he would do his best to return to his original mission. That came as a surprise and relief—since Karl had rarely shown any comparable openness to criticism during group therapy sessions. It made me feel optimistic that we might yet get the seminar back on track.

Intermittently we did, but overall Karl did very little of the process work originally intended, and when the course ended I felt distinctly dissatisfied with the results. In the final meeting of the seminar, I shared some of my disappointment. I didn't feel, I said, that we had done enough with the actual subject matter of the course. The "encounter group" climate had been designed to facilitate more honest intellectual debate on the history of American radicalism, but in fact the exchange of ideas had been minimal.

Perhaps taking this as criticism of the way he had handled the encounter aspects of the seminar (though that wasn't my conscious intent), Karl, with considerable heat, challenged my interpretation down the line. More content work had gotten done than I realized, he insisted; as always, he told the class, "Martin is applying perfectionist standards." To the extent that that goal *had* been compromised, he added, some of my own psychic mechanisms were primarily to blame. Throughout, he said, I had been manipulative, had indirectly exerted control over the choice of topics and the course of discussion even while theoretically rejecting authoritarianism in the classroom.

The ferocity of Karl's indictment startled me. I knew there was some truth to it, but only some. The fullness of the attack felt like a betrayal—and a copout as well. I thought Karl was exploiting his intimate knowledge of my psyche for secondary gain, using my inadequacies as an excuse for not dealing with his own. I felt bruised and distrustful. And for all I know Karl did too, since, if anything, he had invested even higher hopes in the seminar than I had, seeing it as a personal entrée into academia.

The negative effect on our relationship was immediate. I felt far more wary than before of Karl's objectivity and, during group therapy sessions, now tended to hear his comments not as helpful interventions but as self-serving putdowns—the master patronizing his flunkies. He, in turn, mostly acted as if I wasn't there, an expression of pained distress on his face whenever he deigned to talk directly to me. An unexpected conflagration between me and fellow group member Stan finally brought this caldron of resentment to a boil.

The trouble started between Stan and Nelson. The self-deprecating Nelson arrived in group one night with head swathed in a pressure bandage. He assured us it looked worse than it was: the doctor had removed a growth that they thought might have been malignant but had turned out not to be. Stan tauntingly asked him why he felt so sure and then, a steely evenness to his voice, said, "I get a different message from you, Nelson. The message I get is that you're cancerous. You're dying." The quiet savagery of that astonished the rest of us, but Nelson handled it calmly, saying something about Stan obviously being in a bad mood.

But Dick couldn't contain himself. "You really are a shit," he said to Stan.

"You mean I'm not a *nice* boy, like you," Stan shot back, "always acting the way you're supposed to. We all know that's the only reason you gave up sucking cock—because you were *supposed* to."

I must have gasped audibly because Helen looked at me in alarm and quickly moved to squelch Stan through diplomacy.

"You know, Stan," she said, "it doesn't diminish you to say something nice about somebody once in a while. You might find it makes you feel better about yourself."

Stan was not buying. "Oh really, Momsie? You don't seem to get it. I'm not interested in winning any merit badges in here. I'm interested in telling the truth, which the rest of you pansies can't stand hearing."

By now my head had stopped pounding and it felt urgently important that I jump in to defend Dick.

"You *think* you tell the truth, Stan, but all I ever hear is an angry little boy flailing out in all directions."

"Thank you, Miss Muffet, for that profound insight," Stan said with a smirk.

"Miss Muffet?" I looked over at Karl, as if to say, "Don't you think it's time you stepped in and stopped this?" but he look disinterestedly blank.

"Yeah, Miss Muffet," Stan reiterated. "At least Dick *stopped* sucking cock. You can't even manage that feat."

I tried to let that go by. "You don't know you're alive, Stan," I said feebly, "unless you're in combat."

"Beats hell out of words, which is your specialty," Stan countered.

"How come you never shut up, if you hate words so much?" Dick piped in.

"Hey, baby," Stan smiled back, suggestively stroking his genitals, "why don't you lick my private parts, like you want to?"

Dick's features knotted up, as if he might cry. "You don't have any private parts," he said quietly.

"What do you think I piss out of, baby?"

"Out of your mouth," I interjected.

Stan's face suddenly darkened as he whirled toward me.

"Oh, Miss Muffet's back, is she?" He pointed to his crotch. "You want this all for yourself, dontcha? You don't want Dickie boy to get any of it."

"You know what I think, Stan"—I was trying hard for a disdainful tone to offset the rage I was feeling—"I think the next time you feel like a good shit, you ought to try a toilet."

Stan came right back at me: "*Is* there a men's room in this place? It can't get much use."

I was determined to top him. "You know what else I think, Stan?" I said, already regretting the cheap shot, "I think it's *you* who wants to suck cock."

He leaped out of his chair and in a flash was at my throat. Before I could do anything, he dragged me to my feet and landed such a powerful blow to the side of my head that I careened to the other side of the room. Then he was on top of me, pummeling me with his fists. Why isn't anybody stopping him? I thought, unable myself to ward off the fury of his blows. Why in the hell isn't somebody stopping him? His rage finally spent, Stan slowly got up and, adjusting his clothes, went back to his seat. I put my hand up to my nose. It was covered with blood when I drew it away.

"You'd better go into the bathroom and clean up," Karl said. His voice was puzzlingly dispassionate.

I struggled into the bathroom, washed the blood off, sobbing my eyes out. God, what madness! I kept thinking, comforted by the certainty that when I got back in the other room, the others would give Stan the tongue-lashing he deserved—indeed, they probably already were—and would probably even demand that he be kicked out of the group.

Not at all. The room was eerily silent as I sat back down in my chair. "Well Martin," Karl finally said, "I guess you got what you've been asking for all along."

I could hardly believe what I was hearing, could hardly believe that blame for Stan's violence was being placed at my doorstep. "Yes," Karl went on, "what happened here today was indeed your doing; Stan pulled the trigger, but you handed him the gun. Mind you, I'm not condoning violence, and God knows Stan has to learn to keep a rein on his temper. But you, after all, provoked it. You bloodied him with words, and then he, in self-defense, finally bloodied you with his fists. We all use what weapons we have. I've warned you and warned you about how you use words as a weapon. Now the words have finally blown up in your face. Maybe you'll learn from this experience. I certainly hope so."

Nobody else said anything. Dick looked uncomfortable and Helen smiled wanly at me, but everyone else stared either at the walls or at their feet. Karl had spoken. His word was law. That was the way therapy worked—or Karl's version of it. Was it possible Karl was right? *Had* I provoked Stan? *Was* I the guilty party? At the end of the session, after everyone had had time to recover their composure, Helen said she wanted to add a few words to what Karl had said. She turned a loving look toward me:

"Martin, you know how much I care about you, don't you?"

"Yes, I do."

"Then maybe you'll be willing to hear me. *Listen* to what Karl is saying to you. Stop defying him and *listen to him.* He, too, wants only the best for you, though I know that's hard for you to see. But it's *your* problem, Martin, not Karl's. Your problem with authority. It keeps you from getting on the side of your own health; it keeps you from becoming a full adult. I'm begging you, Martin, stop the defiance. Let tonight be a turning point for you."

I melted at the warmth of her words—even as my mind continued to shout defiance. Could someone who cared about me as much as Helen obviously did misperceive what was best for me? Was love different from understanding? I didn't know. I couldn't think anyway. All I wanted was for the session to end. I wanted to go home and comfort myself—because deep down I believed, bitterly believed, that only I really knew how to do that, really understood what I needed. Was that merely the loner speaking, or was it the self-medicating sage? I didn't know that either. I mumbled thanks to Helen and told her I would carefully consider what she had said.

And I did—for weeks. But what I thought about more than anything else was Stan's remark to Dick: "The only reason you gave up sucking cock was because you were *supposed* to." What did that mean? Did Stan and the others who had been in the group before me know something I didn't? Had Dick changed his behavior but not his desire—or does the one gradually transform the other, so that what we do turns into what we want to do? I brought those questions back to the group, heart in my mouth, knowing they were questions about my life as much as Dick's.

When I'd finished asking them, Dick looked in Karl's direction. Karl nodded permission, Dick raised his eyebrows in momentary surprise, then sighed deeply.

"I was afraid it might affect your therapy if I talked about any of this earlier," he began hesitantly, "and Karl agreed with me. However, the time has apparently come . . ." He swallowed his own voice in nervousness.

"It's all right, Dick," Karl chimed in reassuringly. "There's no need to go into all the details. Just give Martin the general outline."

Dick sighed again and went on. "It's like this," he said. "The agreement I made with myself was that I would never *look* for homosexual contact. But if I'm walking down the street, say, and my eyes meet another man's—well, I chalk that up to fate and let myself go with him."

I needed to be sure I had heard right: "So you *haven't* given up having sex with other men?"

"That's what I just said."

"But I thought you were 'cured'—Karl said you had been cured."

Karl jumped in. "Don't put words in my mouth, Martin," he said, a decided edge to his voice. "What I *said* was that in therapy I had brought Dick—and indeed every other homosexual man who has sought my help—to the point where he could *choose* for himself whether he wanted to live a gay life or a straight life. For the first time, Dick had options, he could make a real choice—and what he chose was heterosexuality."

Dick confirmed that with a vigorous nod of his head.

"I still don't understand," I said, feigning more confusion

than I felt, determined to extract as much information as possible. "Had you always had sex with women as well as men, or did that develop during therapy?"

"I found a woman I was able to have intercourse with," Dick said quietly, "and I married her."

"Did you love her?"

"I've grown to love her—very much."

I was in relentless pursuit. "Do the two of you still have sex?"

Dick visibly blanched. "Once in a while," he said sheepishly.

"Once a week? Once a year?"

Karl broke in angrily. "That will do, Martin. You have all the information you need, short of voyeurism. The rest is Dick's business—Dick's and his therapist's."

But I was in no mood to be deterred. "I just need to get this straight," I went on. "In other words, your lust still goes in the same direction it always did—toward men."

Karl now took over for Dick. "Only an adolescent," he said, giving me a mordant look, "would place more emphasis on lust than on love. Dick developed an adult's priorities in therapy, and he acted on them."

I was not going to be vanquished by a flanking movement. "Of course love is more important than lust," I conceded. "But maybe Dick—if given half a chance—could have fallen in love with a man. That way he would have gotten it all in one package."

"Why don't you ask Dick if he's sorry he made the choices he did? Or don't you want to hear that answer?"

Dick didn't wait to be asked. "Martin," he said, giving me an avuncular smile, "you and I both know that homosexual love just doesn't work. God knows we both spent enough years looking for it. It doesn't exist between two men. It *is* lust, and when lust fades, as it always must, there's nothing left to live on."

That threw me a little. "I don't buy that," I said feebly, while frantically ransacking the file cards in my mind to see if I could come up with a relationship of my own, or even a friend's, that I could legitimately present as an example. Panicking, I drew a complete blank, so shaken I didn't even remember my five years with Larry until later that night when I was home and had calmed down. Only then could I begin to penetrate the smug circularity of Dick and Karl's argument: I *had* found love—

homosexual love—at some points in my life. But it hadn't been easy, trained as I and as almost all other gay people had been to distrust our own deepest emotions, to devalue and compulsively discard our own most precious relationships.

Was a comparison between the quality of my relationship with Larry and Dick's with his wife valid? How did I know? How did one measure such things, and who was qualified to do the measuring? Clearly Karl, and the rest of the psychiatric fraternity, felt confident that they were qualified. But were they?

It was all beginning to unravel . . .

# 11

---

# STONEWALL
# AND AFTER

B Y THE LATE SIXTIES the consensus about homosexuality as "disease" was coming apart in the culture as well as in my head. When, in April 1968, Columbia University Medical School sponsored a forum on homosexuality but refused to put any homosexuals on the panel, the newly formed gay student alliance at Columbia picketed the event and declared that it was now time for the discussion of homosexuality to be "pulled out of the morass of psychiatry, 'abnormality' and 'emotional disturbance' . . . and placed into its proper setting as a sociological problem of deeply entrenched prejudice and discrimination against a minority group."[21]

The same issues came up two months later at the American Medical Association's annual meeting in San Francisco. Prior to the event, the editor of the San Francisco Medical Society *Bulletin* had warned arriving doctors "to be on guard against brigades of harlots and homosexuals." And act up the homosexuals did when Charles Socarides, who was emerging as the most influential psychiatric spokesman for the disease theory, took the podium to lecture the delegates on the subject. Socarides spoke of homosexuality as "a dread dysfunction, malignant in character, which has risen to epidemic proportions," and he called on the federal government to establish centers for the "cure" of these dangerous creatures.

Homophile protestors leafleted the convention and called a well-attended press conference. They denounced Socarides's "final solution," demanded that those who opposed the pathological view be represented at future discussions of homosexuality, and urged the medical establishment to purge its research of the antihomosexual bias that had for so long distorted its findings. The editors of *Psychiatric Opinion*, in an unprecedented move that marked another crack in the medical consensus, opened its columns to the president of the New York Mattachine Society for a reply to Socarides which emphasized the distorting role that bias—rather than a particular family configuration (binding mother/absent father)—played in the psychosexual development of the individual gay person.

In that same year of 1968, *The Advocate*, a gay Los Angeles paper, appeared on the stands, and the first congregation of the gay Metropolitan Community Church was formed. Then in 1969 the National Institute of Mental Health's Task Force on Homosexuality, appointed two years earlier and chaired by Evelyn Hooker, made its final report. There was no such thing, the task force said, as a single homosexual personality or lifestyle; gay Americans existed in all classes, regions of the country, ethnic, racial, and religious groupings, and rarely fit the myths and stereotypes invented about them.

But the NIMH report, for all its liberating perspectives, was not yet liberationist. Though it called for an end to discriminatory employment practices and did dissent from the disease model, it did not endorse a gay sexual orientation as a viable choice, urging instead that "an intensive effort" be made to understand the factors involved in producing a homosexual orientation *so that* "effective primary prevention" could be undertaken. In other words, the alternative the NIMH report offered to the pathological view of homosexuality was not a celebration of gay life but rather yet another—this time a "liberal"—cure for it.

The Columbia and AMA protests aside, the organized homophile movement of the late sixties did not find confrontational politics or radical analyses of the inequities of American life congenial. On the contrary, the movement was mostly unsympathetic to the militant impulses and perspectives of the antiwar and civil rights struggles in these years. Gay spokespeople continued to look to the courts for amelioration and to stress the importance of educating and forming alliances with the established nongay experts on gay life, whether in medicine, religion, or law. When, for example, radical lesbian-feminists like Rita Laporte and Barbara Grier tried in 1968 to reorient the politics of Daughters of Bilitis and its publication, the *Ladder*, the old-timers resisted with such force that in the end both DOB as a national organization and the *Ladder* were not converted but destroyed.

Too conservative to join forces with the militant protests of the day, the fledgling homophile movement, ironically, was too radical to appeal to most gay people. To the minimal extent that its existence was even known, it was considered dangerously visible. Identifying to any extent with a gay organization, however moderate, meant risking exposure. Perhaps more threatening still, it meant a more positive redefinition of self that in these years was beyond the psychic resources of most gay people, brainwashed as they had been by decades of negative conditioning. As is often the case, less psychic turmoil is involved in continuing to live with a derisive self-image to which one has long since accommodated, than in undergoing the seismic personality transformations that a more estimable view would entail.

That was certainly my own case. I was less afraid of exposure (I was, after all, exposing myself in my plays) than of giving up a familiar way of thinking about myself. I was in the additionally anomalous position of being strongly identified with the radical spirit and causes of the late sixties—and therefore to the left of the organized homophile movement—while simultaneously wedded to a reactionary view of my own being—and therefore to the right of the homophile movement, with its somewhat more affirming descriptions of gay life. But all this is retrospective. At the time, I wasn't ambivalent—merely oblivious.

And that was true of most gay people. Few had ever heard of Mattachine or DOB, or had heard enough to form an opinion. Of the few who had, negative reactions flowed from timidity and self-hate on the one hand and from disdain on the other— (as was the case with young radicals who were gay but could not abide conservative homophile politics). By mid-1969 homophile organizations still had only a tiny constituency—perhaps five thousand members nationally, with only a few hundred publicly willing to identify themselves as gay.

And then came Stonewall. On the night of June 27, 1969, the New York City police conducted one of their routine raids on a popular Greenwich Village gay bar, the Stonewall Inn. Only it proved not to be routine. After the police had loaded arrested patrons into a paddy wagon, the crowd that had gathered in front of Stonewall responded with catcalls—and then suddenly exploded, hurling bottles at the officers, using an uprooted parking meter as a battering ram, blockading some of the police inside the bar, and then torching it. Reinforcements rescued the officers, but the rioting was renewed for four nights running, with street people and "flame" queens (those in partial drag)—long habituated to defiance, and with no privileges left to lose—in the vanguard, playing a crucial role that the later gay movement has sometimes been reluctant to acknowledge and celebrate.

The Stonewall Inn had become, in the late sixties, my own bar of choice. I loved its cruisy, non-vanilla mix of people, its steamy dancing, and, not least, its proximity to where I lived. Like other patrons, I had taken in stride the occasional raids. I can recall at least two evenings when the light signals suddenly went on (announcing the arrival of somebody suspect), dancing and touching of any kind instantly stopped, and the police stalked arrogantly through, glaring from side to side, demanding IDs, terrifying those not having them with threats of arrest. I remember hearing about another night, when a police raid bagged an illegal alien who, arrested and brought in to the station, threw himself in despair from a window, landing, impaled, on a spiked iron fence below. They worked for hours sawing the metal off the fence, lifting the young man's flesh off the metal. Somehow he survived.

Though I went to Stonewall at least once a week, I was not there on that momentous night of June 27. I've often wondered what I would have done if I had actually been on the premises. I suspect I would have cowered, would have tried to be inconspicuous and deferential, hung back on the fringe of the crowd—or run like hell away from it. One never knows, of course; sometimes the surging energy of the moment can bring an unexpected response, elicit a bravery not otherwise on tap. But what makes me pretty certain I would not have joined the protestors that night is the fact that for quite a while thereafter I did not join the movement that the protest inaugurated.

And almost immediately after the Stonewall riot, a movement did emerge, substantially different from the one that had preceded it. Within a matter of weeks, the Gay Liberation Front had been formed in New York with conscious links to the style and politics of the New Left, and within the year dozens of such groups had emerged nationally on campuses and in the cities. The young gay radicals who flocked to the liberationist banner took it to rallies in support of those they viewed as their natural allies—feminists, farm workers, and Black Panthers. And gay liberationist contingents protested widely against American involvement in Southeast Asia, turning out in especially large numbers for the November 1969 moratorium weekend in Washington, D.C.

I, too, joined the moratorium march of protest—but not under the gay liberationist banner. I thought the day glorious—but because it represented an important shift in public opinion on the war in Vietnam, not because it marked a milestone in the efforts of a newly radical gay movement to broaden its alliances. It was not from timidity that I hung back, for I had little trouble putting myself on the line for causes with which I did identify. In the closing months of 1969 I spoke out forcefully at a campus rally calling on Princeton to disband its government-affiliated Institute of Defense Analysis, enthusiastically joined in forming a Radical Historians Caucus within the American Historical Association, and at the annual convention of the AHA in December 1969 publicly denounced the conservatism of the profession.

I could identify with every cause gay liberationists were now championing—except the cause of gay liberation itself. I could applaud the New Left analysis of American life as exclusionary and oppressive—but could not broaden that analysis to encompass the oppression of a sexual minority. I had long spoken out against the validity of traditional authority—but could not understand how gay liberationists, in opposition to the traditional authority of psychiatry, could affirm their sexual preference as merely an alternate, not a lesser form of erotic expression. I deeply resented the continuing bar raids and street arrests of gay men in New York, but when gay militants now reacted to such episodes with angry confrontational protests—the same direct action tactics I loudly applauded when employed by blacks—I felt merely perplexed.

And when, in June 1970, the newly invigorated gay movement put some five thousand men and women in the streets to march in commemoration of the first anniversary of the Stonewall riot, I remained in my apartment, barricaded by books, deeply immersed in finishing my history of the cultural revolutionaries of Black Mountain College. The following year, viewing the second Gay Pride parade from the sidewalk, I disdainfully characterized it in my diary as "cripples on yet another march to a faith healing shrine."

It *was* the cultural revolution that appealed to me more strongly than any other strand in the New Left mosaic, even if I could not see that gay liberation was a central expression of that revolution. I got into long arguments with left-wing colleagues about the viability of the youth culture, defending it vehemently against their scornful insistence that it was at worst a bourgeois, anti-intellectual diversion that made for political impotence, or at best harmless child's play, irrelevant to the serious business of social reconstruction. To me, the irreverent new youth culture held out greater promise for structural change than either electoral politics or Marxist analysis. As a member of the "in-between" generation, I had never been as attracted to ideology as had the Marxist generation preceding mine, nor as committed to activist politics as the SNCC/SDS generation that had followed. I had trouble working up enthusiasm over theory, Marxist or otherwise, and equal trouble feeling in my gut that—as SDS was currently arguing—our system was so utterly rotted as to warrant total assault.

Attracted as I felt to the new youth culture, I readily conceded that its style was inchoate, that some of its infatuations, like scientology and astrology, were regressive, and that it might never develop into anything distinctive enough to become an alternative value system. Further, I could certainly agree that for the vast majority of people in the world, the older left-wing vision of freedom from material want was still so distantly utopian that perhaps only a citizen of the United States could be provincial enough to doubt its continuing centrality—or arrogant enough to suggest that a more encompassing transformation claimed our primary attention.

Yet I did strongly believe that the youth culture's central preoccupation with the world of the senses and the emotions, its emphasis on participation and sharing, on the spontaneous and casual, the open-hearted and experimental, could prove a potent solvent for our society's hitherto dominant and constricting values of rationalism, puritanism, and materialism. Now and then, when defending the new culture, I would specifically mention bisexuality as one among many valuable elements in its mix—as if to acknowledge, however peripherally, that I *had* a vested interest in supporting it. I never fully articulated that interest, either publicly or to myself, but at least subliminally I sensed that a new set of values had been unleashed that could generate an encompassing appreciation of differentness as something positive, as deserving special respect.

Even aside from my indifference to gay liberation, there were limits to my developing radicalism—peculiarly American limits. I was fairly oblivious to issues relating to class structure and indeed was woefully ignorant of economics in general. Nor was I much more sophisticated about social and ethnic stratifications. My understanding and empathy alike went primarily toward individuals, my interest concentrated on the world of *personal* idiosyncrasy, motive, struggle. It was no accident that I had migrated to writing biography and plays.

And by 1969, I was drawing further into the world of the theater, as both playwright and critic. In the latter capacity, I agreed to do a monthly theater column for Huntington Hartford's new *Show* magazine, which didn't last long, and continued as well to write on theater for *Partisan Review* (not surprisingly, I singled out the work of Joe Chaikin's Open Theater, that prime exemplar of the new culture, for special praise). As a playwright, I had a burst of activity, though I was working against the grain of an academic training that had cramped my inventive powers and trained me *not* to cultivate the subjective voice.

During the summer of 1969 I completed *Payments*, my play about the world of gay hustling based on my earlier involvement with Jim. But I had trouble peddling the script. One producer, a closeted gay man, wrote my agent that *Payments* was "the most fascinating play" he had ever read—but said he wanted "nothing to do with it," indeed felt it should not be staged, that I should "voluntarily retire it." In a similar vein, one of the heads of the Actors Studio took my agent aside and lectured her on her responsibility to "bury" the play—"if it was ever performed, Duberman would be destroyed." Another prominent producer declared the writing "absolutely brilliant" but said he had "some general misgivings about the script succeeding in today's market" and declined to option it. The well-known producer Lee Guber was blunt: "I just don't like the material. Let's talk about something else."

Early in 1970 it looked for a while as if a novice producer might be willing to take the script on. As negotiations progressed, I began to fantasize questions that I might be asked after the play opened about its relationship to my own life. In preparation for that half-longed-for confrontation, I scrawled down on a piece of paper some possible "answers" I might give:

1. It's hard enough for me to talk with clarity about my ideas on public issues, so I'd better put aside my feelings about private ones.

2. I'm all the characters in my plays—and none of them.

3. Almost all the specifics are invented or hearsay, not part of my direct experience.

4. I'm not proud of my psychopathy—and that's what I think it is—but it *is* part of me, and I'm tired of writing about things that aren't part of me.

5. I hate to theorize about myself. It seems to me I've spent my whole life doing that—in and out of therapy. I'm tired of analyzing myself. Let other people do it, if they want.

6. I've lived some of the play, invented some of it. But that's a suspect dichotomy. Living *is* inventing—oneself. Invention—letting fantasy form—is an essential part of living.

Fortunately for my immortal soul—only numbers five or six of the above might have saved it—the production never came off. It wasn't until April 1971 that *Payments* would finally be staged—in a workshop at New Dramatists.

I had more luck with my one-acters, and especially with the nonhomosexual *The Colonial Dudes*, which had several productions in 1969, most notably at Lee Strasberg's Actors Studio, where it was staged to reinaugurate the Playwright's Unit. I was invited to join the Unit itself but after sitting in on a single session never went back, appalled at Strasberg's rambling, egocentric monologues delivered under the guise of explicating a script.

In response to the near-simultaneous production of *Dudes* at the Actors Studio, the Random House publication of my collected essays, *The Uncompleted Past,* and the announced opening in January 1970 of *The Memory Bank,* an evening of my one-acters, the *New York Times* did an interview with me. In the course of it I managed all at once to put down my own accomplishments as a need for achievement "out of all proportion to normal desire," to announce publicly that I was in group therapy ("to get help in understanding myself and to loosen me up to write for the theater"), and to declare that although I remained unmarried at age thirty-nine I was "not as confirmed a bachelor as I used to be." Apparently I still believed that, though as I wrote Ray soon after the double confrontation in therapy with Stan and Dick, I "came within a hair of quitting—in fact it was already settled at one point." Yet I stayed, stayed because Karl persuaded me after a bruising battle between us that quitting would mean I didn't have the guts to persevere when the going got tough.

The battle had begun over seeming trivia back in the spring of 1969. During one of our seminar sessions at Hunter, Karl had offered an impassioned "first-hand" description of the general strike of 1919, which, as he described it, had successfully prevented the Allied governments from supporting an invasion of the Soviet Union. He had himself been present as a toddler, he told the enthralled seminar, when, at one point during the disturbances in Holland, government troops had fired into an assembled crowd of workers. Three of his uncles had been killed in the hail of bullets, one of them falling dead over Karl's own body.

At the time, I expressed surprise at his story and mildly contested its accuracy. Acknowledging that I wasn't widely read in the period, I said I had never come across any reference to a successful, European-wide general strike. Karl assured me and the seminar that his version was entirely true, that it derived, after all, from personal experience. We let it go at that.

But one night in the therapy group months later, Karl, seemingly out of the blue, returned to the dispute, describing our original disagreement to the other members, confirming (as he hadn't during the Hunter seminar) that the general strike *was* absent from the history books and mockingly asking why that might be so.

Kate dutifully took up the cue: "Because they don't want people to know that a general strike of the workers has ever been successful. If that news got out, it might help mobilize workers today."

"Exactly," Karl said, smiling with satisfaction.

I couldn't let it lie. "There *were* sporadic general strikes in 1919," I said. "We're disagreeing only about the magnitude of such strikes and their success."

Karl was eager to pursue the argument. "So you're still trying to tell me what my own experience was during the strike."

I tried to give ground a little. "I'm sure that whatever happened to you that day was traumatic. But isn't it possible that in the eyes of a young child a local skirmish can take on the significance of a world-shaking event?"

Karl was tenacious. "This happens to have been part of my own experience," he shot back, his voice steely. "I was *there*, so I *know* what happened."

It was clear by now that Karl wanted a retraction and an apology. But I held my ground. "I'm sorry, but an event of that magnitude simply could not disappear from history. Sure, the conservative government media might have censored news of a general strike, but at the very least socialist and trade union papers of the day would have carried accounts of it—and later socialist and trade union historians would have come across those accounts and been eager to include them in their histories."

"Then how," Karl asked, "do you explain the fact that the expeditionary army was pulled back from its intended invasion of the Soviet Union?"

"I can't explain it, I'm not a historian of that period. But I can look it up for you, if you like."

Karl ignored the offer. "You admit you're not an expert, and yet you're perfectly willing—indeed eager—to challenge my first-hand experience of the event." He gave me an ice-cold smile, signaling the danger ahead. "Don't you think, Martin, that you might ask yourself *why* you're so eager to tangle with me?"

"I'm not eager. I wanted to drop the whole issue when it came up last spring at Hunter. I still want to drop it. I'm not looking for an argument."

Karl turned to the rest of the group. "Don't you think this is interesting, Group?" he said, his voice dripping with condescension, "Martin starts an argument and then says he doesn't want to argue." He flashed back to me: "In psychoanalysis we call that sort of behavior passive-aggressive."

I felt impaled. Karl had his teeth into this one, into my neck, and whatever I said would be grist for his mill. I figured silence would get me in less trouble than anything else. I was wrong.

"You're pouting, Marty," Kate chimed in. "You're like a little boy stamping his feet. You just won't deal with Karl directly, like an adult."

"I don't think that's right, Kate," I said quietly, furious at what I took to be her effort to curry favor with Karl, but unwilling to fan the flames any higher.

"I think Kate has a good point," Karl said. (Kate beamed, as if she had just been cited Patient of the Month.) "You owe it to *yourself* to express your feelings. That, after all, is what we're here for."

Oh no, I thought, I'm not falling for that one, not tonight. I stayed silent. Karl came at me from another angle.

"How does it feel, Martin, to have someone use your tactics on *you?*"

"What do you mean?"

"I mean, how does it make you feel when somebody—in this case myself—tenaciously refuses to give up a point, insists on winning? How does that make you feel?"

"Lousy."

"Glad to hear it. Maybe now you'll be less likely to pull the same tactics on somebody else."

"Are you saying this whole tangle was a kind of therapeutic game, that you were trying to give me a sample of my own medicine?"

Karl looked utterly pleased with himself. "Let's just say"—his eyes twinkled impishly—"that therapists are entitled to ulterior motives too."

The rest of the group laughed appreciatively. That brought more of my anger to the surface.

"You mean this whole thing was Karl playing at being Martin, so that Martin could better see his own mechanisms?"

"Something like that." Karl smiled enigmatically, as if he held the key to the universe, but had decided not to share it just now.

"I don't believe that's what you were doing," I said, trying to keep my voice as calm as possible.

"I didn't expect you to," Karl said benignly. "You're so defended these days, you can't look at anything that doesn't fit your own preconceptions."

My anger suddenly overwhelmed me. "And how about therapists and their preconceptions?" I said. "Who holds *you* to point? Anything a therapist says is automatically gospel. Anything a patient says is automatically subject to analysis. If you engage in a piece of behavior that's hostile—and *that's* what I think was going on here tonight—you can either deny your hostility, saying the patient is 'projecting,' or you can claim it was calculated 'for the patient's own good.' I say that's bullshit. I say Freud was right—being a therapist is lousy for the character." It had all come out of me like automatic gunfire. I knew I had said far too much and felt immediately frightened at my own daring.

I could see Karl struggling to control himself. He started slowly: "I'll say this much for you, Martin, you've at least gotten some of your feelings out. I'll say this, too"—there was no concealing the fury in his eyes; I knew I was in for it and tried to stop the flow with an innocuous "I suppose I got too many feelings out, some of which don't really relate to tonight."

But Karl went on as if he hadn't heard me. "Even therapists, you know, can get fed up. Even therapists have feelings, and when they're pushed too hard for too long, those feelings spill out." He was now in full cry, almost shouting. "You've been pushing me for months and I'm fed up with it, fed up with you being such a fucking *spoiled brat*. I don't care whether you believe me or not, I'm fed up with your entrenched, little boy antics. You hear me, *fucking fed up!* You told me how *you* feel, now I've told you how *I* feel. And that's it for tonight."

Without another word, Karl got up and went into his inner office, signaling that the session was over. I was so upset that when I got home I made a tape recording (which I still have), going over and over what had happened, trying to understand what the explosion was all about, trying to calm myself down. I talked into the tape for two hours, sometimes sobbing, sometimes incoherent. "Karl blew up at me," I said at one point into the tape, "because I *did* provoke him, because I *am* a spoiled brat." But I said other things, too, said I was *right* about Karl's "invincible self-righteousness," about his inability "ever to admit he's wrong—other than for the occasional Olympian admission that he, too, was 'just human, full of imperfections like everyone else.' "

I acknowledged—over and over, as if trying to convince myself—that despite those imperfections, Karl was a genuinely perceptive human being, a greatly gifted therapist who in many ways *did* have my number, *did* see my bullshit—and therefore *could* help me. But by the end of the two-hour tape, exhausted and confused, I debated with myself whether to quit therapy altogether, uncertain whether the personal antagonism that had developed between Karl and me made therapy impossible, or whether it represented a unique opportunity to map some of my lifelong issues. "Christ," I finally mumbled, "I'm stuck . . . I'm lost . . ."

When I saw Karl for my individual session that week, he showed no signs of doubt or wear-and-tear. If *he* had been through anything, he concealed it well, blandly suggesting we move quickly beyond the acrimonious details of our disagreement and concentrate on the "core issues" at stake—namely, the nature and sources of my "defiance." When I told him that I was giving serious thought to terminating therapy entirely, he shook his head sadly.

"Martin," he said, "you're in danger of using this episode as a pretext, as a way of excusing yourself from doing the hard work of analysis. What happened between us represents a rare opportunity for growth, if you can bring yourself to recognize it as such. Your deepest feelings came to the surface, and some of your most unattractive qualities, and you have to take a hard look at them—that is, if you really *are* determined to grow up. You've reached a critical turning point; now you have to turn. If you don't, you'll always despise yourself for not having had the guts, for quitting when the going got tough."

My mind stalled: I believed every word Karl said and also every counterword running through my head as he spoke. I deeply distrusted him—and myself. I hardly knew whom or what to believe and, in that state of paralysis, decided to do nothing, to go on as before until some clear purpose should manifest itself, to go on with all my heightened doubts, even though, as a condition of continuing, Karl now insisted that I make a *real* effort to stop acting out, so that, as he put it, "my self-respect could be restored and my need to dump my accumulated self-hatred on others could be reduced." It was still not possible for me, in rejoinder, to argue with any settled conviction that therapy itself, with its castigating view of my sexuality, was chiefly responsible for damaging my self-respect and feeding my self-hatred. Instead, I told myself that *all* therapy necessarily involved a harsh breaking down of defenses. There was no other way to expose character defects, however rough the process was on self-esteem.

# 12

# MARATHON

I N 1970, KARL INTRODUCED a new therapeutic technique: the "leaderless" marathon. Without Karl in attendance, the group met for three consecutive days, twelve hours each day. We had two such marathons, the second settling with edgy intensity on "Marty's defiant sexuality." We got off to a comfortable start, airing familiar, entrenched antagonisms. Imperious Stan accused prim Kate of being unapproachable; Frances got in the act by chiding Kate for using compliments as a device to conceal her coldness, a technique Frances was herself adept at; Kate dissolved into tears, drawing everyone together in sympathetic warmth—that is, until Kate, between sobs, declared that I was as ungiving as she, and especially toward the women in the group.

That led to a general clamor, the other women seconding Kate, each with her own version of my perfidy. Helen, the woman I had felt closest to in the group, had recently terminated therapy (though she would dramatically reappear in my life some years later), and on that day I sorely missed the affectionate way she would scold me. The others, using some of the very words Helen had chided me with, forgot the affection and replaced it with rancor. I was told (I take these phrases from a detailed diary I began keeping in 1970) that I was "defiantly holding on to my neuroses," that "I wouldn't have peer relationships with women until I stopped acting out sexually with men and became physical with women instead." What did that mean, I responded angrily, that the only peer relationships are physical ones? Whatever happened to friendship?

Kate was ready for me. "Don't start in again with your tricky words. We all know you're good at words. Why don't you try doing something difficult for a change—like taking a look at the fact that you want *everything*, you want progress in therapy *and* neurotic excitement." Kate had summed up the group view of homosexuality in a nutshell, the view originally sponsored and endlessly reinforced by Karl himself. "Progress" meant movement toward heterosexuality; "neurotic excitement" meant homosexuality.

Dick chimed in: "And you've been *un*lucky enough, Marty, to be getting both—unlucky because holding on to both, you can't go very far with either." His point may have been clotted: what of his own situation, a combination of a heterosexual marriage and a homosexual sidelife? But his message was identical to Kate's: stop acting out.

Judy tried to soften things a bit with a partial compliment: "At least you're no longer acting like the 'nice boy next door' that you were when you first came into therapy, but as I see it, you do still have a lot to work through about women."

"Look, Judy," I said, "I can't deal with big topics like Women and Homosexuals. Let's talk about you and me. Like earlier I heard you and Stan say something quietly to each other about 'it'd be more of an adventure that way, and besides there's a shower.' Now I'll tell you what fantasy that set off in me: that you and Stan are arranging a tryst outside of group, that you're going to have sex."

"You know, you see me as supercunt. You always have. It's one way you frighten yourself off, keep yourself distant. Well, I'm not supercunt. I've got hangups of my own about sex. Like I oversignal, I make myself look more available than I really am."

"Thanks for being so frank. It does make it easier to approach you."

Apparently resenting the détente, Kate jumped back in to say that she disliked my homosexuality—anybody's homosexuality—because it represented "narcissism and rigidity," the qualities she most disliked in herself.

"You're hung up on an old-fashioned view of homosexuality," I heard myself saying, to my own considerable surprise, not having realized the extent to which some of gay liberation's new views were percolating inside of me. "Two people of the same gender *can* form loving relationships. It isn't all sex and narcissistic projection."

"You're doing your usual number, squirming out of a tough spot with an intellectual defense. Besides, I'm talking about *your* homosexuality. Are you going to tell me you *aren't* narcissistic and rigid?"

"No, I can't tell you that."

Kate grinned in triumph. Then I surprised myself again. Turning abruptly to Judy, I said, "I'm sick of 'truths.' I'm sick of analyzing. How about a morning hug?"

Judy instantly jumped up and came toward me. We embraced warmly and then—more than I had bargained for—she sat down on my lap. (She *is* supercunt, I thought nervously.)

Stan knotted up in his famous scowl. With visions of another brawl dancing in my head, I hastened to reassure him: "I'm not trying to bait you, Stan. It's just my feeling that maybe all of us need to act out more *in* group."

Before Stan could respond, Dick jumped in enthusiastically. "Absolutely right, I couldn't agree more! What *I* need to experience is the difference between male closeness and male homosexuality. *I* need to sit on your lap."

And over he came, intent on displacing Judy, who good-naturedly got up. One immediate side benefit was the unfurling of Stan's brow. Dick and I took turns sitting on each other's laps, announced that we felt entirely comfortable *and* nongenital—though I wondered aloud if the two *were* discrete categories: "Isn't it possible that genital contact between two people of the same gender is a natural way of cementing—rather than destroying—emotional closeness?"

"Oh shut up, professor! Dick happily interjected, pulling me down on the floor. Within seconds, most of the group had joined us, and for an hour there was a round robin of back massages and foot rubs. Then we gradually got back into our chairs. "I feel relaxed all the way down," Dick gleefully shouted—"that is, until I said it!" Everyone laughed with relief, agreed we felt good, and decided it was the right moment to take a break.

I went to bed that night feeling as if all had come right with the world—and was promptly flooded with back-to-back nightmares, beginning with Karl telling me that my liver was still bleeding and would continue to bleed until I "did the right thing." Then came a violent murder (mine? or was I the killer?) and a full-scale manhunt with vicious dogs tearing at human flesh. Next up were gorgeous men dancing in front of me and dancing out of reach, always choosing each other instead of me. Instead of waking up exhausted the next morning, I felt full of energy and good spirits, as if I'd exorcised all my demons.

When we began the final session of the marathon that day, the warmth and intimacy of the preceding night carried over. That is, for the first few hours. Then Judy wondered out loud why I couldn't seem to move from feelings of generalized warmth toward a woman (herself) to sexual desire for her.

"But wasn't what happened between Dick and me last night exactly the same thing?" I asked, "and wasn't our ability to *distinguish* between tenderness and sex considered a source for congratulation? If it's a good thing for two men to get close without getting sexual, why doesn't the same hold true for a man and a woman?"

"Oh, you're doing your intellectual number again," Judy said disapprovingly. "With a man and a woman it's *natural* for closeness to lead to arousal. Sex *naturally* comes up between a man and a woman."

Before I could protest this abrupt dismissal of the entire history of male-female friendship, Judy asked if I would answer a "ticklish" question.

"Yes, what is it?"

"When you got home from group last night, did you masturbate?"

"I masturbate almost every night."

"So you did?"

"Yes."

"Did you think about me while you were masturbating?"

"No."

"Who did you think about?"

"Nobody you know. A guy I saw on the street yesterday."

"You see?—there it is, there it is in a nutshell," Judy gloated. "You and I couldn't have been closer last night, but whom do you think about when you masturbate?—somebody you never even met!"

"What's so strange about that? First of all—as if you didn't already know—I don't have sexual fantasies about women, whether I know them or not." I was starting to feel agitated. "Second, as you also know—or should—strangers can set off some of our hottest fantasies, just because they are strangers. For someone who claims to know a lot about sex, you sometimes sound like you're in kindergarten."

We were now both furious. "You're *afraid* to have a sexual fantasy about me," Judy shouted. "You're too chicken to masturbate while thinking about me. You'd rather stay in your narcissistic rut."

"What kind of totalitarian shit is this?" I bellowed. "Are you trying to tell me that any fantasy a man has that isn't about a woman can automatically be labeled 'narcissism'? Are you trying to tell me I'm not entitled to my own masturbation fantasies without checking in for your seal of approval?"

We quickly retreated from the shouting match, and before the marathon ended some semblance of good humor had been restored. But the next day, when I tried to settle in for my usual ten-hour stint on the Black Mountain book, I couldn't concentrate. Fantasies of hairy chests and hard thighs danced in my head, and masturbation did nothing to dispel them. Was Judy right? Was I about to turn to the familiar escape hatch of sex as a way of dissipating the assorted feelings that had been generated between us during the marathon? Was I yet again about to scatter feelings of intimacy or anxiety like buckshot, afraid to sit with them, live them through?

The questions no longer had automatic answers. A new set of counterquestions had begun to form in my head, and they contended for what had once been uncontested terrain. How much sex was too much sex? Who decided that? And on what basis?—on variations in individual need and capacity or on some presumed set of universal moral principles ("sex outside the context of a committed emotional relationship is meaningless," etc.)? Weren't such principles in fact parochial rather than universal, some knee-jerk brand of native puritanism?

# 13

# HUSTLERS

I WAS FEELING MY way toward an affirmation I could as yet scarcely credit. It had something to do with the periodic pleasures of anonymous sex and with the authentic appeal of a variety of sexual partners. Gay men had long acted on that appeal, searching for unadorned sex in bathhouses and backrooms, but had apologetically agreed with the puritanical psychoanalytic police that such "promiscuous" behavior represented an unhealthy compulsion, a profoundly dysfunctional neurotic drive.

The Gay Liberation Front, like the counterculture in which it was embedded, had begun to offer an opposing view, suggesting that nonmonogamous, noncommitted sexual adventuring could do the cramped psyche a world of good, could break down longstanding inhibitions that shackled the personality. It was a view that made immediate sense to me in the abstract, but which I had trouble applying to my own life. Trained to think of my sexuality as criminal, I could barely entertain the notion of exoneration.

Yet in slow baby steps, I *was* learning to think about my sexuality differently. In the period immediately following the therapy marathon, I did indulge in what I then called a sexual "binge," meaning I had three orgasms with three different men in a week. And in the privacy of my diary, I did express concern and shame over having thereby "dissipated" the emotions that the marathon had stirred up. But this time around the shame was circumscribed, fought to a draw by counterfeelings. As I wrote in my diary, "I alternate between thinking I'm simply one of the lucky few able to indulge my sexual appetites and thinking that in fact I'm indulging something else—greed? defiance? self-hate?—under the guise of giving my sexual impulses their play." Before long I was edging toward a more generalized defiance: "Those who suffer most in reputation are not the sexually undernourished (a puritanical society approves the absence or suppression of passion), or the 'creative giants' (whose lusts are forgiven as inseparable from their talents), but rather the *merely* sexual; they can neither be praised for their abstemiousness nor pardoned for their redeeming productivity."

A new set of questions had begun to engage me: "Is an orgasm a day really 'excessive,' and why is the daily orgasm thought less excusable when had with a partner rather than alone?" "Do a variety of partners really preclude 'intimacy' with a mate, or do multiple experiences help put one in touch with one's own fantasies—what might be called *intra*personal intimacy—thus in the long run making one a better mate?" Just being willing to entertain such questions—even if my answers remained equivocal—indicated a growing awareness that social definitions of "normalcy" were not the equivalents of absolute truth, that the ways in which one deviated from majoritarian standards might themselves be a valid measure of individuality and the only reliable path to an authentic personal style—and were thus to be cultivated and prized, not repudiated and reviled.

Yet a lot militated against my coming to terms with these competing value systems, with being able to resolve the debate between them with any ease or dispatch. I turned forty in 1970, an age, in combination with my longstanding deference to the psychoanalytic view of my sexuality, had left a decided imprint; I was hardly an unmarked, impressionable youth, eager for an unimpeded dash to the liberationist barricades. Besides, I had dabbled more and more of late in the world of male hustlers and uneasily doubted if such retrograde activities would qualify for admission under the liberationist banner. Same-gender sex might now be celebrated, but no one was singing the praises of *paid* same-gender sex.

The bars and baths had lost much of their appeal for me. I still liked to dance, and I still liked the good nights when some charming newcomer would guess my age at twenty-eight, but I no longer had the time and patience for desultory beers and chit-chat—especially since they too often ended with my wandering home emptily alone at 3:00 A.M. My sex drive and work drive were both intense, but it began to look as if I might have to choose between the two. That is, until "Ron Cooper" came along.

He was one of the first gay pornographers, using his Greenwich Village apartment to turn out films and magazines that in their day were considered state of the art. Ron relied mostly on California models, and to help them piece out their minimal fees, he would arrange introductions for another kind of shoot entirely. Ron's only real ambition was to get killed, and in pursuit of that goal he had designed a garrulously cool style that allowed only two topics ever to be discussed: cock and money. If you couldn't provide one or the other, you didn't exist—a stance on the world that invited the unendowed, which is to say almost everybody, to beat him to death.

I forget how I met Ron (it was some contact point on the labyrinthine bar circuit), but from the beginning he treated me—as the possessor of a middle-aged cock and limited resources—with unyielding scorn. Only occasionally, and only when his "really important johns" were unavailable, did I get a call from him. And then it would be peremptory: "Kent A., a 'stunning beauty,' is in from L.A. and can see you between three and four P.M.—that is, *if*"—here Ron would laugh derisively— "you can manage to scrape together twenty-five dollars." I didn't always say yes, but soon learned that one negative meant no phone call for a month.

I went through all sorts of moral contortions about this latest wrinkle in my sexual odyssey, filling my diary with fine-spun exegeses on the assorted pros and cons. "Am I hurting anyone? Is any element of force involved? Implicit if not overt force? Rarely, I think. Objective conditions like unemployment seem to play an insignificant role with most of the guys I meet. They're usually into it as a sideline—extra pocket money, thrills, the need for variety and admiration, the (consciously unacceptable) search for an older man." I shakily concluded that male prostitution was not exploitative in the way female prostitution was. Most of Ron's actor/hustlers seemed themselves to control the terms, were usually working class in background but upwardly mobile in their aspirations, and had varied options in life. They had chosen to hustle (I told myself) in order to make maximum money in minimum time, thereby making it possible to avoid the nine-to-five rat race in the name of pursuing careers.

Okay, then, was I hurting myself? I told myself that the hustling scene was better than the old bar search because it minimized the hurt of rejection, which increases with age. That seemed plausible. But then I also had to deal with all the standard theories long employed to "explain" why anybody's erotic preferences ever cross class or age lines, why an E. M. Forster, say, or a J. R. Ackerley develops a penchant for cops, Guardsmen, and lorrie drivers. The standard explanation came in several forms: such men could only feel comfortable when in a position of socially defined superiority; or they so feared intimacy that they had to refuse involvement with anyone of their own background and interests; or they could best fulfill their masochistic need for debasement with certified toughs.

Well, I could certainly be seen in some moods, at some points in my life, as masochistic and as uncomfortable with intimacy, but—as my prior relationships amply demonstrated—certainly not at all points in my life. The standard explanations were far too neat and left out far too much. Like the special appeal of a young, working-class male seemingly indifferent to, even negligent of his own athletic beauty, oblivious to the possibility that he might be considered an object of desire. That sort of casual ease with the body, devoid of overt signs of vanity yet contained and confident, is far more characteristic of working-class men than middle- or upper-class men, who tend to be either phobically unconcerned with the physical, defining their worth instead in terms of verbal or analytic skills, or suspiciously obsessed with it, pumping up muscles and toning up Attitude. To go to bed with a fellow academic was to share not only class backgrounds but also somatic tics. To go to bed with a roofer or a farm boy was, because of their lack of self-consciousness and inhibition, to feel more comfortable with my own body.

Besides, class differences can be overdrawn. Disparities in temperament are too often assumed from disparities in vocabulary, interests, and information—too patly assumed. Surface differences in speech patterns, dress, recreational preferences, reading or motor skills, knowledge of symphony rankings or ball scores can obscure deep compatibilities of personality. Besides, where differences *are* substantial, they can be enriching; opposites *do* attract. I recognized, to be sure, that the move from temporary infatuation to sustained love may well require the presence of significant "likenesses"; if opposition gives the spice, similarity provides the substance. I was not entirely selling myself a bill of goods about the enduring compatibility of people of disparate backgrounds.

Then there was the matter of the cash nexus. Wasn't the exchange of money for sex inimical to any human relating worthy of the name? No, I provisionally decided. To insist on that was tantamount to adopting our society's view that money is of such paramount importance that whenever present in a human transaction, it *necessarily* obliterates all other ingredients in the mix. "Most of us," I argued in my diary, "would want to define a good human relationship in terms of tenderness and caring. I've found those qualities in hustlers about as often as I've found them in any other supposed collectivity of individuals—fellow-guests at parties, street pickups, barmates. Which is to say: not very often, though the traditionalist equation of cash with coldness is about as valid as that between marriage and mutuality."

I further tried to persuade myself that hustling provided a needed pretext and context for contact between older men and younger men, a contact otherwise taboo in our culture, yet one from which both older and younger profited, the one offering (optimally) practical if melancholic insight into how the world works, the other offering physical vitality—and, of course, beauty. When all these earnest arguments left me still uncomfortable, I turned flip: who in his right mind (and puritans weren't) would give up the chance to bed so many beauties? And besides, hustling was a good way of re-distributing the wealth.

But if I could never entirely convince myself that paying for sex wasn't immoral, or that the real reason for my participation wasn't essentially related to self-hate, the hustling scene did open me up to a set of experiences and a variety of people I wouldn't otherwise have known. The appeal of gorgeous bodies was certainly primary, but the high-flying theatrics of the world of hustling ran lust a close second. Many of the actor/models on Ron's cash circuit were simply heightened (if more beautiful) versions of the upwardly mobile young men who crowded the gay bars, exuding anxiety and attitude in equal measure. But some were not, were instead categorically different, either unsophisticated products of farm communities and small towns who had somehow become intent on trying their luck in the big city, or super-sophisticated products of the inner cities themselves, without much formal education but with a surfeit of street smarts. After Ron opened his own club in the Village, with an intentionally cultivated reputation as a "cash-and-carry" scene, the inner city contingent increased.

One thing I began to learn about was drugs: LSD and pot were the specialty of the farm boys, poppers and cocaine the inner-city favorites. In these years, I would argue fervently against drugs as a copout, a flight from feelings, yet I ended up trying most of them. Only poppers (amyl nitrite), with their uninhibited rush, had any real appeal for me. Occasionally I smoked pot or hash, but with limited pleasure—though I felt it my countercultural duty publicly to defend the drug as benign when Princeton expelled seven undergraduates who had been caught smoking. (Such was the pro-pot climate in those years that a psychiatrist at the Princeton Health Services wrote to commend me for my "timely" defense.)

The spaced-out disconnections of pot were not for me—and certainly not LSD or mescalin, each of which I swore off after a single try. My mescalin trip was accompanied with maximum hype. "Pete," an ex-student of mine become friend, was a zealous partisan of mescalin as a breakthrough psychic tool, and he persuaded me that the experience would be transcendent. "It will help you to embrace, *own*, all aspects of your contradictory personality," he told me, "instead of shunning the contradictions or batting yourself like a shuttle-cock between them." I listened mesmerized as, turning the pedagogic tables, he went sternly on: "You're at a breakthrough point in your life, Marty, I've sensed it for some time. But you're unable to break, despite yet more psychotherapy. Mescalin will do what neither suffering nor talk could."

Alas, it proved no more enlightening than either, though there were some stunning moments. Seated on the roof of my building, where I had constructed a makeshift garden, staring into the sunset, Pete and I were entirely, movingly silent. That is, until I noticed, with a sob of guilt, that a wisteria branch I had tied to the trellis looked tortured, its shape grotesquely distorted. I *had* to release the branch at once. "Liberated," it promptly fell over, forcing me to prop it back up again. When I began to expound on the political symbolism involved, Pete gently guided me back down to the living room, where the panting pumpkin walls and the dancing purple pillows soon distracted me.

It was then that I got the inspiration to take Pete, a heterosexual and non-New Yorker, on a stroll down Christopher Street. We lingered for three or four hours, Pete bug-eyed with horror at the "freak show," I calmly analytic. I felt, as I wrote in my diary the next day, "as if I were x-raying the strollers, and all the plates revealed the same stricken symptoms: grieving, desperate faces, haunting discomfort with their own self-mutilated shapes." That homophobic gloss may have said more about *my* inner state than that of the strollers, though that was not an insight—despite mescalin's presumed ability to pierce the veil—which I was proffered at the time.

As for cocaine, when I sniffed my first lines in the summer of 1970, I announced, like any good novice, that it had "absolutely no effect on me"—except briefly to clear my sinuses and to turn me *off* sexually. In that experiment, my instructor was a hustler friend, Derek, who had brought along the coke as "a special treat." At his insistence, I put a little of it around the edge of my cock, but the only effect was to shrivel it further. An indignant Derek, determined to exonerate his favorite drug, announced that *amyl* was the culprit: "You sniff too much of that stuff during prelims," he pontificated. "You should take that stuff *only* when you're ready to come!" I pretended to be chastised, but forswore any further snorting. In later years, I was to find cocaine far more enticing—sexually too.

Until now being gay had meant being with people much like myself, cramped with middle-class guilts and constrictions. Many of the young men I now met were vividly different in cultural and class backgrounds—not less constricted necessarily, but constricted in ways illuminatingly dissimilar from my own. Eddie, the rugged truckdriver who loved being fucked but refused to kiss, taught me something about how arbitrary my own labels were and how anyone, simply by insisting that lips and not assholes were the true organs of intimacy, could keep himself from acknowledging a tabooed connection.

Kelly, on the other hand, sensed (as few of my gay bar pickups ever did) that my surface forcefulness did not represent the sum of my needs, that bed might be one place where I could act out sides of myself not often in play. "Just tell yourself you *deserve* to be submissive once in a while, deserve to *get* fucked now and then." When I seemed unconvinced, Kelly resorted to an astrological vocabulary to persuade me—"*No* wish should be urgent. The planets have their plan. But it's important for you, as a Leo, to learn to *request* passivity." So I did, and a pleased Kelly confided, as if somehow in explanation of his hortatory powers, that he lived with a priest.

Roger turned me on to the excitement of pornography. With borrowed projector and films, we spent hours screening assorted versions of sucking and fucking. "Do note," I instructed Roger, feigning a deadpan professorial lecture, "that in porn the oral (sucking) always precedes the anal (fucking)—a symptom of our culture's surrender to Freudian models, or of the truth of those models." In fact, I found a lot of the films dull—the people interchangeably plastic, the passion feigned. But some of them were a decided turn-on and, ever needing a morally serious gloss before I could surrender to pleasure, I concluded in my diary that visual stimuli were "no better or worse than any other 'artificial' additive to the sex act—musk oil, say, or the sensuousness of soap and a hot shower." But in those pre-VCR years, one had to keep leaping out of bed to change the reels, and I soon wearied of playing projectionist rather than lover.

When I took John home from Ron's Village club one night, I had no idea that his thick leather armbands and heavy boots connoted anything but stylistic flair. But the light belatedly dawned when John, after telling me he was the great-grandson of a Confederate general, ordered me (Yankee boy) to take his boots off and accompanied the order with a tentative slap on the ass. I quickly explained that I wasn't into "the pain thing," and John, like any competent pro, adjusted his routine to a few mild verbal commands, which, to my surprise, *did* turn me on.

That got me to wondering whether I hadn't been avoiding the S/M scene all these years *because* of an appeal I couldn't admit to. As I wrote in my diary, "My cowardice about physical pain may reflect my longing for it—excessive fear as a way of avoiding excessive desire." After a little more controlled experimentation, and with both sides of the S/M equation, I decided that my interest in it was, after all, minimal. But I never quite lost the feeling that I was simply too afraid to expand my sexual reality. Once more I had a suitable moral to draw: "I'm not seriously tempted by S/M because I do my own self-flagellating—I write. Who needs anybody to discipline and punish me when I've internalized it so well, forcing myself to that fucking desk every day, berating myself for any extended time away from it? I've got my own torture rack going. And it doesn't even bruise the skin."

My education had to do with more than sex. Davey, a double for Li'l Abner, told me about gay life in Donaldson, Tennessee, and, when he did, the innocent farm boy turned out to be as sophisticated about strategies for survival as any native New Yorker. Charley, who had recently been kicked out of a Trappist monastery because he confessed to jerking off to muscle magazines, made the goings-on of the cloister sound like a Feydeau farce—which was why I believed it. Manny gave me a long lecture on the Rosicrucians. He was being considered for membership but first had to demonstrate his "worthiness." I hoped for his sake that it wasn't going to hinge on the persuasiveness of the boring "all occult is science" rap he subjected me to for the better part of the night.

Jay, who had a bumble bee tattooed on his cock and had been on the streets and in jail since age thirteen, made most of his living as a second-storey man. He regaled me with tales of his assorted hustles, which included safe-cracking, dealing speed, and handcrafting "antique" torture racks. One client commissioned him to build an electric chair, so he could sit in it *once* and get a (presumably nonfatal) shock. A Vietnam vet named Barney, recently returned from combat, told me horror stories of the war—about "cutting off Cong cocks and shoving them in their mouths," about the village his unit decided to destroy rather than risk occupying, about the old woman who carried around the bottom half of her husband after they blew the top half off, and who gnawed on Barney's arm when he tried to comfort her. When I told him to stop, told him I couldn't listen to any more, he wanted me to say that he had had no choice, which I couldn't, or that he was a monster, which I couldn't either.

Sometimes I'd try to help—with more than cash, I mean. Perhaps I was eager to salve my still-unappeased conscience about being an exploiter, to move the relationships into a more acceptable older brother context. But I did feel genuine concern for some of the vivid young men I met, along with the conviction that a little help might go a long way. So many of them seemed to need nothing more than a lucky break, a chance, a gesture of support to make things right. I soon found out that nobody can be easily rescued, and especially not by an occasional favor, even though well-meant. The damage is often too deep, however much the entrancing surface and the stirring energy suggest otherwise.

I got illiterate Drew into a school devoted to teaching adults to read, but at the last minute he refused to go, suddenly professing lack of interest. I tried to peddle Arty's novel, which I thought showed real talent, about his experiences as one of Roy Cohn's kept boys, but after four different closeted gay editors turned it down, Arty resentfully broke off with me. When Hank went back on heroin after having been senior coordinator at Odyssey House, I got him bumped ahead of a long waiting list into a methadone clinic—only to have him tell me he couldn't risk being recognized and sent back to the involuntary state program from which he'd once escaped.

In therapy Karl scornfully chalked all this up to "acting out my rescue fantasy." Well yes, I responded, but sometimes a rescue fantasy actually rescues somebody, so why not pursue it? "Because," he tartly answered, "it's *yourself* that you're trying to rescue; and you could better do that by getting off the promiscuity merry-go-round altogether." We were back to square one.

"Can't you see," Karl went on, "that all your proliferating contacts add up to no contact? During the marathon you made *real* contact with Judy, and now you're in full flight from it. You can't stand the tenderness, the intimacy."

"Maybe . . . but I don't think so. I think I'm pretty good at intimacy with women. But the generalized warmth I feel for Judy doesn't get converted into lust. Isn't it possible that *you're* confusing the two? Just because I don't want to fuck Judy doesn't mean I'm afraid of getting close to her."

Karl parried my question with one of his own. "You don't see anything suspicious about not wanting to have sex with Judy, even though you do feel strongly toward her?"

"No, I don't. All strong feeling isn't lust. Why aren't we worrying about the fact that Nixon isn't sleeping with Haldeman— though he has strong feeling for him? Or why Erlichman is failing to be aroused by the charms of John Dean? Why not either spread the guilt about having a one-way sexual orientation, or get rid of guilt? As for a man and a woman, why *isn't* affection good enough? Why is it somehow suspect? You seem to be saying that the only *legitimate* feeling a man can have for a woman is lust, that everything else is either a blind or a poor substitute. I can't buy that."

"You're arguing well today," Karl said sardonically, "which means once again we won't be getting any therapy done. Once again you'll win the argument and lose the war."

"I don't know what the war is anymore," I answered, surprised at my own boldness. "Maybe I haven't been fighting the right one all these years."

"And what is the 'right' war?"

"Getting to accept who I am."

"And do you really like yourself as you are?"

Karl remained bland in the face of what was turning into an indictment of five years of therapy with him. It unnerved me. Had he given up on me? That was not what I wanted; I wanted to give up on him. And I wanted him to confess error, to bleed.

"Well," I said, "I wouldn't go that far. What I mean, I guess, is that maybe I'd like myself better if I stopped beating myself up for my sexuality. Maybe—with your encouragement—I've been doing that for too long."

Karl refused to get rattled. "Martin, if you're happy with your sexuality, I say 'so be it.' "

He *was* trying to get rid of me. I didn't look good on his stats, I was lowering his "cure rate." But I had a lot more to say and needed time to say it. I switched back to my hustler friend Hank as a delaying tactic.

"I didn't say I was 'happy' with my sexuality. I was questioning the way you *automatically* dismiss my involvement with Hank as either Florence Nightingale antics or a strategy for avoiding Judy. I think there's more to my feeling for Hank, and more than just lust."

"Tell me, Martin, would you help him if he were an *ugly* addict?"

"I might. Though not as readily. But what does that prove?"

"That his body is what interests you." Karl delivered that line with the quiet emphasis he reserved for a clinching insight. But I had begun to realize his final insights were the most suspect of all, and I ploughed ahead.

"I meet lots of beautiful bodies, but I only try to help a few—the ones I connect with in a special way."

Karl grimaced. He wasn't used to prolonged disagreement and again tried to conclude. "You're going to twist anything I say. But I'll try one last time. You're determined to exonerate your promiscuity by calling it pleasure. I say it's punishment—of yourself."

"Last week you called it tension-reduction—'discharging bad feelings instead of enhancing good ones' was how you put it, quite eloquently I thought."

Karl caught the arch tone and let the "compliment" pass. "Yes, promiscuity is tension-reduction as well as punishment. In any case, it's keeping you from you."

"Meaning the heterosexual me you keep insisting is my 'real' self. But maybe that's been a fiction all along. Maybe I've been keeping myself open to a nonexistent possibility."

Ignoring the rest of what I had said, Karl latched on to the word "open." "In your political writings you talk optimistically about the possibilities of change—that is, other people's or the society's. But there's a deep refusal to change yourself, a nihilistic insistence that *you* can't change. It leads me to conclude that you conceal a fear of personal openness with a political vocabulary that pretends to invite it. Way down, beneath the rhetoric of struggle, you think change is one of two things— easy or impossible. What it all adds up to is that you don't want to do the hard work: you don't want to control your artificial appetites in the name of allowing a deeper self to emerge."

Artificial? Deeper self? Karl was back to reiterating a position I thought I had been successfully challenging. Angry, I reached for a literary reference—wanting to intimidate, not persuade. "Norman O. Brown doesn't agree with you," I said portentously.

"Who is Norman O. Brown?" Karl looked a little apprehensive, which pleased me enormously.

"His book *Life Against Death* is getting a lot of attention," I said, trying hard to rub salt in the wound. "Brown talks about our 'dreams of omnipotent indulgence,' which most people, in assuming so-called adulthood and in capitulating to the 'reality principle,' are forced to relinquish. Only a few of us"—I paused for emphasis—"that is, us gay men who are not tied into traditional relationships, can sustain the initial dream, can remain apart from what Brown calls the sad record of man's 'universal neurosis of repressed pleasure.' "

Karl looked dazed, so I pressed my advantage. "I sometimes think," I airily continued, "that this may be precisely why gay men are considered threatening and called sick—because their sexuality is *not* repressed to the extent true of most people." Then, tongue partly in cheek, I added giddily, "Perhaps that's what accounts for the youthful appearance of so many gay men."

I had overreached, and Karl was quick to seize the offensive. "*Your* 'youthful appearance' is in part an accident of genes, in greater part a reflection of the disparity between your emotional age and your chronological one."

I tried to recover the initiative, calling again on *my* annointed expert: "Norman O. Brown's work suggests that promiscuity is the natural human state, which would mean gay men are among the few who are leading natural lives."

"I'll agree with you on one thing," Karl answered, his equanimity and his argument restored in tandem, "namely, your motto in life: *more*. You insist on constant amplitude, on constant 'events' to distract you from your feelings of emptiness. You refuse to make even a *start* on controlling your appetites, your obsession with sex."

I could feel my anger building at Karl's persistent equation of promiscuity with homosexuality, mounting a reasonable argument against indulgence when his real animus was against *any* same-gender sex. But I had long ago learned to keep my anger at Karl under wraps, and so it came out as a question: "Obsession? Isn't that a little strong?"

"No, it isn't. You said you had sex last week three days in a row."

"I wonder how many times Joe Namath or Bo Belinsky had sex. My guess is that my appetite looks rather modest compared with theirs. And compared with a Charlie Mingus, downright undernourished. Are they 'obsessives' too?"

"They're not my patients. You are. Anyone who wants to grow up has to accept life on life's terms—has to put up with some pain, with some delayed gratification, with *less* of everything."

"In other words, has to agree to repress desire, to join the gray-faced mainstream."

"If you would learn to limit your appetite, it would rapidly come to feel like a liberation rather than a deprivation."

I suddenly thought of a way to pierce the circularity of an argument we'd rehearsed dozens of times. "Should I stop masturbating too?"

Karl looked puzzled, which I considered an advance. "What do you mean?"

"I mean, I *might* be able to control my sexual behavior, but I know I can't control my sexual fantasies. They're always about men. What do I do about that? Do I stop masturbating in order to avoid having erotic fantasies? But come to think of it, that *wouldn't* stop the fantasies—I'd have them even if I didn't masturbate to them. And isn't *desire* the key ingredient?"

"In what?"

"In defining who is homosexual. A homosexual is someone who consistently *desires* sexual contact with a member of the same gender. So if I decided not to act on the desire, that would only make me a *nonpracticing* homosexual—not a heterosexual."

Karl frowned impatiently. "You're doing what you're best at— mounting an intellectual argument. But it still comes down to the same thing: resistance, a refusal to change. Which you don't want to look at."

"And in my view you don't want to look at imprinting. Even if you're right that my sexuality is sick and right that self-denial leads to self-creation, just how much reinventing of the self is possible—especially at age forty and in regard to something as deeply imprinted as sexual orientation?"

"I never said you weren't working against high odds. And especially as regards your family background. Your mother was so overwhelming, it's difficult for you to *want* family and *want* closeness to women enough to give up behavior that does manage to reduce your anxiety and to keep intrapersonal conflict at a manageable level. It's easier for homosexuals to change when the heterosexual vision really does have significant appeal, which is not the case with you. Still, you prefer to believe that you're *caused* because that is less frightening than facing possible options and putting in the hard work to make those options a reality."

"I think my sexuality does more for me than just reduce tension. There's something called physical pleasure, and also the joy of connection. But I suppose you'll tell me those are 'screen' feelings for disgust and self-betrayal."

"The words are yours, not mine."

We paused for a beat. Then I heard myself saying, "I've been reading some of the Gay Liberation Front literature." Karl sat impassive. Another beat. "It's started me thinking about some of this in new ways." I paused again, not for emphasis but on the off-chance Karl might react. He remained still, unmoving. "Started me thinking about the possibilities of change versus imprinting. I think GLF has maybe gone too far in saying it's a mistake for *any* gay person to consider a change in sexual orientation; sometimes the GLF literature even sounds like it's elevating homosexuality into an ideology of superiority."

"I daresay that's characteristic of the literature." Karl had deigned to speak. "In my experience it's characteristic of all liberation literature."

"The point that most impressed me was the contrast GLF draws between being a member of a therapy group and being a participant in a movement involved in political struggle. They call therapy a "game" that *doesn't* transform the individual's life.

Whereas a political struggle *can*, mostly because it insists on grappling with external conditions of oppression, taking the blame for personal misery off the back of the individual and putting it on social bigotry and repression instead."

"Yes, I can see why that message might appeal to you. It relieves you of responsibility."

"No, it removes the *entirety* of responsibility from my own shoulders. It's a message that feels right."

"It's a congenial message for someone eager to stop working on himself."

"On the contrary, I think it's congenial for someone eager to work on himself in a new way—through self-acceptance and through solidarity with others similarly situated in life. In fact, I'm puzzled why I *still* can't fully embrace the message. I've stood up for other oppressed minorities, why not my own? I'm beginning to feel like the Uncle Tom of the homophile movement."

"Maybe it's your healthy side that resists such an easy out."

"No, I suspect it's the extent of my brainwashing—too many years hearing about my 'pathology,' and believing it."

We sat there staring at each other. And then I said it, finally, belatedly, years after I should have: "I've been thinking about quitting therapy. Or at least"—I was instantly backtracking—"my weekly individual session. Maybe I'll keep on with the group sessions for a while longer."

Karl showed no surprise; our whole lengthy, cantankerous discussion had been heading toward this obvious conclusion. But he had one last arrow in his quiver, and the twang from the bow nearly knocked me over.

"I agree," Karl said, "that the individual sessions have become mirthless and should be ended. As for the group, I suggest you think about it while I'm away next month."

"You're away next month?"

"Yes, I'll be telling the group about it tonight. Helen and I will be going on our honeymoon."

"Helen and you will—!"

Karl savored my astonishment. "Yes, that's right, Helen and I are to be married. Ever since she left therapy we've been seeing each other."

"But I don't understand. I mean if you and she—"

Karl interrupted sharply. "No further questions or explanations are appropriate. You'll just have to live with your curiosity unsatisfied."

I guessed that the uncompleted thought was "live with *something* unsatisfied." But I swallowed hard, tried to smile warmly and offered "heartfelt congratulations to both of you." Karl thanked me with a magisterial nod of the head, and then, with a big, patronizing grin said, "So you see, Martin, GLF is wrong to think of therapy as a 'game.' It's real life. Who knows, if you hadn't set your mind against therapy, it might have turned out similarly for you and Judy." Karl got up from his desk, signaling that the session was over.

In group that night there was much good-natured bantering and congratulations over the wedding announcement. "Whoever dreams," I said, trying for a joke at one point, "that one's therapy parents will literally become husband and wife?" Perhaps in retaliation, the group invested me with the job of picking out a wedding present. I chose a piece of Eskimo sculpture, its remote and snowy implications unintentional. We presented it to Karl the following week at our final session before the "honeymoon break." He, in turn, gave each member of the group a gift. That puzzled me; it smacked peculiarly of "farewell." His gift to me was a Giacometti-like matador, drawing a big sword out from under his cape. At first glance, I decided it was meant to represent me "slaying the bull" (that is, my "problem"). Then I noticed that the matador's head hung slackly from his neck and decided the real message was that this guy wasn't going to slay anything.

# 14

# WATERSHED

I SPENT THE NEXT month engrossed in new projects, brooding little about whether to return to group therapy at the end of that time, pretty much sensing the decision had already been made. A multitude of theater ventures happened almost simultaneously. A reading of *Payments* at the New Theater was followed by notification early in November 1970 that I had been elected to membership in the New Dramatists, an organization devoted entirely to helping playwrights get their scripts in shape for staging. Almost immediately I began to put together the necessary pieces for a workshop production of *Payments* in March. Simultaneously, I was writing two new plays, one about transsexualism and one about Oneida (the experimental nineteenth-century community), and also taking part in rehearsals for a production of *In White America* at the American Academy of Dramatic Arts. In the midst of all this, I accepted an invitation to rewrite the book for *Soon*, a rock musical already in rehearsal for a planned Broadway opening in mid-December.

To say that *Soon* was in trouble is an understatement: the direction was muddy, the acting amateurish, and the book non-existent. But the score seemed first-rate, some of the performers (especially an unknown named Nell Carter) struck me as immensely talented, and the producers agreed to tack on an additional three-week rehearsal period. It seemed worth a shot—for the experience and fun of it, and to bring my already crowded schedule to the point of anesthetizing frenzy. A frantic month followed during which I made myself into an instant rock and roll expert. When the preview audiences seemed to like the show, nervous predictions started to be made that we were going to be "the next *Hair*." The critics put an end to that. Though they were divided in their verdict, the worst notices appeared in the most important papers, and to a chorus of tears and recriminations, the producer closed the show after its third performance.

With a mere three theatrical projects left to work on, I promptly began considering a fourth. It seemed impossible to resist: Agnes de Mille suggested that she and I collaborate on a "dance history of the United States." Instantly retooling myself into a modern dance expert, I met with her for a preliminary talk. That went some way toward diminishing my ardor. Though I liked her, I thought she was a terrible listener and decidedly imperious. Nor could I get any real handle, through the sonorous liberalisms, on what she had in mind. But I agreed to an exchange of scripts; I would read her outline, she would read some of my plays.

I thoroughly disliked the outline. It was an inflated rehash of tired subjects (the Salem witch trials, the Triangle factory fire, and so on), empty of any overall design or point of view. I grandly decided that I would "spare" her, would graciously back out of the project on the grounds that for now I was tired of working in the documentary form. Which was true, but I never got the chance to say so. After reading my scripts—I had given her some of my one-acters with homosexual themes, perhaps deliberately trying to turn her off—I got a stern call to pick the plays up at her apartment. A man answered the door, handed me the scripts, curtly conveyed Miss de Mille's thanks for having let her read them, and before I could say a word, closed the door in my face. So ended my fantasy of a new life in tutus.

I still had plenty to keep me busy. Along with my assorted theater projects, I was racing to finish the book on Black Mountain (and to begin a teleplay on the life of Emma Goldman that PBS had commissioned), was involved in various antiwar activities, and—after years of dissatisfaction—was getting ready to resign from Princeton.

I had continued to experiment with the format of my classes and in 1970 had even organized a faculty seminar at Princeton to share some of the new encounter group techniques I had been trying. But I was also feeling more discouragement than before with the possibilities of restructuring teaching and learning in a university environment. I had realized from the beginning that doing away with some of the authoritarian trappings in my own courses would barely make a dent in the system as a whole. But now I questioned, despite student enthusiasm for the courses, whether mere tinkering could hope to overcome the entrenched deference to "teacher," the artificiality of coming together at a set hour each week to talk about a set topic, and above all, the overwhelming passivity that had been ingrained in all of us. My nomination for the Danforth Foundation's 1971 Gifted Teaching Award came at just the time when I was feeling that teaching—at least in a constrictive traditional setting—was a possibly pointless activity.

It dawned on me that I might feel less fraudulent if I were to teach in a less privileged setting. My anger over Princeton's entrenched smugness might have been overly coloring my discouragement with academia in general. I began actively to search for an alternative university.

For a while it looked as if I would transfer to NYU. After a series of meetings with the school's assorted deans, a formal offer had seemed imminent. But then I was asked to give a special convocation on education for the NYU history faculty and graduate students. Deciding not to conceal or modify my views, I spoke openly about my fear that universities had become so entrenched in their procedures that it might be impossible to turn them into true learning environments, that as institutions they might have become fossilized to the point where they had to be circumvented. That convocation cost me the job. As one of the graduate students later reported to me, most of the full professors present expressed outrage at my opinions and came out against the appointment.

But before I had time to feel sorry for myself, two other institutions, the State University of New York (at Purchase) and the City University of New York (Lehman), started bidding for me. The attraction of Purchase was the prospect of a joint appointment in history and theater, whereas Lehman's appeal was in the entirely free hand it offered me to structure (or unstructure) my courses as I saw fit. Lehman finally clinched the deal with the offer of a Distinguished Professorship, which meant less teaching and more money than a typical full professor. The stupendous sum of thirty-four thousand dollars was more than double my salary at Princeton.

I felt my resignation from Princeton could be made to count for something since full professors rarely resigned voluntarily from its august ranks. And so I sent a statement to the *Princetonian* outlining in detail my discontent with the university's hidebound rigidities (and took great pleasure in doing so). The chair of the history department rebutted my statement by slyly implying that my *sole* source of discontent was money. I thought of refuting that by publishing the assorted memos between me and the Princeton powers-that-be over the previous few years, and a *New York Times* stringer tried to tempt me into cooperating with an article about "how established institutions force out their radicals."

But I decided the hell with all that. I didn't want another round of bruising polemics, and besides, the students more than made up for my colleagues' disdain. On the day my resignation was announced, a steady stream of them came into my office to express their pleasure that I was "getting out from under" (one of them broke into a grin on pushing open the office door: "Hey! I hear you're graduating with our class!"). On the day of my final lecture they draped the balcony of the hall with a huge white sheet on which they had written in big letters, PRINCETON WITHOUT MARTY WILL BE FARTY.

Yet the joy I felt in starting over at Lehman was diluted. As I wrote in my diary, "As I ascend the Distinguished Professor pedestal, I think I might miss my Princeton role as rebel and outsider, might wonder what the hell I'm doing at the pinnacle of a profession and as part of an institutional arrangement with which I feel so basically at odds."

But the uneasiness went even deeper than that. I may have been on my way out of therapy, but its negative view of who I was could not be readily expunged. With the Distinguished Professor offer now in hand, I worried (as I wrote in my diary) over "the variance between my public and private lives." Perhaps, I wrote, I felt the variance because I was using *their* measurements—of both achievement and deviance. Even raising that as a possibility was a milestone on my journey to self-acceptance. Yet no sooner had I raised it than I rebutted it: "No, the acute sense of fraudulence that I sometimes feel is deeper than culturally derived formulae. It has to do with *my* realization of being at cross-purposes, of being outside everything I'm involved in, of denying what I enjoy, of letting my words articulate what my emotions refuse to embrace, of confusing self-analysis with self." It was going to be a *long* journey.

Late in November, four days before the therapy group was due to reconvene, and just as I was nearing a decision not to return to it, a letter arrived from Karl. In its entirety it read:

Swiftly and with barely any signs or symptoms a team of competent medical experts has made it mandatorily clear that I must spend my last remaining days in some tropical climate.

Such a location has not been determined, it has all happened so suddenly.

I will do my best to stay in touch.

Fondly,
Karl

P.S. My feeling is that for the present at least I need a period of time to adjust to this news.

P.S.S. Forgive the typed letter but I am just not physically up to handwriting.

I could hardly believe what I was reading, could hardly comprehend the words. My first thought was that Karl had cancer. But then why would his doctors insist on a "tropical climate"? My next reaction was distrust: Karl was making up a medical excuse to cover his desertion—he and Helen had gone to live in Morocco, as he had long said he wanted to. No, no, I quickly countered, that's a *grotesque* reaction, typically self-centered, typically devoid of concern for Karl—my God, their very honeymoon was the occasion for such a tragedy!

Then I looked again at the P.S. It suddenly made no sense. Was Karl suggesting he might resume his practice, that he wasn't dying? But that would contradict "last remaining days." Was he being deliberately vague to abort an orgy of sentimentality? But wasn't vagueness an invitation to fantasy, to paranoid scenarios of abandonment and excommunication? Puzzled, suspicious, I decided that I would go up to Karl's office on the night the group was due to reconvene to see if the others would show up and what they might know or be feeling.

About half the group did turn up, and we went around the corner to Judy's apartment to talk over our reactions. Everyone had received exactly the same letter, and nobody had any additional information, except for a rumor picked up from a patient in another of Karl's groups that he was suffering from something called Raynaud's disease—poor circulation in the capillaries—and that he and Helen had gone to live in South America. Everyone shared a sense of shocked disbelief, and most of what was said centered on concern for Karl and Helen. But to my surprise, Dick did express some resentment at the way Karl had terminated, arguing that no matter how ill he was, he should have cushioned the shock with more information about what had happened and where he was. I said I agreed with Dick.

There was some talk of trying to hold the group together on an informal basis, but I was not the only one who said he wouldn't be available for that. We did exchange phone numbers—previously not allowed—and in the ensuing weeks I met Judy and Dick a few times for lunch or dinner. But the meetings were uncomfortable. I ascribed it to the difference between therapeutic and social climates; the one stressed the most open possible exchange of the deepest possible feelings, the other put emphasis on describing surface activities. Whatever the reasons, I didn't continue the contact. Probably I wanted to be entirely clear of therapy and its associations.

But one thing I did get from my few meetings with Judy and Dick was an acknowledgment that Karl was fallible. Dick even confessed that when Karl and I had tangled over this or that issue, he had often thought I was in the right. Well why hadn't he said so at the time, I asked, instead of letting me dangle in the air, letting Karl fix all responsibility for the disagreements on my "defiant" personality? Dick had no answer for that. He shrugged and mumbled something about not wanting to jeopardize his own therapy. I was furious at these belated revelations, furious that for so many years the rest of the group had dishonestly united behind Karl's view that *he* was above criticism and *I* was contemptibly misdirecting my feelings.

It was a useful fury. It made it possible for me to ignore a call I got from Karl's secretary about three months after his original letter. She informed me that Karl was feeling much better, though he still tired easily, and said I was invited to correspond with him via cassette tapes. She gave me a New York address to send the tapes to, saying they would be forwarded by persons unnamed to a place unspecified. I declined the opportunity. And that was the last personal contact I ever had with Karl. But it was not the last word I had about him.

In 1977 my phone rang one day, and there on the other end of the line was Helen. She had divorced Karl, was back in New York, and wanted to see me. We fell into each other's arms at the restaurant—it had been something like eight years—and for the next three hours she riveted my attention with an astonishing tale.

It began with her own history with Karl. It seems they had become lovers soon after she entered therapy, and Karl acknowledged to Helen that she was just one in a long line of female patients he had had sex with. He justified it as "therapeutic": it made the women "feel feminine," thereby "freeing them up for future relationships." Within a few years of their becoming lovers, Karl had encouraged Helen to divorce her husband, coaching her on tactics for "taking" him for all she could. The tactics had worked, and Helen emerged from the divorce a wealthy woman. Soon after (at just about the time I entered therapy), Karl, who was separated from his own wife, moved in with Helen.

By the mid-sixties, according to Helen, Karl had tired of his practice and had decided to retire. He fancied himself a writer— one of several sources of the profound antagonism he felt toward me, Helen added parenthetically. He plotted the retirement carefully over a period of years, gradually storing up illegal gold holdings and undeclared funds abroad. To avoid possible complications with the IRS, he fastened on Costa Rica, which had no extradition treaty with the United States, as the best place to live. He had long had a *mild* form of Raynaud's disease and elaborated that into the melodramatic letter he sent his patients.

Once they were in Costa Rica, the marriage had quickly disintegrated. Karl's ambition to write came to nothing. He drank increasingly, had affairs, and, ultimately, became abusive toward Helen—the whole heterosexual nine yards, I thought to myself bitterly. Helen explained that she had cared deeply for me but at the time had been too besotted with Karl to read his megalomaniacal character rightly or come to my aid more often. She had wanted to see me to make amends and had generously thought that if I heard more about Karl I might have an easier time freeing myself from any residual power he might have over me.

By the time I saw Helen in 1977, Karl's influence on me had long since crumbled, but I could have dearly used her information when therapy terminated in November 1970. At the time I initially felt elation, as if literally let out of prison. But I soon realized that I was in no shape simply to embrace freedom; I trailed so many negative attitudes about myself that the process of peeling them away still continues to the present day.

# 15

---

# AFTERMATHS

I N THE MONTHS IMMEDIATELY following the end of therapy, my anger focused almost entirely inward. I castigated myseif in my diary for the "greedy, manic" way I "dash and gobble, dash and gobble—and then try to conceal the emptiness by pretending all those scattershots and gulps result from 'a variety of creative impulses.' I never waste time—which is how I waste life." As my play *Payments* moved toward a workshop production at New Dramatists early in 1971, I decided that one of its least endearing characters, "Paul," was a thin disguise for myself: "the man who fully understands the pathology of his behavior and yet is unable to change it; whose self-indulgence ends in isolation; whose energy is devoted to remaining dead center; a man peculiarly American in his unyielding adolescence, his charming, manipulative, destructive greed."

I berated myself, too, for letting my political activities slacken off at just the time that events demanded heightened commitment. The American invasion of Cambodia in May 1970 and the killing of students at Kent State had galvanized protest around the country. I shared in the general outrage, but didn't do much to express it other than by joining in a few demonstrations and signing a few indignant petitions. I also made an incomplete stab at tax refusal, signing a War Tax Resistance pledge stating that I would not comply with a new excise tax designed to fund the war effort, and agreeing to withhold 20 percent of my federal income tax (the WTR's recommended figure). But when I discovered that I was due to get a tax *refund* that year, which would automatically abort my plan to withhold federal payment, I made no further effort at tax refusal.

On another occasion, I tried to use my designation as a prize-winner to make a political statement, but the effort again came to nothing. Early in February 1971 the National Institute of Arts and Letters notified me that I had been given a three-thousand-dollar award "in recognition of my creative work in literature." Delighted though I was—and needing the money—I decided to refuse the prize if, as I thought probable, the government was in any way involved as a sponsor. I was aware that the likely notoriety that would come to me from turning the prize down would be worth even more than the cash, but I decided the act of refusal was right even if my motives were less than perfect. But then the Institute assured me that it was funded entirely from private sources and had no ties of any kind with the federal government. And so, once more, my career projectory remained undeflected by a political gesture that had been perhaps calculatedly inept.

I didn't attempt even an inept gesture in support of those gay activists who, following the lead of the antiwar movement, began to adopt confrontational tactics in 1970. Directly invading the citadels of bigotry, the activists "zapped" psychiatrists lecturing on the "disease" of homosexuality, interrupted a taped television interview with Dr. David Reuben, author of the homophobic (and best-selling) *Everything You Always Wanted to Know About Sex But Were Afraid to Ask*, and, most importantly, carried out a variety of guerrilla actions at the American Psychiatric Association's 1970 convention in San Francisco.

In the most dramatic confrontation at that convention, the activists disrupted an APA panel featuring Irving Bieber and then created pandemonium at a crowded session on the use of aversive conditioning techniques (electric shock) in the treatment of sexual deviation. As some demonstrators yelled "torture" and "barbarism," others demanded that homosexuals themselves be heard. They were shouted down with epithets of "paranoid fool," "maniac," and "bitch," and the session was hastily adjourned. Some of the enraged psychiatrists—not used to having their authority challenged—demanded that the APA refund the cost of their plane fares to San Francisco. And one of them called on the police to shoot the gay demonstrators.[22]

As I can see in retrospect, a necessary prelude to becoming an activist myself was taking some of the anger I vengefully turned inward and putting it where it belonged—on a repressive culture, and on Karl as its representative. By 1971 that shift had begun, my anger at Karl building slowly but steadily. In the privacy of my diary I mulled over my therapeutic history, reconsidering whether my grievances against Karl were indeed as trivial and as entirely of my own "infantile" making as he had long insisted, expressing them for the first time without worrying about "the explosive retribution that followed on the few occasions when I had dared to say them directly to Karl."

Gradually, I let the anger surface. I recalled Karl's vanity, his related need to put me down, his refusal ever to acknowledge the privileged position and unequal authority that he held in the therapy group, and the uncompromising certitude with which he stated his opinions (announcing, for example, that "Lincoln was *clearly* psychotic!"). I remembered, too, the equal certitude with which he would sometimes reverse his opinions, always denying that the latest ones contradicted his earlier views in any way. Thus, over my protest, he had vigorously denounced women's liberation when it first surfaced as "sick," but later, shifting to guarded approval, he explained that the movement had "cleaned up its act."

The more my grievances ripened, the more puzzled I felt as to why I had let Karl browbeat me all those years, let him reduce me to a compliant, docile boy. Part of the answer centered on the profound self-distrust that I brought with me into therapy, and my attendant eagerness to be told what to do and how to please. What also made a forceful contribution to my thralldom was Karl's ability to reveal issues about my character that I knew were real. The fact that he exploited those insights for his own vain and homophobic purposes did not invalidate them. And his charismatic intensity—he was far from the conventionally uninvolved, imperturbable therapist of the day—seemed to add weight to his insights. Further, members of the group (and especially Helen and Dick) with whom I had formed strong bonds and trusted, seconded Karl's views and lovingly urged me to yield to them, persuasively certain that they were for my own good.

But I was not simply the victim of other people's mistaken agendas. I had been mesmerized by Karl's potency and was covetous of it. Aware and flattered that this electric, compelling man seemed to feel competitive with me, and even (to an extent he could never admit) intimidated by my verbal and writerly skills, I had wanted to believe that regardless of who "won" the contest, this powerful figure dispensing love and approval would make good on his promise to anoint me with his blessing, to certify me.

Trying to clarify some of these feelings further, I decided to sample several of the new consciousness-raising groups that had begun to appear in New York.

The first convened at the invitation of Joe Chaikin, the head of the Open Theater and a recent friend. Seven men gathered in Joe's apartment one morning in March—most of the others in their twenties and all but one either gay or bisexual—to talk about the prospects for forming a men's consciousness-raising group. The session went on for about three hours. Most of the talk centered on homosexuality, and most of it closely reflected my own emerging views. As I wrote that night in my diary, one of the gay men "seemed a touch too certain that homosexuality had nothing to do with neurosis, and another seemed a lot too certain that it had everything to do with it, but there was little glib glorification à la Gay Liberation or guilty self-hate à la the 1950s."

I had only recently set my feet on that in-between path and might logically have found camaraderie in joining a group that seemed to share my perspective. But instead, I told myself that men's groups were gimmicky—women's liberation without any genuine sense of shared oppression—and that the particular men who had shown up weren't sexist enough to bring out my missionary zeal either. Like most people who offer themselves for rites of self-improvement, they stood in far less need of it than those who don't. Besides, they simply didn't interest me much as individuals.

In retrospect, I suspect the deeper reason was that I didn't feel that I deserved the comfort. The man who claimed homosexuality had nothing to do with neurosis might, after all, persuade me to his view, which was still too advanced for my shaky liberationist spirit. Explaining my decision not to join to my old friend Ray, I professed to disdain the current penchant for lurching from group to guru, for "cluttering rather than enriching life," and haughtily concluded that faddish New Yorkers "changed their vocabularies more than their lifestyles." Having delivered myself of that judgment, I promptly signed up for a daylong "marathon on sexuality," sponsored by Anthos, the East Coast branch of Esalen. Whereas the men's group might have encouraged me to accept myself more, I must have sensed that Anthos would urge me to persist in making myself over.

The marathon started at ten o'clock on a Saturday morning and was scheduled to run until midnight. Fourteen people gathered (at sixty-five dollars a head), led by the organizer of the session, the therapist "Alfred Steiner." Among the other participants, several quickly made themselves prominent: Joan, age twenty-seven but with a child's nervous straightforwardness— and a case of severe colitis; Mike, a stockbroker recently released from Bellevue and recently separated from his wife (who he felt *certain* was a lesbian); Estelle, a loud, upfront woman in her late forties whose son was a masseur at Esalen and whose recent roommate, as she proudly announced, was a drag queen/prostititute; Roger, in his late twenties, tightly knit, piercing eyes, bisexual, accustomed to turning on everyone of both genders; and Janet, an Anthos regular, an aggressively comfortable two-hundred-pound hug addict.

As the opening exercise, Steiner announced, we would "pass the hat," each in turn telling what his or her expectations were for the marathon. Earlier, friends had asked me why I had signed up for what to them seemed a gimmicky, perhaps even destructive one-shot encounter session with no chance for followup, and I had answered that paradoxically that kind of limited liability might allow me to take some chances that had proved too threatening in an ongoing therapy group. I had also said something "jocular" about needing "an electric shock" to dynamite my overly defended psyche.

But when the hat came to me, I heard myself saying that I had signed up for the marathon "to confirm the hopelessness of my homosexuality, to prove I was irrevocably imprinted."

The other members tsk-tsked at the notion of "hopelessness," so antithetical to the Anthos spirit, but no one tsk-tsked over my negative characterization of homosexuality. Steiner said that before the marathon ended he would disprove my "foolish" belief that I had *no* sexual feelings toward women—if, that is, I showed the requisite "guts."

After the hat had gone round, Steiner peremptorily told us to take off all our clothes. There was some initial resistance— Susan, an uptight, virginal nurse of twenty-two nearly sobbed with fear over what her mother would say. "Don't tell your mother!" Steiner shot back. "You either take off your clothes *now* or you get the hell out of this marathon—money fully refunded." A tearful Susan slowly peeled off garment after garment, as the other group members murmured encouragement. I was none too happy myself with the prospect of nudity, given my habitual discomfort with my body. But since I had recently been going to a gym, even I knew that I was in presentable shape; gradually, just slightly in advance of Susan, I managed to strip down.

Steiner then divided us into four-person subgroups, with instructions to pat and feel each other's bodies. Roger was part of my group and his presence unnerved me. Attracted as I was to him, I agonized about rolling over on my stomach to let him and the others poke and explore what I considered my "unaesthetic" side (meaning thinnish legs and a scar from an operation twenty years earlier). I was even more unnerved when Roger seemed indifferent to my bodily "imperfections." Reconvened as one group, each of us reported on what we had felt while patting and being patted. When my turn came, I confessed my lust for Roger, who, with unwavering indifference, blandly responded that he felt no sexual attraction toward me but did like me, and especially liked how "calm" I was. (So much for *his* insight! I thought with bitter satisfaction.)

Joan then announced that her colitis was kicking up and said she had to go to the bathroom. Steiner brusquely told me to accompany her: "Joan needs to get over her anger at men— that's what her colitis is all about." Having a man stare at her while she groaned her way through a bowel movement didn't strike me as a likely cure for hostility, but not wanting to make undue waves, I dutifully followed Joan into the bathroom. While she sat grim-faced on the can, I affected a sophisticated lounging pose, à la Ronald Colman, trying not to press my naked body too close to the ice-cold tiles. We chatted away about how much we were getting out of the marathon, how wonderfully it was breaking down our defenses.

When we reported back to the group that we had grown fond of each other in the can, Steiner reacted as if inspired. "Aw' right, Martin," he barked, "here's your chance! If you *seriously* want to find out whether you're as sexually uninterested in women as you claim, then I suggest you and Joan go into the adjoining room and you let Joan try to turn you on. Take Estelle with you, so she can relieve Joan. Between the two of them, I guarantee results." Joan looked as reluctant as I, but Estelle was on her feet in a flash. "Come on, kids!" she bellowed cheerfully, "let's give it a whirl!"

So off the three of us trooped into the next room, where for an hour we touched, fondled, and cuddled, Estelle sucking away nobly at my limp cock, Joan obligingly letting her breasts get hard at my touch. None of it was unpleasant. Despite some initial nervousness, and whether through denial or disinterest, I felt calmly detached (*defensively* detached, both Karl and Alfred Steiner would have insisted). I congratulated myself on not having been too uptight to go through the motions, and all three of us generated considerable affection for each other. But limp my cock remained. When we reported this back to the group, Steiner decided, grumpily, that my failure to get excited merely proved that *those* two women didn't turn me on. Within his own frame of reference, Steiner was proving as dogged as Karl.

I stayed another few hours, participated fully, volubly exchanged confidences, opinions, and interpretations, let myself get hugged and patted several dozen more times and then decided to cut out, having become alternately bored and appalled at the callow exchanges, the simulated feelings. But when I started to put on my clothes, expecting to deliver a quick, polite good-night, Steiner stopped me in my tracks. "The least you can do before you chicken out of the group," he said, his lips decidedly curled, "is to express your feelings about each person in this room, *starting with me*."

As I silently mulled over whether I wanted to take on the exercise, and in what spirit, Steiner denounced me for "pussyfooting." Throughout the day he had taken any pause for thought as a betrayal of feeling, demanding, as if we were all unambiguous need machines, that we instantly say, "what it is you *want!*" In that same spirit, he now yelled, "Whatsamatter, Martin, don't you have the guts to tell us your *real* feelings?!" And so I did. I told him that I didn't like him very much, though I did envy his self-confidence. But given his bullying strut, I added, maybe it really wasn't self-confidence at all.

Steiner jumped up, eyes blazing, yelling that I had "no power to hurt" him, denouncing me as passive, devious, unwilling to help myself. I don't need any more abuse, I thought to myself. To Steiner I simply said, "You may well be right," and went for my coat. My last vision of Anthos, as I stood waiting for the elevator to arrive, was Janet, stark naked at two hundred pounds, rushing toward me, begging me "not to betray" myself by leaving, pressing me up against her. I thanked her for her concern and stepped gratefully into the arriving elevator.

I expected to feel uneasy the next day, to guilt-trip myself yet again, as Karl had trained me to do, at having "run away when the going got tough." But instead, I woke up feeling confirmed in my judgment that the marathon had been a fraudulent kind of instant therapy. I realized with a start that I had lost the habit of automatically blaming *myself*.

Or perhaps, more accurately, I had begun to find different grounds for doing so. As I wrote in my diary the day after the marathon, "I did come away with one clarification: the new model that's gradually been emerging in my head—paralleling the shift in cultural attitudes of recent years—is that I should be able to enjoy individuals of either sex, that my 'problem' is best defined not as homosexuality, but as the exclusivity of my homosexuality." Increasingly in the next few years, I would come to feel that bisexuality might be the ideal standard against which a "healthy" sexuality should be measured. But even in 1971 I realized that assumption could itself prove tyrannical, could prove the latest in a long series of party lines used to disparage and police individual choice.

And I was able to say exactly that one night when an ex-student of mine with whom I had become friendly after his graduation, told me he had been having sexual fantasies about me. Though he'd never had sex with a man, he wanted us to go to bed. Instead, we had a long talk. I told him for the first time that I was exclusively homosexual (he had been assuming, it turned out, that I was bisexual). I also told him that I didn't think either of us felt any real lust for the other and that it would be a mistake to have sex: we didn't live close enough (he was currently in medical school in Boston) to be able to work through any repercussions that might follow.

I raised the possibility that in pushing for us to go to bed, he might simply be trying to get his credentials in the counterculture. He bore, I thought, the special burden placed on cultural radicals of his generation to prove not "masculinity" (my generation's burden) but rather liberation from its confining definitions. He readily acknowledged that he felt downright guilty about never having made it with a man, convinced that his "residual puritanism" was responsible. Just as I had begun to question whether my *exclusive* homosexuality (rather than homosexuality itself) might be pathology, he had begun to regard his exclusive heterosexuality as a sign of blocked growth.

I told him (as I summed it up in my diary that night) "that I wasn't at all sure the current cultural definitions of sexual health would hold up any better than earlier ones had; that I saw no logical progression from men hugging more to sucking each other's cocks; nor that the progression had to take place before caring could be certified." He seemed relieved. We had a long hug at the door.

Yet it was easier for him to shake the notion that everyone *should* be bisexual than it was for me—even though I could see, as I wrote in my diary, that "only my perfectionism continues to demand that I measure myself against a bisexual ideal, that I reject any personal limitations (real or imagined)." I was still referring to an exclusively gay orientation as a "limitation," which meant that for me, being gay remained a suspect, lesser condition.

Ray and I would talk about that over long dinners. He had recently taken a teaching job in the New York area, and so we were able to spend more time together than we had in many years. Ray and I had come from much the same background and had had similar therapeutic indoctrination, but Ray was a bit less wary about gay liberation and the "new homosexuality" than I was.

After one such evening, I summarized our conversation in a long diary entry:

I found myself repeating arguments I already know are confused and unconvincing, like citing Erik Erikson's work on the "natural" life cycle as somehow proof that homosexuals are aborted in their growth at some early phase, never becoming "whole." But I know Erikson isn't sacrosanct, no more than Freud before him. And having to fall back on concepts as vague as "wholeness" hardly satisfies me that I've done more than parrot, albeit with an academic gloss, majoritarian definitions of normality.

Ever since the Gay Liberation Front emerged and I've thought about trying to tie in with it in some way, I've been paralyzed by ambiguity. What it seems to come down to is that I've internalized for so long the social definition of homosexuality as pathology and curse that I'm unable to embrace a different view, though I'd desperately like to. . . . The best I can honestly manage is to insist that I'm "caused," my imprinting so deep as to preclude any change in sexual orientation—yes, a change I'd still grab at, if perhaps a little less certainly than before. I've "progressed" to the point where I can (occasionally) relieve the guilt and shift the castigation from me to society. . . .

Yet the progress was real and ongoing, even if not linear, even though marked by retreats and hesitations. And as in the past, it was my playwriting and my experiences in the theater that did the most to fuel the advance. In April 1971, *Payments* (about the world of male hustling) went into rehearsal at New Dramatists. Its stormy course moved me further along the path of a public coming out—and further persuaded me of the need for it.

Some of the problems that arose during rehearsal would have been standard for any play that called for a large cast and had a complex structure that included double scenes. The production was further endangered by a bare-bones budget and limited stage facilities. All this created stress enough, but the most intractable problem proved the unwillingness of "Andy," the actor cast in the leading role of the bemused bisexual, "Bob," to com-

mit himself to the role. The closer we came to the first performance, the more Andy clammed up, terrified that he and the
role would become synonymous, that his career might be
compromised.

As Andy froze, I began to sweat. "It was bad enough," I wrote
in my diary, to "publicly expose my hang-ups but much worse
not to have them validated as art." The workshop audiences
would be filled with personal friends and possible angels—a
double-barreled potential for disgrace. My worst fears seemed
realized after the first performance, when the actor Jimmy Coco,
with whom I played poker in a weekly game, took me aside and
whispered with alarm in my ear, "What did you do—swallow a
brave pill?"

Nor did matters improve with subsequent performances. Another friend chewed me out privately for "needlessly trivializing
myself through thinly disguised public confession." A third left
the theater during intermission—as did a quarter of the audience at each performance, the remainder sitting stony-faced
through the second half. There were a few enthusiasts, the most
vocal being the British director Peter Glenville. He came back-
stage to congratulate me on my "courageous" play, saying that
"it makes *Boys in the Band* look like the homosexual world's *No,
No, Nanette.*"

But at the end of the five-performance run, it was clear that
no commercial producer was willing to touch *Payments*. The few
who had nibbled tentatively at the manuscript version hastily
backed off when confronted with the reality of a live production.
I tried to be philosophical, telling myself in my diary that "the
failure to find a producer for *Payments* might prove a blessing—
I'll have gotten the play out of my system, and without the cost
of a public humiliation." But in fact the opposite happened.
Having all but announced my homosexuality, and having lived,
more or less, to tell the tale, I felt less timid than ever about
further exposure.

And so the following month, when I got a phone call from a
gay publicist friend inviting me to take part in a panel discussion
on "Gay Activists and the Arts" at the Gay Activists Alliance, I
at least hedged, saying I would welcome the chance to learn
more about the organization and would make up my mind after
that. GAA had recently come into existence as a breakaway

alternative to the Gay Liberation Front, and would shortly su-
percede it. Whereas GLF had believed in organizational spontaneity and decentralization, the activists of GAA opted for a
more orderly and traditional Robert's Rule structure; and
whereas GLF had argued that sexual liberation had to be fought
for in conjunction with a variety of other social reforms and in
alliance with other oppressed minorities, GAA believed in a
single-minded concentration on gay civil rights and eschewed
"romantic" excursions into revolutionary ideology.[23]

Within days I had a letter from the publicist friend confirming
that I had agreed, which I had not, to join the playwright Ron
Tavel and the writer Merle Miller on the GAA panel. My first
inclination was to go along with it and participate. But when I
told Ray, he expressed surprise that I would let myself be
"shoved" into a public commitment for which I felt unprepared.
"What an irony," he said. "You're more pessimistic about the
'homosexual condition' than I am and more skeptical about the
organizations peddling gay power, and yet you're the one who
winds up sitting on the platform. I think you're being foolish."
I decided he was right, and I extricated myself from the commitment, reiterating to the publicist friend my interest in learning more about GAA.

I spent the summer of 1971 chained to my desk, churning
out chapter after chapter of the Black Mountain book, cutting
distractions to a minimum, promising myself that come mid-
September a new life would begin: the book would be completed, I would start teaching at Lehman, and I would even be
living in a different apartment (my landlord had announced he
was selling the brownstone I currently lived in). But I did let
myself take a break from work over the July Fourth weekend
and go off to Fire Island with Ray.

Throughout the weekend, I sounded an elegiac note, mixed
with a fair amount of self-pity. Trying to minimize my usual
uneasiness while on vacation and separated from my work, I
concentrated on the known pleasures of the beach and avoided
the known anxieties of competing in the sexual sweepstakes with
glamorous twenty-year-olds (most of them, thanks to the endemic drug-taking that had settled on the Island, more acces-
sible than ever for anonymous sex but not for any other kind
of connection).

But the beach itself made me melancholy. Walking it at sunset, trying to clear my head of Matthew Arnold-like clichés about "the eternal note of sadness," I nonetheless found a profound loneliness flooding in. "This," I wrote in my diary, "looks more and more like the name of the game for me. No more thrashing around in therapy, trying to make it with a woman. No confidence left of anything lasting with a man. But God, I need someone to touch me like they want me a lot, to tell me they're glad I'm around. It's when I'm away from New York, stripped of my usual insulation of people, props, work, that being alone hurts this much. Well, at least I do have the insulation of work. I guess a lot of people don't have any insulation. So they go nuts—or grow up." Starting to cry, I gave myself a stern lecture about ingratitude, about how (as I wrote in my diary) "disgustingly self-pitying I am. I *do* have caring people in my life. I expect too fucking much."

Remembering that my old friend Harry—he of the manifold bed partners and family millions—had a house in Cherry Grove, I dropped over there one evening, hoping to get a boost in spirits. Instead I got more disconnection. Harry had sealed his life off long ago—and with impeccable wrapping. Surrounded, as always, by perfectly formed twenty-two-year-olds, he was now surrounded as well by a cloud of pot smoke and given to giggly exclamations of "groovy!" and "dynamite!" Hoping to catch the spirit, I dutifully puffed away, but the net effect was to make me still quieter, still more in need of talk and cuddling. When Harry's group headed out to dance at the Ice Palace, I went along, but my mood remained glum, and later, in my diary, I censoriously put down "the preening peacocks trying to outdo each other's exhibitionism, the glittery poster-boys parading their symmetrically perfect, essentially asexual bodies." I reproachfully added that "this sex-drug madhouse makes me feel sexless—and a tower of maturity, the 'sexual hysteria' for which I sometimes berate myself laughably tame in this context of meat racks and round-the-clock orgies."

I carried my ascetic mood back to New York—and straight into the arms of Swami Satchadananda. I had been hearing more and more about the wondrous serenity that yoga induced, and when I learned that the Integral Yoga Institute was two blocks from where I lived, I trooped over for a beginner's class.

The first session did indeed relax me, though the thousand years of Western rationalism in my head rumbled now and then at the "Oms" and at the general air of beatification, and though I was alarmed to see none other than Estelle, she who had chomped on my cock at the Anthos sexual marathon, turn up in the same class. Her flesh bulging out of her baby blue bathing suit, her eyes as manic as ever, Estelle smiled at me in a slightly reproving way, as if to say she hadn't forgotten my refusal to get hard, had taken note of the fact that I was chatting with the beautiful man on the mat next to mine, and had serious doubts whether either of us could profit from the mysteries of the East.

Had Estelle been able to read my mind during those first few weeks of yoga, her dire predictions would have been confirmed, for my mood remained poised between suspicion and mirth. I mocked the repetitiveness of the sessions, claimed the process needed speeding up by a goal-oriented Westerner able to grasp the *through* line. I decided the Indian chants sounded Hebraic, and especially when Estelle was overpowering the rest of the group with the loudest "Om, shanti" in the room. And I refused to shut my eyes when instructed to "place the concentration inward," determined to see if anyone was getting their legs higher off the ground than I was.

But as my body toned up and my angst toned down, I became a convert. A teenaged girl whistled at me from her bike as I walked along in a new tee shirt. Two handsome men in one week stopped to cruise me on the street. I had long been vain about my mind, but now it felt wonderful to be exulting in my body. "Perhaps," I wrote in my diary, "I'm beginning to locate an *appropriate* self-image, since in the past I've been overly impressed with my rational skills, overly apologetic about my emotional needs, and overly shy about my body."

Eager to parlay the good feeling, I shifted to crunchy granola for breakfast, toyed with the notion of eating only organically grown foods, and even renewed my vow (again soon aborted) to stop taking a sleeping pill at night. By late August I had promoted myself to an intermediate yoga class, determined to master the headstand *at once*, slowed in my zeal only by the realization that in this case the end result of overachievement could be a cave in the Himalayas.

I felt better than I had, physically and emotionally, in years.

On my forty-first birthday in August, I wrote in my diary, "I wish I'd felt this good about myself when I was twenty. But that sounds retrospective, which I don't feel at all. With Princeton, Black Mountain and therapy all off my back, or nearly so, I feel a new beginning, a wide opening-out." Ten days later, still fired up, I wrote, "I feel like I'm pacing the deck during the last weeks of a long, long overdue voyage. God, how I want to get off this ship, throw overboard all those trunks stuffed with memorabilia, and stretch, *stretch* my legs on some unfamiliar (but not *too* unfamiliar) shore."

But I couldn't sustain the good mood. And perhaps that was predictable. It was naive to think that a few months in the lotus position would be enough to transform me into a yeah-sayer. The journey back was going to have to take as long, or nearly so, as the journey out. Too much good feeling too quickly was threateningly unfamiliar, in the nature of a burden—and could not be borne for long. I needed a respite, a way back to more familiar ground, comfortably troubled. And the way presented itself in the usual form: a beautiful young man, this time named Danny.

# 16

## DANNY

D ANNY CAME FROM A working-class family on the outskirts of Poughkeepsie. He had grown up as one of the local roughnecks, high-spirited and energetic, more interested in athletics than school, and more interested in risky adventure than either. Immensely shrewd, with little education but with a mind as agile as his instincts, and ambitious to stand out, he had become a drug dealer while still a teenager, making and spending considerable sums. By 1970, at age twenty-two, he had gotten tired of the drug trade—which was fortunate, since the state police had picked up his trail. Down he had come to New York, with no money, swaggeringly confident that he could parlay his rugged good looks into an acting career, migrating quickly, as "an interim measure," to the world of male hustling.

We met through Ron, the male madame, and after our first toss, I wasn't even interested enough to get Danny's phone number. A month later he rang my doorbell: "just passing by and wondering what you're up to." We talked this time for a couple of hours, followed by sex ("on the house"). He filled in some details of his prior history—how he had played at being paralyzed in an army hospital for a year in order to qualify for a permanent disability pension—and asked my advice about getting some training as an actor. I suggested the Herbert

Berghof Studio as the best starting point and told him I'd be glad to go over the catalogue with him if he wanted to come by with it. He made it clear that his "thing" was women, and I saw no reason to doubt that, even though in bed he was decidedly present—aroused and not at all coy about showing it.

He started to drop by regularly. I told myself that it was simply a matter of being glamorized by my contacts in the theater and that *under no circumstances* should I fantasize about getting involved with him. With that warning duly registered, I promptly started to get involved. Initially I helped him choose courses at Berghof and took him to see some plays. Then one day my doorbell rang and up came a gleeful Danny clutching $350 in cash—from a hash deal, it turned out. He asked me to hold $300 of it for him toward his Berghof tuition ("you're the only guy I trust, including myself"). As a reward for taking on the function of private banker, I was given a big hunk of the hash. "I've been wanting to do something for you," he said, "and this is my first chance." I had never smoked hash, but with my heart melting, that was neither here nor there.

As Danny and I began seeing more and more of each other, Ray took me aside for a scolding. He had had dinner one night with Danny and me and had decidedly disapproved of the growing attachment. "You're going to end up getting treated badly," he sternly warned. "Danny's gravitational system is heterosexual. You've got to understand that and get out while you can. You should aspire toward something better for yourself."

"Isn't that a little abstract?" I said defensively.

"No more than your fantasy life," Ray countered.

"Oh look, I'm not *deeply* involved, I just enjoy his company. I love his energy."

Ray looked solemn. "Dear heart, your life has been on a decided upswing of late. Are you *sure* this isn't a form of self-sabotage?"

"Of course I'm not sure. But I'm not imagining his interest in me. This is *not* one-sided."

Ray drew a deep breath. "Danny is responding to your attention and generosity. That is not the same as love."

"Who's talking about love?" I said, trying to feign indignation. "I enjoy his company, period." I was now repeating myself, a sure sign I felt on shaky ground.

"You're enjoying locker-room camaraderie. You two *are* a lot alike—high energy, defiant, demanding. But buddies are not lovers. I implore you: make him a friend, or a surrogate son if you're feeling maternal, but *stop* thinking of him as a potential lover. Can't you *once* try to resist what you know is bad for you?"

That sounded superior and gave me an excuse to get angry. "Well listen to you! You sound exactly like Karl! Just what I need in my life—another policeman! How do you know what's good for me or bad for me? It could be Danny is the only kind of lover I'm capable of having—meaning, somebody occasional, different from me in age and background, and even, maybe, in sexual desire. We get what we want. And maybe Danny is all I want."

Ray exploded. "Don't hand me that crap! You've had much more than that in the past and you could get it for yourself again if you'd only give yourself a chance—Christ, what a smarmy mix you are of self-indulgence and self-betrayal!"

That cut like a whiplash, but I was already in too deep with Danny to let myself feel the sting for long. As storm signals gathered over the next few months, as Danny would fail to show or call as planned, would cover his tracks with patently unconvincing excuses, would hint that he was getting involved with one of the women in his class at Berghof, I did my best to look away, telling myself that I had no right to monitor his activities or demand a fidelity that had never been part of the bargain. After all, I would indignantly remind myself, we *weren't* lovers, and even if we were, so foolishly antiquated an expectation as faithfulness would be beneath us. Besides, I told myself, the surest way to lose Danny would be continually to express my insecurity, to accuse him of caring more for somebody else or to accuse myself of being lovable only to the extent I could offer theater connections or cash.

Periodically, when my own arguments began to wear thin, I would stage a showdown. I would tell Danny that I was thinking of getting out of the relationship, of backing off from a situation where the odds and obstacles seemed so great, where I wasn't getting enough of what I needed. To which he would reply with some variation of "just what is it that you need?" and my honesty would lead me shamefacedly to confess, "probably just what I'm getting."

Then we would laughingly patch things up, and Danny would tell me that he had "never felt this way about a man before," that he had never let *anyone* this far into his life. We would agree that what we had was in fact terrific, that we loved each other's company, loved having sex together, loved the way we complemented each other. As I wrote in my diary one night, after Danny had taught me how to play pool in a Forty-second Street dive, "It's great that we know such different kinds of things: Danny, the physical and mechanical, street stuff, the woods and outdoors; me, the informational, urban, cerebral, cultural. And it's great, too, that each of us is looking for ways out of (or at least supplements to) the bags we've been in so long—that's why we enjoy each other so much: the differentness. After pool we came back to my place, smoked a joint and lay around on the bed cuddling and talking, neither feeling much like sex. We're so comfortable with each other, and so appreciative of each other. Of course, all the obstacles and dangers remain—but the ship's too far out to sea; I've forgotten what the reefs look like."

By now it was mid-September, the manuscript of the Black Mountain book due, my first class at Lehman College imminent. The involvement with Danny had put me somewhat off stride, but only somewhat. It was a long-standing pattern with me that when something unexpected got added to my life, I not only refused to cut back on prior commitments but insisted on carrying them out with a little extra panache. What I was trying to prove, I suppose, was that nothing or no one could really disorder my life, no matter how many demands were made on it. By redoubling rather than redistributing my energy, I could avoid repose, inflict self-punishment, profess martyrdom.

And indeed, I got the Black Mountain manuscript completed by late September—turning in over a thousand pages, as if to compensate for being a few weeks overdue. To celebrate, Danny and I went out to Fire Island for a weekend, tramped back and forth on the beach, talked about our peculiar chemistry—our similar personalities and dissimilar backgrounds, our common reactions to events and people, but our widely different reference points for them. He told me again that he "didn't think" he was homosexual, that his feeling for me was "something special that just happened." I agreed with him, and not just because I wanted to believe that I was unique and he was straight. At sunset one night, he put his arm around me and said, "I have a feeling, Marty, we'll always be part of each other's lives, even if we're at opposite ends of the earth." That sent a chill through me; it sounded predictive—that is, about opposite ends of the earth.

Back in New York, I enumerated my assorted blessings: the relationship with Danny was in a good phase, the book was off my back, and my first classes at Lehman had filled me with enthusiasm. "None of that Princeton blandness," I wrote in my diary, "or, among the radical students, that sad, despairing we've-had-it-all-but-damned-if-we-know-what-else-we-want blues. These Lehman students are often from lower-middle- or working-class families and *haven't* had it all. They're raucous, rough-edged, high energy; my kind of driven, city-pocked, tough-tender types. Yeah, the facilities stink—I'm sharing an office with two other faculty members—lines and crowds everywhere, even an overhead subway nearby that rumbles through every few minutes. That's all right: it's part of home."

In mid-October, aroused at the government's continuing refusal to end the conflict in Southeast Asia, I spoke at an antiwar moratorium at Lehman, glad for the chance to reactivate myself politically. I talked in my speech about the entrenched power of the state, then about the appeal of the antistate philosophy of anarchism, then about the inspiring life of the anarchist Emma Goldman. The segue was not accidental. After the few days off at Fire Island, I had turned directly to completing the script on the life of Emma Goldman that PBS had earlier commissioned and had become deeply absorbed in the project, overwhelmed by the drama and integrity of Goldman's life, angry at the psychologizing about her that in my view had long delayed her appreciation.

I got so angry that I went into print about it, aware that in publicly attacking the accuracy of "psychological explanations," I was venting my own accumulated grievances against them—and advancing my own liberation from them. Writing to the *New Republic*, I protested the critic Kenneth Lynn's recent article arguing that it was "unmistakably clear" Emma Goldman's "political militancy had been rooted in sexual resentment," and specifically resentment against her volatile, sometimes brutal father. That aspect of her experience, I wrote, was indeed "unmistakably clear," but the link between it and a life in radical politics was not. Conservatives had long used psychology as a weapon for devaluing commitments and lifestyles antithetical to their own, and as a convenient device for not looking at the societal conditions that spawn revolt. "The social ills Emma Goldman encountered *warranted* radical protest," I wrote, "and must themselves be included in any 'explanation' of her activities. The question really begging for explanation is not why Emma Goldman spoke out, but why so few others did."

I was, of course, lecturing myself as well as Lynn. Though I had been drawing steadily closer to speaking out against the oppression of gay people, I still held back, feeling more and more impelled to break my silence yet, almost mysteriously, not quite able to. But it had begun to dawn on me that the Black Mountain book might itself prove the appropriate forum. In it, I was attempting a new, more honestly subjective approach to historical writing and in my draft introduction had already written, "Since all balances are to some extent a betrayal, I've felt the final responsibility of letting myself be known." In that draft I had also suggested that rejecting "the traditional pretense of nonexistence" would "make historical writing a considerably more risky enterprise than is currently the case. 'Risky' not because the past would be revealed less, but because the historian would be exposed more. To try to show up in one's work instead of distancing oneself from it, to remove the protections of anonymity" would, I predicted, prove "searing."

As I started to revise the manuscript in the fall of 1971, one episode in Black Mountain's history jumped out at me as a readymade opportunity to declare myself. In the mid-forties, the theater director Bob Wunsch had become head of Black Mountain. Wunsch had always done everything possible to conceal his homosexuality, cultivating instead the image of an asexual loner. But sometimes, after supper, he would drive off in his small roadster to the nearby city of Asheville. There, one evening in mid-June 1945, he was arrested while parked in his car with a marine. The charge was "crimes against nature."

In those days in North Carolina, that charge carried a mandatory penitentiary sentence and Wunsch—with an instinct for self-punition characteristic of pre-Stonewall homosexuals—promptly pleaded guilty. Apparently some influential Asheville friends interceded with the judge, the indictment was changed to trespassing, and Wunsch was released with a suspended sentence. But his ordeal was far from over. Instead of taking Wunsch's side and offering him comfort, most of the people at Black Mountain—a place that prided itself on being "in the vanguard"—felt he had behaved disgracefully. When he offered to resign, the offer was accepted. Worse still, he was allowed to sneak away in the middle of the night without so much as a kind word, let alone an offer of assistance.

When I came to revise my description of that episode, I found myself choked with anger, and I wrote this: "It's hard to think well of a place that could cooperate as fully as Black Mountain did in an individual's self-destruction—indeed to have assumed it as foreclosed. But perhaps I exaggerate—a function of my own indignation as a homosexual, a potential victim."

This was a more definitive coming out than anything I had previously said in my plays. But it was not yet published. It remained to be seen whether I would lose courage and remove the passage before the final manuscript was due to go to press; or whether developments in my own life would move me far enough along in my commitment to a political struggle for gay rights that I would let the passage stand.

I drilled into my head the latest countercultural rhetoric about the need for "freedom" in relationships, about spontaneity being the only obligation, but it didn't have much effect on my behavior. As Danny continued to be Danny—late, forgetful, irresponsible—I continued to act as if I could make him over into someone who better suited my own needs, even though I still had trouble defining those needs. (Did I *really* want a mate? Did I myself want to commit to any sort of domestic arrangement?) Knowing my own ambivalence, convinced from my own inability in therapy to change according to someone else's specifications, I tried hard to repress the tyrannical therapist within myself, to refrain from demanding that Danny meet *my* specifications for "right living."

But it was a battle I frequently lost. Sometimes I magnified Danny's "infractions" into proofs positive that he didn't care about me, that he was using me, that I was a mere convenience. If he broke an appointment or showed up an hour late or failed to call at an appointed time—all of which he did with infuriating frequency—I would make an instant murder trial out of petty larceny. Alternately, I would assume *all* the blame for our blow-ups, would tell myself that I was insanely sensitive, a neurotic overreacter who exploded in advance of any detonation. But self-castigation didn't wash either. That I sometimes overreacted was indisputable; but so was Danny's uninquiring conviction that his inability to sustain closeness represented a hip lack of possessiveness. He would assure me that he never *meant* to hurt me, but his puzzled innocence only demonstrated how unconnected he was to his own fear of intimacy, and to the effect of his distancing act on others.

As always, I turned to Ray for clarity, and he, as always, gave me a bit more than I wanted. "Why did you choose Danny," he would ask with feigned innocence, "if you didn't want someone who behaves as Danny behaves? You chose somebody with a bastard streak—let us not even speak of the fact that he is a heterosexual bastard, lest you be accused of outright madness—and then you complain bitterly that he acts like who he is. Really, dear one, do take a little responsibility for your own mechanisms."

If I would protest that Danny had many positive, endearing qualities and that I had fallen for him despite the fact that he could *sometimes* act like a bastard, Ray would snort with derision: "Yes, of course, dear. He's the sweet, compliant, cuddly mate you've dreamed of *all* your life—earning his way through school by occasionally turning tricks or drug deals. Once he graduates, I don't doubt he'll straightaway build you that picket fence."

"Don't be arch. I'm in serious pain."

"That I don't doubt—though it's essentially self-induced." Becoming entirely serious, Ray would then warn me that unless I was prepared to stop seeing Danny—which he advocated—I would have to accept certain limitations in the relationship: the intensity and the vintage Hollywood expectations were far greater on my side than Danny's; he had never had a homosexual attachment and might not be either desirous or capable of one; and I had to get rid of the notion that with time and patience I could find some formula for coaxing Danny into a degree of involvement that would match the intensity of my own—an impossibility so long as Danny saw himself, probably accurately, as basically heterosexual. "Besides," Ray would add triumphantly, "even if you somehow *could* create a comparable intensity in Danny, you would then, in direct proportion, lose interest in him, since central to *your* intensity is his unavailability."

For his peroration, Ray would fix me with his Ancient Mariner look: "You've invested Danny with all the magical endowments of the stereotypic male—the vigorous, boisterous roustabout, the All-American hellraiser stud—a persona you have long coveted for yourself and had hoped to incorporate by taking him hostage. As if that wasn't stacking the deck enough, you then turn to this same limited man for comfort and connection! Now that *is* perverse!"

"You make it sound hopeless. I'm miserable."

"What would it look like if 'hopeful'? It would mean a Danny other than who he is—which means less attractive to Marty, unless *he* became someone else as well. Yes, as you said—hopeless."

When I would then look weepy, would say I knew he was right but didn't see how I could survive a total break with Danny, Ray would quickly rush in with reassurance, insisting I *would* survive, reminding me that I existed quite apart from my obsession with Danny, that the obsession represented only *one* thread in my fantasy life. Yet analyzing Danny's hold over me did not automatically loosen its grip. Ray urged me to let will power do the work of conviction: "Just try applying some of that enormous discipline you use in your work to putting Danny first on the margin and then entirely out of your life." Ray prescribed a steady stream of garden parties and gorgeous men, whether paid for or not: "Break your machine-like productivity, let in some time and air, make yourself available."

I took his advice about the gorgeous men, even though I stayed half-hard through most of my escapades, entertaining fantasies of Danny during foreplay instead of attending to the Hero currently at my side. But I did not take Ray's advice about easing off my work schedule; it was the only survival tactic in which I had any confidence. I poured myself into finishing the script on Emma Goldman, scheduled a production of three of my one-act plays at New Dramatists to follow immediately thereafter, and accepted a variety of book review assignments. That enabled me to tell Danny that I was so tied up with work I couldn't see him as often as before and, further, to insist on precise meeting times instead of the haphazard droppings-by whose will-he-or-won't-he-show traumas had previously left me a basketcase. "It's not a question of punition," Ray would reassure me, "just simple self-protection."

But Danny wouldn't stand still while I played out my plot for gradual disentanglement. As I made myself less available, he seemed alarmingly unaffected, staying cheerfully busy with rehearsals, "odd jobs," and assorted Berghof ingenues. And when I did see him, I was thrown into confusion, my careful resolutions instantly dissolving, the scenarios of redemption and change instantly resurgent.

As a stay against backsliding, I started to compose kiss-off letters in my head, fearful that Danny was about to write one of his own, convinced that if a break was going to occur *I* had to produce it, had to be able to see myself as the person actively doing the leaving. But the letters I concocted were vengefully moralistic: "Look, Danny, I love you. But you don't want to be loved. If anyone tries, you'll hurt them till they stop trying. So okay—I'll stop." Or this punishing variation: "You don't want to be at the center of my life—don't, that is, in any way that includes mutuality and consistency—and so my job is to get you out of it."

But then an outside event finally conspired to produce the break I couldn't quite precipitate on my own. Of the several young women (several dozen in my fevered imagination) Danny had been dating at Berghof, he began to mention Linda frequently, if sheepishly—as if uncertain whether our relationship allowed for enthusiastic reportage about third parties. Linda was from Great Neck, was utterly middle class, energetic, smart, controlling—was, in other words, a female counterpart of me. (What was the point of being bisexual, I wondered, if that meant sleeping with different genders but duplicate personalities?)

I stayed cool about Linda—once the three of us even went to dinner—telling myself that Danny needed her and better a her than a him. But then came the weekend when Danny said he had to bury himself in rehearsals, yet left at my place the script he was supposedly working on round-the-clock. Thinking he would need it, I took it over to his East Village apartment—and found him and Linda packing for a weekend in the country. I managed a graceful exit, but decided the time had finally come to face the music: Danny and I were never going to be committed lovers, and my strategy of gradual disentanglement was only prolonging the agony. As I wrote in my diary, "I have to get out of this mess. Danny's power to make me suffer is incredible. I gave it to him, but Christ, I want it back."

So I composed another letter, and this time sent it. The first draft was too gushily "understanding," dangerously close to being a disguised invitation for him to dash over and reassure me. The second version was just two lines long: "It can't work out between us. Don't call or contact me." Somewhere I must have hoped that Danny would nonetheless come barging over, swear eternal devotion, and rush me off to the rabbi (with Linda serving as reluctant ringbearer). But instead, he followed my instructions to the letter, and I heard not a peep from him.

I raced to my anodynes of work and sex, but neither sustained me. No sooner had I finished the 250-page script on Emma Goldman in late November 1971 than the Feds slashed the PBS budget because its programming was "too radical," and PBS in turn axed my script. There was some vague talk of producing it the following year, after the political climate had cooled off, but that wouldn't help me staunch the Danny-wounds *now*. With the workshop of my one-act plays at New Dramatists still two months off, I turned to the presumed solace of sex. But my libido seemed to have quit, and at one point, unable to get any comfort from my standard routines, I contemplated experimenting more with sadomasochism, on the assumption, as I wrote in my diary, that I needed "to act out, to discharge, all the accumulated masochism from the relationship with Danny; real punishment may alleviate imaginary crimes, and the crimes atoned, I might be free for an involvement where punishment is not unconsciously sought."

That turned out to be highfalutin bravado. I did manage two half-hearted S/M scenes, which collapsed in nervous laughter and which persuaded me that the answer to life's problems did not, for me, lie in scenarios of contrition. While awaiting that answer, my spirits erratically improved. But I missed Danny terribly, and I missed the qualities of energy and warmth within myself that he had brought out. On my worst days I could barely refrain from putting in a call to him, from begging him to come back—and on *his* terms. Every time my phone rang, hope flickered; and the downstairs buzzer felt like an electric shock. On those days I would repeat over and over that all a reconciliation could lead to (assuming Danny would even agree to one) would be ultimate disaster and *maybe* some interim pleasure. "Don't knock it," a voice in my head would whisper back. "When does life ever offer more than that?" But I did knock it, and hard, telling myself that something better *was* possible.

And then it dawned on me where "something better" might be found.

# 17

# NEW BEGINNINGS

A FRIEND HAD RECENTLY mentioned that someone he knew had joined a Gay Liberation Front consciousness-raising group and had been finding the experience "invaluable." I had been learning more about GLF from a new book that had just come out—Dennis Altman's *Homosexual*—and suddenly, with all the force of an imperative, the idea of joining the consciousness-raising group seized hold of me. I called the friend, who said he would check out whether there was an opening in the group and would get back to me. While awaiting word, I continued to read Altman's book and on finishing it, wrote in my diary:

> Deep, deep in my gut I continue to believe that homosexuality is sickness, inimical to growth and adulthood. But now I'm at least ready to consider the possibility that much of the "sick" behavior homosexuals demonstrate is a function of their self-hate—like my involvement with Danny, a man I sensed would prove unavailable and abusive—and that the self-hate, in turn, is a function of growing up in a society (and being for so long in the hands of a therapist) that equated sexual deviance with pathology. What I feel in my gut about homosexuality being a disorder is still stronger than the dim new possibility that it may not be. But I'm finally at the point

where the new possibility has registered, and I want to open myself up to it more.

It took two months before a spot could be found for me in a GLF group. (Are that many people presenting themselves for liberation, I wondered, or is there only one group?) Ten of us gathered in an East Side apartment, and after the session I confessed bitter disappointment in my diary:

> Lord!—the impulse to be savage is strong. I wasn't, to put it mildly, impressed with the level of awareness—of self or others. The organizers' rap was fuzzy to the point of incomprehension, full of the jargon but none of the evidence of liberation. And the people who showed up seemed a standard crop of needy, aging homosexuals, looking for new friends and support. There's nothing wrong with that—I've been known to do it myself, half of every day. I don't want to feel this sardonic and superior—I'd hoped for a far better experience. To be sure my reaction isn't merely self-protective, I will try to attend at least a few more times.

But I never did go back, which suggests that my disdain was due in part to fear—of learning to think better of myself, of being forced into a political commitment I didn't feel fully prepared for. Yet I can't entirely write off my reaction as "preliberation consciousness," as the fortified smugness of someone still not ready to leave the closet. Being gay, isn't, finally, a guaranteed bond between people. "Sisters and brothers" may be necessary rhetoric for building a political movement, but it isn't sufficient for building friendships. Even the common bond of being gay often turns out, on closer inspection, not to be so common after all; there are as many ways of being gay as being black or female.

As proof that I was not simply hellbent on beating a retreat to the closet, I began to read absorbedly in the limited liberation literature then available and could feel the impulse building in me to write about my experience as a gay man—something more, that is, than I had already written for probable inclusion in the Black Mountain book (itself delayed in publication as the result of a cleaning woman in my editor's office throwing out the marked manuscript copy on which he had already put in several months of work).

Reading the liberationist literature brought confusion along with clarity. As I struggled to accept the new, positive perspectives on being gay, I continued to feel uncertain whether self-acceptance wasn't itself a copout, a retreat from the hard work of change. Wasn't it true—just as Karl had said—that the insistence on an unconflicted identity ("I am a homosexual") was antithetical to a world view that I otherwise championed—namely, that neither individuals nor institutions have fixed essences that remain immutable over time? Only *conservatives* argued that all effort to change the world (or oneself) was chimerical, a misguided attempt to tamper with the intrinsic nature of things.

I began to share my assorted doubts not only with Ray and other gay friends, but with a few straight friends as well. With four of them, I came out—itself a milestone: openly naming oneself sharply limits the possibility of retreat.

Three of those four straight friends were women. Even then I sensed—which later experience would amply confirm—that women were far less threatened by homosexuality than men. I had had the early example of my sister, Lucile. She had known since the fifties that I was gay and had always given me the same message: "I don't care who you love as long as you are happy"; and through the years she had periodically run interference with my mother, gently answering her nervous questions, subtly preparing her for the day when I might publicly come out.

The three women friends I now told were not only supportive, but shared with me their own feelings of anger *as women*. We bemoaned all the time we had earlier lost in disguises and games and together began to discover those parallels among the oppressed that were beginning everywhere in the culture to forge new alliances. The one straight male friend to whom I came out was a hippy-ish type who on hearing the news instantly announced that he wanted to go to bed with me—a consummation I resisted as programmatic rather than gonadal.

All of this helped me to cope with the loss of Danny. And then, late in December 1971, auditions began for the five-performance workshop of my three one-act plays scheduled for mid-January at New Dramatists. As always in the theater, where a glut of aspirations (and even talent) competes with a penury of outlets, the turnout for auditions was huge, requiring nearly round-the-clock readings. Nothing could have pleased me more than having my energies so entirely absorbed—unless it was the psychic pleasure in meting out all the little nos to one beautiful actor after another, to all the approximate Dannys, as they performed for me, tried to court me, failed to please me.

We cast an unknown young actor named John Travolta in the first of the three plays and managed to fill out all the other roles with equally promising performers. But a workshop setting, in which nobody gets paid and everyone has to scurry for outside odd jobs to survive, is beset by scheduling conflicts and the play usually ends up underrehearsed. Certainly ours did; and when, on opening night, Travolta decided to calm his nerves by smoking a joint just before the curtain went up, the resulting missed cues and memory lapses made a shambles of the evening. Matters improved enough in subsequent performances to bring in several nibbles for moving the plays on for a commercial run. Ultimately, I went with an offer from Edward Albee and Richard Barr, who were scheduled to take over the John Drew Theater in East Hampton during the upcoming summer season—with what would turn out to be catastrophic professional, but liberating personal consequences for me.

In the short run, I got an offer from "Victor," a sometime movie producer, to write a screenplay for him revolving around a pro football player; O. J. Simpson was scheduled to star in the film and Ossie Davis to direct it. I disliked Victor on sight: he seemed a grandiose and petty tyrant. But the money was good, the notion of working in film appealing, and the prospect of once more being frantically busy enthralling. Me and pro football hardly seemed a natural match (other than on grounds of erotic fantasy), but I soon came up with a concept—the game as an arena for class and racial conflict, and as a metaphor for fascism—which allowed me to ease my conscience and plunge ahead.

Along with trying to bat out a screenplay in the requisite eight weeks, I was meeting on a nearly daily basis with my editor (and close friend) Hal Scharlatt, to go over revisions on the Black Mountain book. Hal was one of the few left in publishing who still insisted on actually editing a book rather than simply processing it, and he held me to a rigorous line-by-line accounting. (Though his perfectionism greatly improved my manuscript, his lifelong pattern of relentless overwork may have contributed, alas, to his death a few years later, while still in his thirties, from a heart attack.)

The next two months were a happy nightmare of impossible deadlines, harried conferences, maximum mania. Trouble soon developed on the movie front, but I welcomed even that as needed distraction from the Danny-blues that still occasionally assailed me. Victor became convinced that Ossie wanted to make a one-dimensional allegory about super-Black beating the White Man and his Machine, but because of Ossie's box-office appeal Victor hesitated showing him the door. He tried to turn me into an ally, but I knew dynamite when I saw it and pretended to be a screenwriter mole inept at front office manipulations. Ultimately Ossie walked anyway, after Victor attempted his own rewrite of Ossie's material. After frantic scurrying to find a replacement, the project collapsed.

I didn't care. The film had never fully engaged me, the money was in the bank, conferences with Albee and Barr had begun for the production of my plays in East Hampton, and having found a new apartment in the Village, I was already kneedeep in negotiations with painters and plumbers and shoulderdeep in emptying drawers and cupboards of ten years of debris.

Then in mid-May 1972, just as arriving galley proofs on the Black Mountain book had absorbed what little free time I had left, I got a phone call from an old friend, the historian Howard Zinn. Would I join REDRESS, a group of "notables" mobilizing in the Capitol to protest the war in Indochina? Four days hence the group would be presenting a "petition of redress" to Congress demanding that it use its power over appropriations to vote an immediate end to the war. The point of the demonstration, Howard added, was to show that prominent, middle-aged artists and professionals—not just college students and radicals—were willing to be arrested to dramatize their discontent with the war. Oh God, I thought to myself, why can't we present the petition *next* month when the galleys will be done and I'll be comfortably settled in the new apartment?—a thought that immediately prompted me to say yes.

In retrospect, I was glad I did. The action in Washington proved something of a milestone in showing me that I could put myself directly on the line for what I believed in—whether anti-war or pro-gay issues—and not only survive, but feel better about myself. When I got back from Washington, I scribbled down some exhausted, shorthand notes that summarized what had happened and what I felt I had learned from it:

Meeting in the DuPont Plaza Hotel, the night before the demonstration. About 200 people. Lots of exuberance and argument over tactics. Robert Brustein, Arthur Laurents and Judy Collins especially vocal against civil disobedience. Larry Rivers full of beans, insisting we must get arrested, must all wear Afro wigs. Decision left to individuals.

Next morning at 7:00 a.m. A cab to Union Station to check my suitcase into a locker for safekeeping, just in case I get arrested. I have some of the galley proofs of Black Mountain with me and the only copy of the corrected manuscript. Then I join the others for the march to the Congress, where we wait outside the Senate chamber to present the petition. Gerald Ford comes out to lecture us: "We must talk about *realities*, not killings." Speaker Albert accepts the petition mechanically, without comment. When Congressman Rosenthal appears, Bob Lifton eloquently says to him, "We feel this is an extraordinary constitutional crisis; we ask for an extraordinary response from Congress—*not* business as usual." Chief of Police gets out his bullhorn, two feet from our faces. The familiar speech from the '60s: "Awright, you have 15 minutes to clear the premises." About half of our group quietly leaves. Isn't it *my* Congress, *my* government? Fucking bullhorn ringing in my ears. Blinding camera lights. I'm getting angrier *and* more frightened. Judy Collins sits down on the marble floor; last night she spoke *against* civil disobedience. Others are sitting—Barbara Harris, Kenneth Koch, Bob Lifton. I sit. Judy starts singing "All we are asking is give peace a chance." We all sing. The police start removing us one at a time. Bella Abzug remains—the only Congressperson to stay behind. She looks as if she's going to cry. She hugs each of the women as the police move them past her.

My turn comes. A huge policeman grabs me. Handsome,

I think to myself. Pictures taken; a line; another line. "Can you cash in a Metroliner ticket?" I ask my policeman. He smiles at me.

We're led down the steps of the Capitol, the marble blinding in the sun. The zipper on my fly is open; it broke as I sat down. I'm shocked to hear applause, to hear my name called out. I feel a flush of pleasure. I feel righteous. Then I remember my zipper.

Standing in the full paddywagon. I talk to Noam [Chomsky]. He seems calm, he's describing something to me at great length. Can't remember a word of it.

I'm leaning over to Dr. Spock. "Excuse me, Doctor, but . . . what do you think will happen?" Spock cheerful, simple, hearty; an everyday affair with him. He tells me about likely procedures ahead, his voice firm, fearless. I hear every third word, but his voice, not his words, is what I need.

I'm in a cell with Cleve Gray, Bob Klein and Kenneth Koch. Two metal slabs and a narrow space alongside. It's about 5:30. The heat is terrible; feels like 100 degrees. Tom predicted during the lineup that we'd be out in 3 hours. A sardonic young movement lawyer, Ellen, moves glacially from cell to cell; "*now* what?!" smirked on her face. Hours later: "Any more questions?" Ellen asks. Kenneth Koch: "Beloved Ellen, answer *one* of the earlier ones!"

We're given some half-frozen Spam sandwiches. "Left over from the last demonstration," someone quips. A plastic orange drink, too. I knock over half a cup of it. Nothing to clean it up with except for a few of Kenneth's Kleenexes. Everything is sticky for the rest of the night. Kenneth spots cockroaches. If it's masochism or an ego-trip that brought me down here, why aren't I enjoying it more? Marcus Raskin yells out from a cell, "Don't you sometimes wish you were *for* the war?"

Lifton, in the cell next to ours, starts a theoretical discussion with one of the young organizers in the opposite tier. It irritates me. Kenneth starts needling Lifton: "Too bad you forgot to invite a prominent bondsman, Bobby dear. Next time, a *little* better organization on the legal end—mmm?" Lifton laughs: "Ah-ha, the backlash against the leadership has begun!" He sounds *too* content.

"About 2:00 a.m. we hear a bondsman is in the prison and those who want to get out can. Hardly seems any point by then, but I'm in a panic over the manuscript in the railroad station locker disappearing—local organizer has told me that thieves are constantly breaking in, nothing likely to be there after a few hours. About 40 of us (out of 95) line up outside the cell tier to be released. They let us down into the processing room one at a time. When I reach the head of the line, the surly young white guard says to me in a Southern accent:

"You all professional men?"

"Yes."

"What's *your* profession?"

"I'm a writer."

"What you write?"

"Plays and history."

From the floor of the cell directly opposite our lineup, where he is curled up in a ball, I hear Dr. Spock's barely audible voice: ". . . and cheap novels."

The guard leans down to Spock. His voice becomes almost gentle.

"Doctor, you sure you don't want out?"

"No, it's too late. I'd only wake the friends I'm staying with. No, I'm fine."

On release, several of us pile into a cab, first stop Union Station. My suitcase is still there! The manuscript is okay! Rapturous joy. Then on to the women's prison. We pile out. Judy Collins is sitting on the steps (she was released last night at 7:30 p.m. but is waiting for the other women), chatting happily with the guards who have gotten off duty. They adore her. So do I.

At the Dupont Plaza, I implore a sleeping pill, having earlier thrown away my own so as not to embarrass the action if searched. So, it turns out, has everyone else—except Howard da Silva, who produces my own favorite Doriden. I want to hug him. Asleep about 4:00, up about 7:00, feeling reasonably alert.

On the bondsmen's orders, we appear at the courthouse at 9:30 a.m. They start arraigning us at 2:00 in the afternoon. Judge Goodrich rules that he *will* entertain *nolo contendere* pleas. The movement lawyers tell us how lucky we are not to have gotten another judge; the penalty could be six months. One by one, we're arraigned. Each of us gets the same sentence: 2 days or $25. Finally my turn comes. At the last second I decide to take my suitcase with me, certain the ordeal is about to end.

After the judge passes sentence on me, I swing happily through the doors behind the bench, expecting immediate release, applauding crowds. Two crewcut roughnecks grab me, throw my suitcase off to the side and thoroughly frisk me. Then I'm led into a windowless room with seven others. The guard tells us more paperwork has to be done. Ten minutes later, we're put in an elevator and taken down to a large bullpen. All the other men are there. After more red-tape, they start releasing us in batches of five.

Then the releases stop. No explanation. About 25 of us are left. We catch snatches from the guards: "papers not in order"; "looks like they ran out of money"; "at six o'clock, they're gonna be *all ours*." A new movement lawyer arrives. He tells seven of us that he saw our papers on a pile marked "recommitted to jail." For the first time, I feel something like panic. It's Memorial Day Weekend. With the courts shut down, one more night could mean five. Dick Avedon reassures me: "They're just having a little fun with us. Don't worry, the power of the privileged will prevail."

He's right. An hour later the movement lawyer returns to tell us we *will* be let out; he contacted the judge and he has sent down a direct order for our release. Steven Cohen, one of the young staff arrested, says he feels it would be a copout on his principles to leave. The lawyer socks it to him: "The guards will almost certainly beat you up after you're left alone—and then will put you in a 20 man cell to be raped." Steve blanches, then reluctantly agrees to be released.

As we're let out of the elevator into the main corridor, 15 or so of our group are waiting there for us with hugs and kisses. I rescue my suitcase yet again, then grab a cab with Felicia Bernstein and Dick Avedon to the airport—my fear of flying gone. We have double drinks before takeoff, chat furiously all the way home.

Safely back in the apartment, I took stock in my diary: "Did we make any impact? A little, maybe; very little. God knows Congress isn't about to assert its power over appropriations to end the war. But when nothing else is left to do, I guess you do what little is available. Beyond that, I learned a lot personally: that I'm more cowardly than I even thought, but that I *can* give up my controls—and survive. I say 'I'm not cut out for jail.' But who is? I remember the frightened young black prisoner they took away just before they released the last of our group. He'd never been in jail either; he was just as frightened as I was, but unlike me, didn't get out. And no one was there to worry about him.

"I learned more, too, about the psychology of concentration camps—the eagerness to please one's guards, the fury at other prisoners who threaten to make waves. If I hit that level in 48 hours, I shudder to think what I'd be like in 48 days—or months. The only thing that frightens me as much as the fragility of my own defenses is the unshakable density of the government's. But one risk begets another: I know I feel *more* available than before for political protest, and more convinced that risks have to be taken, including the risk of being arrested and jailed. I feel good that I finally got off my ass; bad that under pressure I proved mostly liquid jelly. But you have to start somewhere. And with the example in my head of some of the remarkable people I met, models of untheatrical valor, maybe I can slowly work my way out of my silken cocoon."

# 18

# DANNY REDUX

I SPENT THE NEXT month buried in a swarm of carpenters, galley proofs, and cartons. Before moving into the new apartment, I decided I liked its empty, spacious feel and vowed not to clutter it up. But within weeks I was indulging in an orgy of consumerism—too many new towels for the racks, too many plants for the terrace. When I looked around at what I'd done, I realized I'd set up a *home*, as if to compound my loneliness or force myself somehow to end it. As I wrote in my diary, "Trying to inhabit the new apartment is harder than furnishing it. Everything is in spanking order—I'm in disarray."

I began to get wrenching thoughts again of Danny. "If it hadn't been for my terror of pain," I wrote self-accusingly in my diary—forgetting Danny's own disabilities—"he'd still be in my life." And so one night in mid-July, passing Danny's tenement building in the East Village, I gave in to the impulse and yelled up at his window. His head popped out. He gave me a broad smile and threw down his key. Within minutes it felt like we'd never been apart. He was reluctant to talk much about the past but did say he understood why I had broken off: "You were in love with me and I couldn't handle it, even though I have strong feelings for you." He said he "doesn't ever want to get in a comparable situation again," but agreed with me that our lives were, in some uncategorizable way, intertwined. He said he'd come by the next day. I tried to stay calm.

Within weeks, the familiar pleasures and limitations of the relationship resurfaced. We quickened each other as much as ever, but I kept a cautious lid on my expectations and Danny on his arbitrariness. I congratulated myself on the absence of lust this time around, hopeful that my libido wasn't simply playing possum, tricking me so it could trick him into the belief that all obsession had fled and we were headed toward the smooth shore of friendship. The equation—no erections, no intensity—was simpleminded, but it allowed me the comfortable illusion that the situation was entirely under control.

In the meantime, trouble was brewing in East Hampton. Rehearsals for the evening of my one-act plays were due to start in mid-August, but now, two weeks before, the production seemed suddenly in jeopardy. My close friends "Jane and Dave Robins," in whose East Hampton home I was going to stay during the rehearsal period, reported that a protest campaign had begun in the community against the "summer of smut." Albee and Barr had already produced three evenings at the John Drew Theater (mine was scheduled as the fourth and final offering) that had alarmed the priggish locals, Joe Orton's irreverent *What the Butler Saw* causing nightly walkouts. Since my one-acters (*Metaphors*, *The Guttman Ordinary Scale*, and *The Colonial Dudes*) were alternately explicitly or implicitly erotic, and *Metaphors* homoerotic, Jane and Dave predicted that the protest would mount.

Barr himself confirmed the trouble a few days later. He called to tell me that "in an effort to circumvent unpleasantness," he and Albee had withheld my scripts from the John Drew Theater's board of trustees until two days previously and that, having now seen them, the board had refused to sanction production.

"Can it do that?" I asked. "I thought you and Edward were promised absolute artistic freedom when you agreed to take over the John Drew this summer?"

"Yes, we were," Barr answered tersely.

"You have it in writing?" I persisted.

"Yes," Barr said, more tersely still, this time with an edge to his voice.

"Well then, the board is involved in a clear breach of contract."

Ignoring my comment, Barr asked if I would be willing to have one of my plays—*The Colonial Dudes*, the least erotic and threatening of the three—appear on a substitute double bill with one of Edward's. I said I wouldn't, not because I didn't admire Edward's work and not because I thought all three of my plays had to be done as a unit, but because to negotiate with what was a transparent act of censorship implied the act had some justification. Barr gruffly replied that his own impulse was "simply to close the theater and walk away." He said he would confer with Edward and would let me know their decision—and then hung up before I could respond.

"Clearly," I wrote in my diary, "Barr is not prepared to press the legal or moral case—'The heart's gone out of me,' he said at one point. His overriding impulse is to bring the unsuccessful season to as quick an end as possible. With an ally like him, I feel almost as insecure as with a certifiable enemy. I find myself in a state of disbelief—can this be happening in 1972 in a 'sophisticated' community like East Hampton? It sets me to thinking about the Black Mountain book, and whether my overt declaration of homosexuality in it isn't going to produce serious repercussions for me. I am, after all, vulnerable as a city employee."

All hung fire for the next week. Barr didn't phone as promised, and when I left messages for him, didn't return them. After three days of no word, Roger Hendricks Simon, who was scheduled to direct my plays, finally got through to the sympathetic general manager of the John Drew. He reported that Barr was doing little to force the board's hand, apparently hoping the cancellation would stick. But the manager predicted that it would not. Though the board did indeed "despise" my scripts, feeling that "the plays are not right for this area, that their 'freaky' subject matter would attract the 'wrong' kind of theatergoer," it would nonetheless be forced to let the plays proceed. It was either that or face substantial financial loss, since the board had a contractual obligation to pay cast and staff salaries whether or not the plays opened.

The prediction proved accurate. Two days before the plays were scheduled to go into rehearsal, the board reversed itself. Barr phoned with the news. "Well, we won," he said in a dispirited voice, as if describing a pending execution. Then, recovering animation, he issued his instructions: I was to use *thoroughly* opaque slides in *Guttman* (the play was set in a sex research lab in which volunteer subjects were shown assorted nude slides to test their responses) so as not to "needlessly offend community tastes." Then, from left field, he barked, "You know, Martin, you need to decide whether you want to go to jail for political causes or develop as a playwright." It was clearly not going to be a peaceful month at the beach.

Barr appeared for the first rehearsal dressed in storm-trooper leather, lest his proclivities and intentions be in doubt. He left in the middle of the runthrough, noisily, unnerving the actors with shouted demands to Roger, the director, that the order in which the plays appeared *had* to be reversed and the new opaque slides *had* to be installed immediately. I told Roger afterward that both demands reflected Barr's (not the John Drew board's) quirkiness and that I would not agree to either; the plays were already in their appropriate playing order and as for the nude slides, the board had not attached any conditions when reversing its decision. Roger sensibly advised me to stay cool: "Barr is sore as hell and dying for an excuse to cancel the production."

Having issued his orders, Barr then disappeared for ten days and we were able to get down to work. We had assembled a wonderfully talented cast, James Woods (in *Guttman*) being the standout. He throttled the script, forced its experience to combine with his own, wouldn't accept a line or a direction until he was able personally to justify it—thus forcing me into rewriting (and much improving) the play's ending. But by the end of the first week of rehearsals, my own work on the scripts was completed and I was left to idle in the theater or, far worse, to be thrown back on the purported pleasures of East Hampton.

They eluded me, even though I was staying in great splendor with my friends Jane and Dave Robins. They owned a huge house near the beach (Dave was a wealthy realtor), complete with Olympic-size swimming pool, corridors of rooms, and a full-time staff of four on call for everything from meals to towels. So long as it was daylight and I had something to do that looked like work (like sitting in the theater watching other people work), I was okay; but at night I felt footloose and blue.

Jane and Dave took me with them the first few evenings on their nightly round of sumptuous socializing, but that experience quickly paled. At one 1972-style chalet, the guests splayed out on the perfect lawn in perfectly matching pastels, as if each had been assigned in advance a place on the coordinated color chart, Jane aggressively introduced me as the playwright of *those* plays. The response was predictably civilized. One ascoted older gentleman, as if responding to a dare, sniffed that as a regular subscriber to the John Drew he *would* attend the season's last offering. And a modish middle-aged matron archly observed— just before passing on to the goose pâté—that "East Hampton is *indeed* a lovely place, and we hope it will always remain that way."

Fortunately I had a few friends in the Amagansett arts community, and I managed a little restorative time with them. One afternoon I biked over to the purportedly gay Two Mile Hollow Beach and ran into Terrence McNally and his lover, the actor Bobby Drivas. They confirmed that thus far the Albee/Barr "season" had managed to alienate everyone—the town conservatives over the nature of the plays chosen, the John Drew management at the poor financial showing, the intellectual/creative element at the amateurishness and self-celebration (one play by Albee, two directed by him) of the first three productions. Biking home, I passed in front of the theater and saw that a sign had been affixed to the announcement of my plays: RECOMMENDED FOR MATURE AUDIENCES ONLY. Whoever can they mean? I grimly wondered.

The night of the technical rehearsal, Barr and Albee (the latter there for the first time) glided silently into their seats about an hour after the runthrough had begun. For the next two hours Barr paced the aisle and audibly grumbled at how long the tech was taking—"It should have been—*hrrumph*—simplified." At its completion, he let loose with a barrage of complaints about the acting and direction, ending, before he stormed out, with a renewed insistence that the slides be changed. Albee had said little, but he reappeared at the theater for the next day's runthrough. During earlier discussions in New York I had found him much as he was usually described: owlish, furtive, smothered. But now, without his fawning entourage, his manner was pleasant and simple, and he made a number of helpful suggestions.

Two days before the first performance, I got a call from

Danny in New York saying he would like to come out to East Hampton for opening night. I was delighted, and Jane confirmed that—with their corridor of empty bedrooms—it would of course be okay for Danny to stay overnight. But something in her manner—oblique, abrupt—warned me that it was not going to be quite that simple. As if further to test the ground, I suggested that if their twelve-year-old daughter, who had returned from summer camp the night before, wanted to watch the runthrough that afternoon, I would take her along with me to the theater. "No," Jane tersely responded, her expression a mix of embarrassment and severity, "her father has forbidden it." That startled me, but I let it drop.

The next morning, Jane greeted me with the news that she had talked to Dave on the phone—he spent weekdays in the city—and that he had decided reservations should be made for Danny, due that evening, at the 1770 House in town; such an arrangement, Jane said, would be more "comfortable" for all concerned. Up to that point in our relationship, the Robinses and I had never talked openly about my being gay, though it had long been apparent that they knew. Now, hearing Dave's decision, and trying to hold my anger at bay, I told Jane that I thought a talk between us was long overdue. She looked terrified, mumbled something about having to pick flowers for tonight's dinner table, and fled to the garden.

I followed, determined to force *some* discussion. Cornered between the zinnias and the rosebushes, Jane stammered out a few explanatory words: "Dave and I are the squarest people I know. . . . Why, we don't even allow unmarried *straight* couples to share the same bedroom in our home. . . . Dave still has trouble believing that *you're* homosexual . . . and after all, we do have two teenaged boys in the house. . . ." I swallowed the impulse to scream in her face that her two sons were too fucking ugly to interest me, and that she and Dave were stuffed shirt bigots. (Fifteen years later, ironically, a Robins family member turned out to be gay and has become a prominent activist.)

What I said instead, holding myself to that tone of sweet reasonableness that I was only beginning to understand was a form of self-sabotage, was that I thought she and Dave were over-protecting their children and patronizing their adult guests. But it *was* their home, I said, and I couldn't tell them what its values should be, especially since those values were apparently so entrenched that no amount of argument would dislodge them. I made it clear, though, that if I were to respect their feelings, I expected them to be considerate of Danny's, that if I saw any trace of mistreatment of him while he was in their home, I would have to leave it—that in fact I might decide, in any case, to stay with Danny in the hotel.

"Just so you'll get the facts straight," I added, "Danny and I had no intention of sleeping in the same bed. We've only recently picked up our relationship again, haven't yet slept together this time around, and I doubt if we will out here. Besides, Danny prefers sleeping with women."

Jane scrunched up her face in disgust. "Oh dear, that's worse," she said. "Dave thinks bisexuality is even more bizarre than . . ."

Seeing my face cloud over, Jane let the sentence go unfinished and rushed away toward the house. I made no effort to follow. My legs had started to buckle; I was losing it. I stayed in the garden for an hour, pacing back and forth, trying to get my emotions under control. When I wasn't raging at the Robinses, I was raging at myself. Had I been too "understanding"? Should I have simply let Jane have it, stormed out of their house forever—not even showing up for the opening night party they had planned? What about Danny's feelings? What did I owe him? Should I stay with him at the hotel?—did he *want* me to stay with him, or would he consider the whole thing a manipulation on my part, a way of forcing myself back into his bed?

I hadn't resolved any of this when it came time to pick Danny up at the train station. On our way to the theater, I told him what had happened, and he turned immediately distant, tied into an angry knot—at me, it seemed, more than anyone, at being treated like Marty's (vermin) boyfriend, a role he thought he had just extricated himself from. And to make matters worse, when we got to the theater, all was in disarray. Barr, it turned out, had unexpectedly turned up at the afternoon runthrough and had terrorized everyone with last-minute complaints and demands. It proved too late to soothe egos and reinspire confidence. That night the thoroughly demoralized cast turned in a disastrously bad opening performance, highlighted when a woman stood up in the audience, shouted, "This is shit!" and stormed out of the theater, leaving a stunned cast fumbling for cues and a shaken audience mumbling in mingled sympathy and outrage.

Torn in my conflicting allegiances to the cast, to Danny and to myself, I finally decided to go to the opening night party at the Robinses, and Danny reluctantly agreed to join me. But furious at being an unwanted guest and at being viewed as part of a gay couple, he kept icily apart—ostentatiously spending the evening exerting his charms on one of the women in the cast. At the end of the party, he refused to let me come back with him to the hotel, refused even to let me walk him there. Dispirited and miserable, I lay in bed sleepless that night at the Robinses, wanting nothing more than to mow down Jane, Dave, and Danny all together in one murderous burst of machine gun fire.

Next morning I got up early and knew what I had to do— get the hell out. I picked up a still sullen Danny at the hotel, and, in a rented car, we drove out toward Montauk looking for a place to stay. Once settled into a motel and a safe distance placed between ourselves and the assorted humiliations of East Hampton, we both began to revive. The next few days we rested on the beach, waterskied, had sex, and evenings drove to the theater to catch the performances. They were infinitely better than the one on opening night, but it was too late to salvage the run; the local critics published negative reviews, and the cast played to nearly empty houses.

Barr and Albee never again appeared in the theater, apparently content to wash their hands of what the *Hampton Times* called a "disastrous season." But it was a Katharine Bennett, in a letter to the *East Hampton Star*, who summed up community reaction:

> Even though the Duberman evening was suggested for mature audiences only, I believe it is an insult to any audience. I see no reason why "smut" should be foisted on any audience! . . . The author must have a completely perverted sense of humor. . . . There is no room in a good society for that which tends to drag it in the mud.

I was able to shrug off that view as the expected bigotry of the homophobic mainstream. But what I could not shrug off was that the "liberal" Robinses, widely known for their generous sympathies and philanthropic largesse, and he a boyhood friend of thirty years' standing, had in fact treated me as vaguely unclean, a threat to the morals of their teenage sons, a kind of criminal. It stuck in my craw—and stayed in my craw, a milestone in my awareness of the depth of contempt for homosexuals that existed even in so-called progressive segments of American opinion, and of the need openly to combat that contempt. I made the decision then and there to let stand the "coming out" passage in my forthcoming book on Black Mountain. And I wrote a letter to Jane and Dave that was designed to burn many more bridges than that of a single friendship:

> There are a few things I'd like to say. First, I want to thank you for your kindness during my two-week stay. I much appreciate your generous hospitality. But I have to add that it stood in stark contrast to your behavior in regard to Danny—so stark that I felt I had to leave your home in order to protect my own feelings of self-worth. It is—as you rightly pointed out—*your* home, and it's run according to your values, which you're under no obligation to defend or even discuss. But I do feel that not even in one's own home is one entitled to treat a friend as if he were an active (or at least, potential) criminal. Given how different and entrenched our views are on the subject, it's probably futile to discuss the matter at length. But I would suggest that homosexuality and *not* premarital sex (as you insisted) is the central issue. You could, after all, have offered Danny a bed in some other room in your house.

Jane wrote back immediately:

> We were delighted to have you visit us, and equally pleased that you enjoyed your stay.
> The point you raise about Danny is a difficult one and, frankly, we may have over-reacted—as most square, child-oriented families are wont to do.
> We certainly have no desire to impose our morals on you or your home; on the other hand turnabout is fair play. We

have never had an unmarried "couple" in the house—and had you not introduced the issue, it would not have arisen.

We certainly had no intention to hurt Danny's feelings or yours, and, if we have, we are genuinely sorry.

It was a letter that in other circumstances I might well have considered conciliatory and might well have answered by gratefully suggesting that we meet for a restorative dinner. But I was not in a grateful mood. An implacable anger burned in me. Rage that had accumulated from decades of mistreatment condensed in a single episode. And I let the anger course through me unchecked. I wanted to vent, not forgive, wanted to tell the heterosexual world, in the persons of Jane and Dave, that I was finished with being scorned and demeaned, finished with being the object of their smug superiority. And I did:

Since the reply to my letter came from you alone, I don't know whether to associate Dave with its sentiments. I can only assume, as with the hotel reservations for Danny, that he exercises primary control over decisions and leaves you with primary responsibility for consequences.

In any case, let me say to *you* that although there is much in your note that I find offensive (particularly the implication that Danny and I somehow posed a threat to your children), the tone is conciliatory—and where a deep division exists over values, that's perhaps the most to be hoped for. It would seem to me a shame if a friendship of such standing was permanently ruptured. I would rather risk that, though, than have my choice of partners in bed be treated as the equivalent of moral delinquency. Society has propagandized that view for too long—and homosexuals have internalized it for too long. I can't afford to have "friends" who act toward me in a way that reinforces my already over-developed tendency to self-punition; that kind of encouragment can reliably be left to enemies.

If you (*and* Dave) feel capable of that kind of adjustment, then perhaps in time, when the hurt's subsided, we can again see each other. I hope that will prove to be the case.

It did not. Jane never answered my letter, and the friendship never resumed. But that price seemed a small one to pay for the gain in self-esteem.

Which isn't to say that henceforth my path followed some pulp scenario of unbroken surges to the light. Hardly. The path remained so indistinct and strewn with debris that it often seemed more like a cul-de-sac. But the grim set of experiences in East Hampton did, for the time being, fill me with an uncomplicated sense of purpose. I told Hal, my editor, that the "coming out" passage in the Black Mountain manuscript, now in final page proofs, definitely stayed. I told him, further, that for my next book I was strongly leaning toward an autobiographical account of "growing up gay in America"—an account now realized, nearly twenty years later.

# 19

# IN PRINT

O N SEPTEMBER 18—YOM KIPPUR, the Day of Atonement, I portentously noted—I picked up the phone and called the *New York Times Book Review*. Using the fact that I was a frequent contributor and knew most of the senior editors, I suggested I do an essay on the literature—both psychoanalytic and movement—of homosexuality. The editor with whom I spoke cautiously asked whether the piece I had in mind would "avoid the pitfalls of being merely confessional." I said a certain amount of autobiographical detail would be essential to the article's integrity: I had to make it clear that I was speaking as someone "in the life." But I would be saving most of the personal material, I added, for a followup book. The *Times* got back to me a week later with a go-ahead: two thousand words and six weeks in which to write them.

That same week I went to my first Gay Activists Alliance meeting at the Firehouse, the group's headquarters in Greenwich Village, and presented myself, age forty-two, for an orientation session designed especially for "beginners." The two oldtimers (meaning in their late twenties) who ran the session earnestly testified for the benefit of us novices as to how GAA had "made them whole persons," proud of their identity as homosexuals. I thought that rhetoric skindeep and smug; the equation of homosexuality and identity, I wrote in my diary that night, "seems to me derived from the very culture GAA denounces as oppressive. It equates an individual's choice of bed partners with the whole of his being, and suggests that if one loses guilt about the former, one automatically comes into possession of the latter—as if identity consists of a firm defiance of social norms. Besides, external persecution is not itself a *sufficient* explanation for all inadequacy, hurt, disaffiliation."

At the general meeting following the orientation session, I heard still more that made me squirm. One of GAA's leaders, due imminently to move to the West Coast, gave a farewell speech in which he stressed that "this is a movement based on love." Love? I muttered to myself. That's a rare commodity, and any organization that claims to trade in it must be not only naive but on its way to extinction. Besides, wasn't the expectation that all gays should love one another as mindlessly destructive of individual impulse as the larger society's homophobic insistence that no gays *can* love?

The next speaker hardly quieted my doubts. He rose, in giggly high spirits, to deny the current rumor that he had broken off his love affair with Jim and to affirm the rumor that he was concurrently having an affair with Tom. He then justified the public announcement "as a moral lesson in rejecting the old culture's insistence that you can only love one person at a time." As I grumpily wrote in my diary that night, "Despite my own increasing attraction to public disclosure, I still hold to an 'old-fashioned' equation that links total lack of privacy to a low capacity for intimacy, which in turn reflects a deficient identity."

Before long, I would myself argue that our cultural training (and not some intrinsic modesty) had taught us to place sacred connotations on "privacy," and for perhaps no better reason than socialized shame about the body. I would also question whether the notion that sexuality is best confined to a monogamous relationship wasn't itself the narrow reflection of a sex-negative cultural norm. But for the moment I was still not ready to embrace the organized gay movement, choosing, on this my initial exposure to it, to focus on its perceived deficiencies, to emphasize my gingerly doubts. I did see much to admire that first night at GAA: the easy good spirits and camaraderie, the dedicated earnestness. But I had not yet seen enough to transform me, and certainly not overnight, into a fully committed activist. Over the next few months, I did drop in at the Firehouse from time to time, but as an outside observer, as a man writing an essay for the *Times* about a movement from which he personally remained cautiously distanced.

In those months I was much more assiduous about keeping up my involvement in REDRESS, the antiwar group. Following our initial petition action and the arrests in the Capitol in the spring of 1972, REDRESS had continued its activities, and I had become part of its steering committee. I attended regular meetings, helped to organize a weekend-long conference to mobilize action against the government's renewed bombings of North Vietnam and to publicize the finding of the international war crimes tribunal that the *conscious* culpability of the United States for criminal actions went back at least to 1965.

But still more of my energy went into maintaining the precarious relationship with Danny; I was more relentless in pursuit of that unattainable fantasy stud than in affiliating with a gay movement whose new perspectives on machismo might have helped rid me of the fantasy's allure. As I wrote in my diary, "It struck me that I may have internalized Karl's negative attitude about homosexuality so thoroughly that it's no longer possible for me to have a sustained relationship with another gay man. Instead I seek out straight (or semi-straight) partners, try to become by indirection, by incorporation, the kind of man Karl insisted I should be."

Following the debacle in East Hampton, and as if to atone for it, I intensified my efforts to help Danny with his career, introducing him to casting agents, coaching him on his script preparations, even auditioning him for a production of my own one-act plays at the Manhattan Theater Club (while cushioning his possible disappointment with the advance warning that the role had already been all-but-offered). Danny gave a surly, flat reading and blamed *me* for having inadequately prepared him.

The more I did for him, the less he did for himself, putting off getting photos made, signing up belatedly for new acting courses at Berghof, incompletely memorizing scripts, sliding perceptibly, as such macho types are wont, into a passivity they insistently, if unconsciously, seek all their adult lives as a reprieve from the stony demands of their manly mask. But it is not a ieve, once found, for which they feel or express gratitude. ie more I became a kind of unofficial agent for Danny, the iore distant and sullen he became, as if the dependency he had so instinctively lapsed into was somehow part of a deliberate plot—of which gay sex was the other part—to unman him.

And the more Danny withdrew affection, the more I coveted sex. Up to now we had been congratulating ourselves on the maturity of our relationship, on how, as our feelings for each other had continued to deepen, our need for genital contact had lessened. We had "transcended" sex; we no longer needed to use it for confirmation. But I had never really bought into that theory. Sometimes I really did feel that hugging and kissing—which Danny and I did plenty of—were all I needed and wanted, that sucking and fucking were somehow a redundancy, even a diminution, that not having to use his cock had freed Danny to discover his emotions.

But more often I realized that we had tacitly agreed to phase sex out not simply or primarily because lust had diminished and gotten converted into a more generalized warmth, but because Danny couldn't live with a sustained sexual relationship with a male (and possibly with a female either). Our hands-off policy had represented a truce, a capitulation to the fear that having sex regularly could well prove explosive, forcing Danny to break and run. I hadn't earlier felt able to handle that prospect. But now, as I edged toward publicly revealing my homosexuality in the Black Mountain book and in the article for the *Times*, a paradoxical strength was building in me: if I was strong enough to stand up to the likely repercussions of coming out, I was deserving enough to get more emotional comfort for myself—more than Danny was ever likely to provide. Building new bridges was proving the best way of burning some old ones.

The conflagration took place in Jamaica.

We went there for a week's vacation and stayed one day. I had booked us into the Half Moon Hotel, which on first glance was clearly the wrong place—a wealthy compound with a family orientation. After unpacking we went into town, started talking in a bar with two young local men who got us stoned on potent grass and then took us—me with my heart in my mouth—for a wild ride into the hills for "more ganja." That mission accomplished, we found ourselves, heads reeling, in another bar where

Danny started to talk to a prostitute and announced he wanted to make it with her back in our hotel room.

I protested, and he finally, reluctantly, gave up the idea. But later, back in our room, he lashed out in a towering rage, saying I had brought him to Jamaica to fuck him, that I treated him like a faggot hustler, that he couldn't be around me and feel like a man. And that's all he would say. When I tried to apologize—I wasn't sure for what, but the impulse was strong—he shouted that he would kill me if I said one more word. Stunned at his savagery, I believed he would and kept my mouth shut. The next morning he said he was returning to New York, and I decided to go too.

On the plane, Danny still refusing to talk, I had plenty of time to think the nightmare through. I tried excusing him. I told myself that since I wasn't his lover, I had had no right to monitor his sexual behavior, or even comment on it. I told myself that neither of us had arrived in Jamaica in good shape. Danny had had a promising nibble to audition for one of the leads in a new play at the Public Theater and had reacted with a combination of terror and hauteur, saying almost simultaneously that he "wasn't ready" and that he was going to "knock 'em dead." I, in turn, had reacted to his good news with a mixture of genuine happiness for him and abysmal fear for myself, certain that if his career took off, he wouldn't need me any more. The certainty had seemed confirmed when, the night before we left for Jamaica, he said to me, "You have a special place that nobody can ever take." That had made me feel a little safer, but a lot sadder: "special place" seemed to convey such a sequestered, carefully delimited role.

Thinking about all this on the plane, I berated myself for trying to convert friendship into romance and then, on top of it, managing only a self-centered version. But that wouldn't wash. None of my faults excused, or even fully accounted for, Danny's brutal, nonnegotiable behavior, his refusal to consider anyone else's feelings as comparable in importance to his own. By the time I got off the plane, I had decided it was the last time we would ever see each other. I was cutting him out of my life for good.

It was not, of course, that simple. For months I wandered around feeling bereft, functioning mechanically, meeting my classes and going to REDRESS meetings, but coming home at night to break up in tears, to curse myself for having made the wrong decision, to wonder all over again whether Danny and I couldn't find some formula for making the relationship work. But although tempted almost nightly, I did not reach for the phone.

And my resolve held, even when Danny finally called me one night. He wanted to tell me, he said, that he had broken his ankle in a fall and was therefore effectively out of the running for the role at the Public Theater. It sounded as though my invincible, disaster-prone he-man had been doing his own form of grieving. But even in misery his voice managed to remain pugnaciously detached, and though I recognized the call as an appeal for rescue, I resisted the urge to race over to his apartment with money, groceries, and moral support, confining myself to a distant "I hope things get better for you soon." "If I reach out a hand," I wrote in my diary, "he'll grab it just long enough to pull himself out of the quicksand—and pitch me over his shoulder into it. I may derive peripheral pleasure from suffering—somehow it confirms my existence as a superior being capable of being victimized by love—but I'm not a true masochist, I don't seek out pain as a primary source of gratification, sexual or otherwise, don't require abuse before I can accept pleasure."

Knowing that routine activity would eventually restore some actual animation, I stayed busy, frantically busy. I was unable to write, but I did throw myself into antiwar activity, trying to organize the Lehman campus, forming a "hostage committee" with Muriel Rukeyser, Andrea Dworkin, and Karl Bissinger (of the War Resisters League). Our notion was to become the nucleus for a group of "prominent" Americans who would offer to go to Hanoi (*if* Hanoi thought the tactic useful) as hostages to discourage further bombings. It was a madly grandiose scheme—the U.S. government wouldn't *dare* bomb Hanoi, if Andrea, Muriel, Karl and Marty stood defiantly in the town square!—but of a piece, perhaps, with the madness of Nixon's bombing raids, as well as a gauge of how, *in extremis* over the break with Danny, I found melodrama topped with the prospect of self-destruction entirely plausible.

On a less fraught level, I joined a small group of gay activists in working for the election of Jim Owles, the ex-president of GAA, to the New York City Council. The Owles campaign marked the first time an openly gay man had run for elective office in the city, and I hoped to find myself enthusiastically caught up in it. But once again, a feint in the direction of the gay movement left me with the feeling that it and I were in irreconcilable places. I was still loading the dice, of course. Political campaigns, be they straight or gay, are not the place to look for high-toned theoretics, but I chose to feel surprise at the sloganeering and preferred to act sniffish (where ordinarily I would have laughed) at the campy complaint of one gay politico that the candidate was "not sufficiently muscular" to draw the needed votes.

The moment had nonetheless arrived when I would be irrevocably "out." In October 1972, with the publication of *Black Mountain* imminent, I called my mother to give her advance warning in case a reviewer should mention the passage declaring my homosexuality (and her friends rush to their phones to offer "commiserations"). She took the news remarkably. After a few nervous questions ("You don't go into *details*, do you, dear?"), she said, "I'm proud of you for doing it." "And I'm proud of you for saying that, Ma," I answered, after catching my breath. "That should be the reaction of anyone with *sense*," she replied with unpersuasive vehemence. "It's a new world. Who knows any more what 'normal' is."

But mothers are more generous-hearted than reviewers. The press response began well, with Edgar Friedenberg in the *New York Review of Books* saying the book "cannot be overpraised" and Judson Jerome in the *Saturday Review* calling it "perhaps the most intimate, tender history an institution has ever inspired." But then the dreaded *New York Times Book Review* weighed in, and my worst fears were realized. The *Times* chose Herbert Leibowitz, editor of *Parnassus*, a poetry journal, to review the book, and Leibowitz wrote a patronizing piece in which he took care to mention my homosexuality but only as one more of those "tendentious" personal intrusions that marred the narrative: ". . . his feelings as a homosexual . . . including his . . . 'fantasies and needs,' however sincere, ends up much ado about very little." (Several of the scholarly journals later picked up the same theme more emphatically. "Duberman has thrown the cardinal principles of historical writing to the wind," the reviewer in the prestigious *American Historical Review* wrote, "by letting himself get 'personally involved' with his subject."}

I could have borne impassioned disagreement from Leibowitz—even welcomed it, given my penchant for controversy and my conviction that the book, like any innovative work, would have its importance confirmed by the range and heat of the response to it. I could have respected argument either with my decision to come out or, more generally, with my conviction that historians had to stop hiding behind presumed and false notions of "objectivity." But Leibowitz did none of those things. He treated the revelation of my homosexuality offhandedly, as merely confessional, an inappropriate, trivial, unwise bit of exhibitionism. (In a book he wrote in 1989 on autobiography, Leibowitz, curiously, takes Gertrude Stein to task for *failing* to discuss in print her lesbianism!)

Upset though I was, I tried in my diary to take the high road:

> I suppose it's good for me. Now I have some sense of what it means for an "average" homosexual publicly to declare him or herself. Somewhere I must have believed that the talent of the book would protect me from the repercussions of coming out—even more, that the latter would be treated as yet another index to the depth of the talent (or at least the honesty). Anyway, I told myself I knew the risks, wanted to take them, and was prepared for the consequences. If all the while I deceived myself into believing that the worth of the book would automatically confine the nature and extent of the risk—well, I'm undeceived, and have to at least try to curtail the whining. Too bad my sense of worth is so wrapped up in achievement. Maybe this will help me unwrap. What I hope it doesn't do is propel me, out of fear of remaining in an unaffiliated twilight zone, into a more active commitment to Gay Lib than I might otherwise feel. If discussing my homosexuality was legitimately a function of my search for greater integrity, as I like to believe, then I can't surrender the integrity for a mustard plaster.

But I had trouble remembering that high resolve as the blows continued to land. The party for the book took place only a few days after the *Times* review appeared and was more like a wake than a celebration. People stayed away in droves and the small crowd of about fifty (two hundred having been expected) consisted mostly of family, friends, and the publisher's own people. While I was still feeling bruised about that, the *Village Voice* published a review that sent me reeling. It was written by James Leo Herlihy, a sometime friend who was himself gay, and the author of *Midnight Cowboy*. He was in fact the man who had originally urged me to do the book. Jim now complained at length in the *Voice* that it was one thing to reveal my own homosexuality but that it had been irresponsible of me to reveal Bob Wunsch's (the arrested rector of Black Mountain).

The charge rankled. My extensive efforts to reach Wunsch while writing the book had failed and, given his advanced age, I had assumed him dead. I further told myself that there was no way I could have made Wunsch anonymous at the point of his arrest without making him anonymous throughout the book (or inventing a reason for his disappearance from it after Mr. "X's" arrest)—neither a viable possibility, given Wunsch's prominence in the narrative. My only other option had been to omit the cause of Wunsch's arrest, but to have done that would have seriously distorted the record, especially since I had included personal revelations about other leading figures at Black Mountain.

Herlihy didn't object to any of the other personal items in the book, and so his real animus seemed to be against my—or anybody's—coming out. ("What I want," he had written in his review, "is for each of us to mind his own sexual business, historians included.") Yet as far as I knew Jim had never gone to any great pains to conceal his own homosexuality, and in the upshot I was unable to throw off the baleful feeling that I hadn't sufficiently thought through all the moral implications involved. As best I could understand it, I had been so absorbed in deciding whether or not to reveal my own homosexuality in conjunction with discussing Wunsch's, that *his* homosexuality became obliterated as an issue. Wunsch never did reappear, and no one besides Herlihy accused me of doing him wrong. But my unease at having opened someone else's closet door never fully dissipated.

I had difficulties of another sort with a closeted gay reporter

from the *New York Post* who asked to do a "profile" of me for
the paper. He turned out to be English-born, Aubrey Beardsley-
like in manner, and lived in a Village apartment (where we did
the interview) dominated by huge silver ferns and a plastic purple couch. None of which, contrary to expectation, predisposed
him in my favor. Neither Jewish intensity nor the confessional
mode appealed at all to his fey Oxbridge sensibility, and at one
point, as I was recounting my assorted struggles with homosexuality, he said in an enervated voice, "I had thought of committing myself to it at one point, but the scene was *so* heavy."
Before the two hours were over, he had softened considerably
(and indeed the piece he ultimately wrote was sobersided and
straightforward), but he did icily remind me as I was leaving
that "not everyone can enjoy the luxury of self-revelation." It
was a point well taken.

Reading an interview in *Psychology Today* with Carlos Casta-
nada a few days later, I found myself writing down this passage:
"The more you are known and identified, the more your freedom is curtailed. When people have definite ideas about who
you are, and how you will act, then you can't move." Had I
made a mistake in coming out so publicly? Why were the blows
and praise alike landing with much more impact than I would
have predicted? "Probably," I wrote in my diary, "because I've
offered a piece of my life for validation; I'm seeking permission
to be alive. I guess I'd be less anxious if I was as accepting of
my homosexuality as my coming out seems to suggest. Why
can't people understand that coming out is a *strategy* for self-
acceptance, not its equivalent. I meant to take a few steps out
from the shade tree—and suddenly find I'm in the middle of
the Sahara, each breeze coming through like a gale. And here
I am working every spare minute on the 'gay lib' piece for the
*Times*—preparing to whip a gale into a hurricane (or is that,
meteorologically, weaker than a gale? If so, maybe *that's* what
I'm doing)."

The article for the *Times* would have been difficult to write
under the best of circumstances, but with bullet-reviews rico-
cheting off the walls, I had to draw on all my (considerable)
reserves of willpower to get through it. "Doubtless," I wrote in
my diary, "I wouldn't be so worried if the theories about homosexuality that I'm beginning publicly to expound coincided

more fully with my own convictions—but in fact, they coincide mostly with my aspirations." Yet, when I completed the article in mid-November, I felt proud of it, felt it was informed *and* personal. In condensed form, it embodied much that I had lived through up to that point and summarized much that in recent years I had begun to rethink.

"After months of reading the 'scientific' and 'movement' literature on homosexuality," the article evenhandedly began, "I'm convinced that no one is in possession of sufficient knowledge at this point in time (though almost no one concedes this) to warrant the confident generalizations heard on all sides— and especially on the scientific side." I then went on to argue that so-called scientific discussions of the "causes" of homosexuality not only centrally contradicted each other, but in the past had been primarily designed as a "political tactic to perpetuate barbaric legal and social discrimination, and as a convenient intellectual outlet for heterosexual condescension."

Even if the experts *could* agree on the causes of homosexuality, I wrote, "they would not have thereby demonstrated that it is a 'sickness.'" Not only had no measurable physico-chemical pathology been adduced for homosexuality, "but the behavioral traits often employed as substitute proofs of illness—self-contempt, protective clowning, guilt, dependence and passivity—have been drawn primarily from clinical sources, from homosexuals who present themselves for 'treatment.' These traits are far less characteristic of homosexuals not in treatment and in any case reflect a pattern of 'victim' symptomatology regularly found among all oppressed minority groups."

Most scientists, I continued, brought to their research a model of "normal" behavior that derived from the assumptions of their own culture. For most American scientists, that meant the sex-negative assumptions of Judeo-Christianity, as well as the strong tendency in the national character "to brand as sick that which is merely unconventional." In our society, I wrote, "differences of all kinds have come to be equated with 'deficiencies,' and deficiencies—for we are rigorously rational and ameliorative— must be 'explained' and 'cured.'"

The Western model of "normal" sexual development, I argued, presupposes instinctive biologic forces that propel all individuals through similar "stages" culminating (unless the "wrong" environmental forces intervene) in the "healthy" end product of monogamous heterosexuality. But as even a cursory glance at crosscultural data reveals, this Western model is a moral, not a scientific construct, based on assumptions and distinctions that can themselves be viewed as aberrant—that is, confined to a small minority of the world's cultures. But denying its own parochialism, the arrogant West has proceeded as if its values were—or should be—universal ones.

And as part of its missionary fervor, I wrote, Western science has pursued the causes and cures of homosexuality with a zeal that has been almost comic—were it not for the tragic number of lives destroyed in the process. Same-gender love and lust have been variously ascribed in the West "to possession by devils, to self-abuse and to neurological or glandular disorders; and its 'cures' have ranged from being burned alive, to chastity, to 'transference,' to electric shock. If the causes of shifting social reactions to sexual deviation had been studied with anything like the fervor invested in searching for the causes of deviation itself, we may have had relief long before now from punitive laws and moralistic vocabularies."

Understandably, I went on, the recently emergent gay liberation movement was furious at this history of "scientific" fraudulence and social oppression, and had already spawned a considerable literature in opposition. Singling out Dennis Altman's *Homosexual* for special praise, I concluded my essay by underscoring the importance of several of Altman's themes. As had Altman, I argued that the current divisions within the gay movement between the radical Gay Liberation Front and the reformist Gay Activists Alliance represented healthy diversity, "and in any case serve expressive if not instrumental ends."

I also joined Altman in repudiating the easy assertion sometimes found in gay liberation circles (indeed throughout the counterculture) that promiscuity and the ability to appreciate varieties of human eroticism were the equivalents of liberation. And, like Altman, I cautioned gay liberation against the temptation (generated by the desire for quick self-confirmation) to replace an older set of myths about sexuality with a new one. I thought Altman was perhaps being a bit prim in shying away from the possibility "that selective promiscuity and cycles of erotic variety" might represent genuine ingredients in a liberated sexuality, but I agreed with him that "sexual adventuring" would not in itself guarantee a new human consciousness.

In asserting, finally, that "we homosexuals" had "unique testimony to offer on the human condition," I was not only publicly affirming my identity as a gay man but doing my best—since that identity was recent and incomplete—to invest it with proud-hearted import: "Basic inquiries," I asserted, "originate on the margin, not from the center," and we gay people should therefore be loath to claim that our lives are identical with everyone else's; rather than passing ourselves off as 'jes' folks," we had the obligation "to develop our outsider's special insight into socio-sexual norms." I also cautioned the gay movement "to remember that there are basic racial and class inequalities in American life, and if gay (or black or female) separatism now seems an essential stage in consciousness-building, it is not in itself the optimal goal. Eventually—and here the difficulties can hardly be overestimated—a coalition of the oppressed must be forged."

When the *Times* article appeared, I expected a mixed reaction to it and felt reasonably calm at the prospect. The die, I knew, had been cast, and I was content that I had tried my best to sift the evidence with an honest eye. But what I hadn't expected was a drubbing from the gay activist side. Jean O'Leary and Ginny Vida, two leaders of the recently emergent Lesbian Feminist Liberation, wrote a letter to the *Times* (which was not printed) protesting my failure to give sufficient weight to lesbian writing. They had a point. I had briefly mentioned the two most prominent lesbian books then current—Sidney Abbott and Barbara Love's *Sappho Was a Right-On Woman* and Del Martin and Phyllis Lyon's *Lesbian/Woman*, but most of my article had indeed been devoted to discussing gay male literature. By this disparate emphasis, I had inadvertently helped to confirm the growing conviction in lesbian circles that gay men would never extend equal recognition and status to them—a conviction which in 1972 was propelling many lesbian activists into separatist organizations.[24]

One of the books I *had* discussed in the article was Lige Clark and Jack Nichols's *I Have More Fun With You Than Anyone*, characterizing it as "merely self-congratulatory, as nonchalantly bypassing the myriad issues that other liberationists find enigmatic and troublesome." Clark and Nichols came at me with both arms swinging. Using their regular column in *SCREW* magazine as a launching pad, they denounced me as the *Times'* "homosexual lackey," a man of "phoney erudition" who "didn't read the many books he reviewed" and "passed over most of the important ones with condescending shittiness."

Clark and Nichols's friend, Dick Leitsch, who had been an influential figure in the Mattachine Society, took up their cause in his own column in *GAY* (begun in late 1969, it, along with *Gay Power*, was one of the first local newspapers to aim at a homosexual readership). Characterizing me—tellingly, I thought, for someone who didn't know me personally—as one of those gay people "who have allowed the preachers and psychiatrists to brow-beat them into feeling guilty and unhappy," Leitsch declared that he felt "not pity but contempt" for us. He claimed that I was temperamentally incapable of appreciating Clark and Nichols, two men who "*like* being gay and view their homosexuality as an *advantage*, a joyful experience they wouldn't exchange with any of those smug heterosexuals." Leitsch advised me to put my Puritan scruples behind me and join the liberationist chorus in shouting the happy words, "If it be sin to love a lovely lad, Oh, then sin I!"

Well, I wasn't quite up to that (besides, lads didn't turn me on). Nor was I ready to embrace the assorted other forms of salvation recommended by the batch of correspondents who wrote me in response to the *Times* article. Several devotees of Aesthetic Realism—Eli Siegel's "philosophy of living"—assured me that their group had had great success in converting homosexuals and suggested I present myself for cure. Another letter writer recommended megavitamins, and a third—after reproaching me ("I do think we have enough anti-Semitism without people named Duberman justifying such a sickness")—enclosed a list of "legitimate doctors who could help to fix your condition."

Several academics came out to me in private letters, but guiltily added that they could not bring themselves to go public. To all of them, I sent a similar reply meant to be comforting: I had felt that I *had* to come out, for urgent expressive reasons I didn't pretend fully to understand, and had only done so from a protected position—tenured and with a long list of publications, it

was unlikely I would suffer any serious professional consequences. "But," as I wrote to one woman teaching at a small
college on the West Coast, "I would certainly not generalize
from my own situation. This is New York, and I don't think it's
merely provincial to feel that New Yorkers tend to be more
enlightened than even big city dwellers elsewhere. Maybe I un-
derestimate mid-America, but my guess is that a national ref-
erendum would at the least deny us the right to teach."

I took a different and sharper line with a straight colleague—
a prominent historian—who wrote me a long, pontificating letter about how every society had to "protect itself against sexual
irregularity." According to him, laws that criminalized homosexuality were "not merely instruments of repression but a
moral and educational force—they tell people what society
thinks they ought to do and not do." He acknowledged that
"many people will violate the established norm," but felt that
such "purely personal behavior" could be tolerated "only so long
as it does not upset the norm itself." Every society, he concluded
"has the right to make moral judgments, and I get alarmed
when I hear that it does not."

I tried to deal with him on his own calmly rational terms, not
yet having fully learned the lesson that many blacks had in the
early phases of *their* struggle—namely, that courtesy and earnestness rarely succeed either in maximizing outside support
or in accommodating internal rage. "Of course," I wrote back,
"the majority views sexual regularity as essential if society is to
continue to function *as it is*—and it has the power to pass laws
to that effect." But I did not see, I went on, why we had to
accept society as it is: "You suggest that many people will violate
the norms. Well then, why continue to honor the norm as desirable and immutable when it seems at odds with human nature
(or the nature of many humans)?" Why *must* we allow society
to pass judgments on sexuality? I asked. "To preserve its 'health,'
you seem to say. What health? I don't see much around me."
To be sure, society *will* continue to enforce its values, but that,
I insisted, was "a function of power, not right. I'm old-fashioned
(and utopian) enough to want to see those two kept separate."

But what did I intend to do about it? How much time and
energy was I prepared to give to the gay movement, and what
form should that involvement optimally take? Should I make

my contribution primarily through my writing, or should I enlist as an activist soldier in organizational work—and if so, which organization? There were no obvious answers to such questions, or none at least that were likely to manifest as skywriting in the heavens. I would have to do what I had been doing—inch along at a personal pace somewhere between a limp and a shuffle.

# 20

---

# AFFILIATING

AFTER TWENTY YEARS OF building brick walls between me and my sexuality, I knew more about bricks than about what I wanted to put in their place. Before the publication of *Black Mountain* and my *Times* article, I had vowed not to let my fear over severing one identity and set of affiliations propel me into forming closer ties with the gay movement than I actually felt. And in the months following those publications, I held to that resolve. A number of invitations to lend my name or presence to this or that enterprise arrived, but to all of them I gave essentially the same answer I sent the Mattachine Society when it asked me to join its board of advisors and speak at its public forum: "I feel I've said all I have to right now in the *Times* piece, and don't want to waste people's time by merely repeating myself."

But I made an exception when Bob Liebert, the Columbia University psychiatrist who had written sympathetically about gay liberation, invited me to share a platform with him and two gay students from Columbia to debate Irving Bieber—the psychiatrist whose 1962 book, *Homosexuality*, had caused me so much personal anguish—before an audience made up of college counselors. At first I hesitated, telling Liebert that I "had no wish to become any sort of spokesman for the gay movement," but he persuaded me that an audience of counselors was an important one to reach. In the upshot, the experience of debating Bieber proved one more of those small, incremental steps that add up, bit by bit, to a consolidated commitment.

Bieber turned out to be a Central Casting version of the portly, pompous psychiatrist, contentedly patronizing everyone else on the panel, imperviously repeating his own circular arguments. When he announced that he had never known a homosexual man who had a "loving, constructive father," one of the gay undergraduates grabbed the microphone to declare that he had had just such a father. Bieber smiled unctuously and told the young man that as an experienced clinician he had long since become familiar with such "distorted self-evaluations." He offered to give the young man a "proper" battery of tests should he be willing to present himself at Bieber's office. At that point, *I* grabbed the mike and in a tone that matched Bieber's in unctuousness, politely offered to test *him* for "advanced symptoms of homophobia" if he would trot round to *my* office. Bieber looked astonished at my insolence and disdainfully moved on to another topic.

Our dispute continued a few years later, in print. In 1975 the *New York Times* commissioned me to cover the trial for reinstatement of Leonard Matlovich, a tech sergeant in the Air Force who had been relieved of his duties after publicly coming out as gay. In the course of the article, I referred to the "inadequacies" of the "binding mother/absent father" theory of male homosexuality associated with the views of Bieber and Socarides. Both men responded with blistering letters to the editor. Bieber accused me of having "clumsily attacked psychoanalysis" and of being unqualified to make judgments in a field where I was "strictly a layman."

Socarides, too, lambasted me for "venturing into an area beyond [my] expertise" and for "irresponsibly mislead[ing] the public . . ." ("Only in the consultation room," Socarides thundered, "does the homosexual reveal himself and his world." He claimed that psychoanalysts "have been in the vanguard of those protecting the homosexual against persecution" (and indeed back in the fifties, homophiles *had* viewed psychiatry as an ally against statutory prosecution and police harassment), and he pronounced himself deeply affronted at my suggestion that therapists had themselves become the persecutors of gay people.

It gave me real pleasure to answer both men. Who, I asked, is the layman when discussing homosexuality? "It is surely time to ask whether gay women and men might not themselves qualify as 'experts' on their own lives. Perhaps Dr. Bieber remembers the time when white liberals—always with the best intentions—tried to explain to blacks the meaning of their own experience. Perhaps he also remembers the aftermath." In response to Socarides I added, "It was the 'experts' in foreign affairs, with their presumptive monopoly on insight, who got us into Vietnam. And it is the same pervasive deference to 'expertise' that causes people to turn over to others the power to run their own lives—to the 'qualified' politicians, industrialists, priests, *et al.*"[25]

If Bieber, during our 1972 debate at Columbia, ran true to form, my own reaction did not. I was filled with an anger that I could neither entirely control nor fathom. When he continued to insist that only he and his colleagues were fit to detect "pathology" and that pathology was intrinsic to homosexuality, I finally bellowed that he hadn't heard a *word* of my arguments, historical and anthropological, disputing those contentions. And when he responded with a pitying smile, I bellowed again. I was startled at the depth of my rage *and* my willingness to express it. Bieber became Karl—smug and oppressive, the arbiter of health, the destroyer of worth.

Yet for a while longer, I continued to seek that worth by affiliating with the left in general rather than with the gay movement in particular. In February 1973 I accepted an invitation from *Liberation* magazine to join some forty or so people at a two-day conference in Voluntown, Connecticut, to discuss "Where the Left Is At." The winding down of the war in Vietnam was no guarantee that the country had ended its war-provoking posture in the world, and Nixon's overwhelming victory in the presidential election, followed by his call for "an end to the era of permissiveness," had seemed to forebode a domestic repression as well.

The two days in Voluntown did little to inspire confidence that the left would be able to respond effectively to Nixon's agenda. Indeed, we had trouble finding connections among ourselves. Was there a "common enemy"? Who or what did we need to overthrow—capitalism? traditional sex roles? racism? imperialism? Failing to find new links, the conferees mostly fell back on old jargon. One Hispanic man, fed up with talk of "vectors of the labor force" and "the viability of commodity exchange," sensibly concluded that "if a worker was here, he wouldn't understand a fucking thing that's being said."

And yet some occasional words of wisdom, and even of hope, were offered, particularly about the long-range promise of the gender protest movements that were challenging entrenched, hierarchical forms of power. And the women at the conference provided a visible example, caucusing and staying together throughout the two days, in symbolic contrast to the men, who wandered around in isolation, briefly formed subgroups for impassioned, angry talk, then fragmented off again into isolation.

But what surprised and comforted me the most was the frequency with which the gay movement was mentioned and its importance to the gender revolution stressed. In a conference where everyone and everything was attacked at least once, I heard not a single hostile reference to gay liberation. Perhaps that was itself a form of patronization, a way of saying that gays didn't matter enough to take issue with. But I thought not, I thought I was witnessing at least the beginning—it would prove a long, and is a still continuing, struggle—of a new attitude on the left toward gay people, a welcoming into the ranks of opposition.

Meanwhile, REDRESS was deep into its own plans for a two-day conference that spring on issues relating to the pending peace, and I threw myself into its preparations. The conference drew some three hundred people and an impressive array of movement "heavies" that included Dan Berrigan, Rennie Davis, Grace Paley, Dave McReynolds, and Daniel Ellsberg. I myself chaired the sessions on amnesty, which concluded with a call for *total* amnesty inclusive of deserters and carrying no penalties or conditions. But the conference failed to come up with a program for implementing its policy decisions, settling instead for an orgy of resolutions (More teach-ins! Protest Thieu's visit to Washington! Oppose covert warfare! Work for reparations!), and for a grab-bag of recommendations that ranged from wearing Amnesty buttons to convening an international tribunal to try "the criminals in Washington."

I came away tired of rhetoric and thoroughly dispirited. I needed to take some concrete action and soon decided to implement an idea Muriel Rukeyser had earlier suggested to me: a petition drive to nominate for the Nobel Peace Prize "all those Americans who were asked to fight and kill in the Vietnamese War and refused." I placed notices soliciting signatures in a variety of publications and before long had a flood of responses that ultimately allowed me to forward a petition with some four hundred names to the Norwegian Parliament (a petition about which I never subsequently heard a word).

Despite all my activity, I felt that I was treading water, waiting for something to clarify that I could not even name. I had publicly labeled myself a "gay man," yet still had not formed any consistent, ongoing affiliation with the organized gay political movement. I sensed that such a commitment might prove a mechanism for discovering more about who I was, or wanted to become, but I feared it might also demand of me what any organized movement demands of its participants—that in the name of stressing common intersections and fighting effectively against common oppression, they put a lid on individual expressiveness. As Emerson put it long ago, "We descend to meet." To participate successfully in political protest, individuals must, at least publicly, cease to be as fully individualized as they know they are. They must be willing to downplay the reality of their own *varied* internal impulses and desires in the name of presenting an unconflicted identity that can more readily lend itself to needed political simplifications.

Having already, in coming out, given the straight world an opportunity to label and minimize me, I was reluctant to let the gay movement accelerate that process. But in holding aloof, in telling myself that I—anyone—was much too complicated to be summed up in terms of sexual orientation, I was also denying myself the sense of belonging that can put an end to isolation and its miseries. One part of me, I suppose, didn't feel that I deserved that kind of comfort, and another part, wedded to the self-image of "one who suffers," felt superior to it.

And the insistence on remaining apart did prolong the misery.

I turned back to the male madames and the hustler bars for solace—and got excitement instead. I started to take Placydyl at night to sleep—and promptly had technicolor nightmares. I remember waking up in a sweat from one of them, unable to shake the dream (as I jotted it down in my diary) that I had been "caught in the army as a homosexual. Had planned to play it safe and escape. But waited until it was too late. I almost talk a kindly older officer into letting me go, but a brutal younger one discovers my diary. He brands me with a lead plate on my chest. I flee in white pajamas, running down corridors through EXIT signs. Finally out on street. All in tropics. Wake up. Certain they're about to capture me again."

I described the dream to Ray, and he dismissed it impatiently as "your basic crime-and-punishment scenario—and here I thought you had finally let some new air into your life!" When I told him in mournful proof of the *lack* of new air, that I'd recently become enamored of a young guy from Ohio, married with two children, whom I'd met on the hustling circuit, Ray turned serious. And he turned downright censorious when I related details of how I had already been plying the latest Hero with favors.

"Sounds to me," Ray said, resuming his choric function in my life as substitute therapist, "like you're setting up the same deadly pattern you had with Danny. You've already laid yourself out, a dancing waiter at some fantasy feast, offering a lifetime platter of desserts. And before this guy has even picked up a menu, or said he was hungry—to say nothing of proving he has a credit card. You frighten people off by being too intense."

"Too intense about what? My need for affection?"

Ray snorted with derision. "Don't flatter yourself, dear. If anything, you come across as self-contained, as someone who doesn't need affection—or anything else—from another person. No, you frighten people off because they sense you want to steal their identity—just like some imperialist explorer pursuing the natives with a camera. Which is strange, come to think of it, given your tenacity in standing up for your own opinions; indeed you can be a bore about it—but let's not get sidetracked on that. My point is, you see yourself as eagerly sympathetic to these needy studs, but what you're really eager for is to become like them—my God, when you were with Danny you even took on some of his physical characteristics: you walked as if you had a poker up your ass!"

"You're far smarter than any of my shrinks," I said, hoping a compliment might deflect further analysis. "Unfortunately I'm too old to profit from your insights. My patterns are fixed. Which is what I was trying to tell you—the way it is now is the way it's always going to be for me. I'm too old to change."

Ray laughed. "You've claimed *that* ever since I've known you—and gone right on changing. The claim of immutability—of nothing changing—is a pose, dear, a way of refusing to countenance age and death. You'll go on changing. You always have."

As if in proof of Ray's point, I embarked within days on several new courses of self-improvement—desiccated liver pills recommended by a friend for depression, granola and honey for morning invigoration, and, for a *very* brief period, an effort to learn the martial art of Aikido. It had been described to me as a way to "clear the head and tune into the body; to go with rather than oppose another person's power; to relax enough to let the rhythms flow." That struck me as exactly what I needed to improve my life. I especially liked the notion—after being at loggerheads with Danny for a year and a half—of not meeting force with force, but rather learning to accommodate (and thus neutralize) it.

After the first Aikido class I was delirious with excitement. It was, I raved to Ray, "ballet without the tension, yoga without the mysticism, karate without the violence."

"Fine, dear, lovely," he said, "I *told* you you would never 'settle' for being what you already are. But don't you think getting thrown to the mat by two-hundred-pound black-belts might be just a *little* strenuous for someone—ahem—approaching middle age—however much I recognize the fantasy appeal of surrendering to brute force!"

I assured Ray that I would take it slowly—and promptly bought a heavy-weave judo gi made in Taiwan. The trouble was, it weighed more than I did and I had to soak it in the tub to see the end of my fingertips. During my second class, the teacher warned me that I was being "too cerebral," that thinking led to anticipation, which led to tension, which led to getting hurt. "Hmm," I mused, "he's just spelled out the paradigm of my life," which made me more certain than ever that Aikido was the perfect counterweight for it. I left the class feeling elated exhaustion. But by evening body aches and diarrhea had set in, and by morning I could hardly move or stop crying. Aikido, I quickly concluded, was not for me after all. Ray warily suggested that perhaps I ought to stop trying to "fix" myself. When I gave him a dangerous side look, he quickly shifted to camp, giving it as his *absolute conviction* that the desiccated liver pills would all by themselves produce the desired transformations in my life.

Another channel proved more promising. I had been bouncing ideas off my editor, Hal Scharlatt, for a new book on growing up gay in America, and we decided I should try typing up the diary I had periodically kept and seeing what came to me along the way in terms of commentary and asides. What came, along with commentary, was intense anger at the way I'd been abused and cooperated with that abuse. I'd allowed myself to be treated, especially in therapy, as an abstract collection of symptoms to be ameliorated rather than as a specific person to be actualized. I'd learned to think the best of my persecutors, especially my therapists, and the worst of myself. Told that, like all homosexuals, I had no capacity for intimacy, I'd turned by my midthirties to seeking connection in hustler bars—a bit like looking for snowballs on the equator. Hoping to win approval, I had directed a docile face to the world and, to demonstrate that I had the right to exist, had lacerated myself into producing a nonstop series of articles and books. My spasming colon and insomniac nights had recorded all too accurately the costs of a life based on self-flagellation and concealment.

Typing up this sorry record day after day, gut churning with resentment, was just what I needed to move me further along in claiming a better future for myself. And so when, one day in April 1973, I got a phone call inviting me to join a group of gay academics who had begun to talk together informally about our situation in the university world, I accepted enthusiastically. About twenty people gathered in an Upper West Side apartment, most of them graduate students and junior faculty, and most of them not yet "out" professionally. They were eager to hear about the repercussions of my own public debut. "Mostly positive," I told them, but warned that my protected position could hardly be compared with their own and suggested that the safest and most effective tactic for others might be some form of collective declaration.

We then got to talking about whether as a group we had some special function to perform and after lengthy discussion came up with several: we could pressure the American Association of University Professors and other academic organizations to protect the rights of openly gay faculty; we could serve as a support network for the many isolated gay people on campus; we could pinpoint needed areas of scholarly research; and we could originate pilot programs for course work in gay studies.

What had started as desultory conversation became an animated, three hours of serious talk mixed with lots of good-humored banter ("No, we can*not* call ourselves the National Association of Gay Scholars—the acronym is NAGS!" "How about Queer Profs?"). By the end of the evening, I knew for certain that I finally had found a home—and an ideal way of tying into the gay movement. The group excitedly decided to meet again in two weeks, and I could hardly wait, eager to throw myself into the kind of organizational work for which I had always claimed temperamental distaste. For my zeal, I was subsequently awarded the job of drawing up a statement of purpose and cheerfully accepted the chore after Jonathan Katz, Seymour Kleinberg, and Bert Hansen volunteered to work with me on it.

From this point, we began to meet frequently, soon named ourselves the Gay Academic Union, and soon after that decided to plan a national conference for the fall on "The Universities and the Gay Experience" as a way of announcing ourselves and providing a rallying point. The speed with which we formed the organization, mapped out strategies, and debated national, even international, ramifications led one of the few women in the group to say, acerbically, "You guys may be oppressed faggots, but you show the same comfort with power and the same confidence that you'll gain access to it as any other gathering of men I've ever witnessed." She was not at all sure, she added, that she liked the pace or approved the tone.

And indeed from then on the issue of how and whether women would affiliate with GAU became a constant and contentious topic. Within a few months of our organizing, forty or so people were attending the meetings, with twenty to twenty-five showing up regularly. But very few were women. The men agreed from the start that women should have equal representation on GAU's steering committee, but claimed the principle was difficult to implement: women were scarce in academia, and open lesbians scarce among women. Some of the men vocally disclaimed any interest in making a special effort to encourage women to join GAU, an attitude that several of the women who did attend the meetings rightly took to be sexist.

To try to combat the sexism, a dozen of us met separately for an evening of frank talk about whether men and women *could* hope to work together successfully in GAU. We all acknowledged some variant of sexism within ourselves. Several of the men admitted that machismo turned them on erotically even though, politically, they fervently disapproved of it. Other men conceded that their preference for the company of women hinged on endowing them with stereotypic "compassion" and "sensitivity." Some of the women acknowledged that they tended automatically to see *all* men as the enemy, even though many of the men in GAU had shown genuine sympathy for the feminist struggle.

Andrea Dworkin, with whom I'd gotten friendly as a result of our activities in REDRESS, gave an angry, intransigent rap against women working in "integrated" organizations. When some of the other women replied that the goal *was* feasible and in this case desirable because the consciousness of most (though certainly not all) of the men in GAU was higher than the mean, Andrea insisted that "our sense of primary emergency does not coincide; For women, feminism takes precedence as an issue over homosexuality." But why should that prevent us, I asked, from combining forces where our concerns genuinely did co-incide—as surely they did on campuses, where gay men and lesbians shared similar discrimination because of their same-gender sexual orientation?

Besides, I added, to the nodded agreement of several others, feminists and homosexuals did share a common rebellion against the heterosexual male master *and* a deep-seated wish to become like him—here I had Danny distinctly in mind—to play his macho role, to incorporate his macho body, to offer ourselves, thrillingly, to his macho mistreatment. Even if the hope that we could work together was slim, didn't we owe it to ourselves to seize the possibility instead of presuming failure? At some point gay men and lesbian feminists *would* be able to combine their efforts, and that point might just be now.

I would subsequently come to feel still more strongly that a psychic alliance between lesbians and gay men did exist, even though the two subcultures were in some important ways at variance (for example, in the greater value many lesbians placed on monogamy and permanent pair-bonding). Lesbians, in my view, were far more nonconforming in their gender roles and much more marginal in the culture than were heterosexual women, and that gender nonconformity and cultural marginality were precisely what connected lesbians to gay men. That connection, however, was infrequently recognized and rarely got translated into sustained political alliances.

What prevented the alliance from maturing, in my opinion, was a growing denial on the part of many gay men—and particularly the white, middle-class contingent that would soon come to dominate the organized political movement—of their own marginality and gender nonconformity. Many of these middle-class men might not in fact play stereotypic male/female roles in their relationships, or might luxuriate in the anonymous, promiscuous pleasures of the baths or the backroom bars, yet would publicly insist—and even in their own psyches continue to believe—that they were "jes folks." The wish to buy into heterosexual white male privilege would increasingly come to take precedence for many gay men over an honest avowal of the actual dimensions of their differentness. Seeing that eagerness to conform to traditional male roles and institutions, many politically-minded lesbians would choose to keep a wary distance—and to ally instead with the feminist movement.

After months of further discussion, the women in GAU finally proposed that we list the organization's *first* purpose as the desire "to combat oppression against women." Several men angrily attacked the proposal. The women, they said, were "demanding impossible proofs that they were welcome," and their proposal, if adopted, would make GAU a mere appendage to the feminist movement. Despite the opposition, the resolution was voted on and carried by a large majority. Even so, the gender issue continued to agitate the group. At the following meeting, one of the men who had opposed the resolution patronizingly announced that he hoped its passage "would ensure *no* further discussion of the woman question—we have *important* work to do." Some of the women took that comment as proof that the men in GAU had no intention of honoring the commitment they had just made, and a few, including Andrea, walked out.

Despite the continuing tensions, plans for the fall conference slowly matured, and many of us found the process of working together—on balance—deeply satisfying. Often the meetings were joyful, the combination of laughter, respect, and high purpose setting a tone unlike that of any other gathering of academics I had ever attended, typified as they usually are by posturing and point-scoring. Often excitement ran so high that we rushed to complete each other's thoughts, quickened by a similarity of experience and perception we had never fully appreciated before, astir at the confirmation that we were not singular freaks but part of an emerging community willing at last, nervously willing, to talk about our desperate secrets, to end the separation in ourselves and in the society between our private and public voices, to embrace our differentness as an enrichment rather than a shameful deficiency.

The camaraderie carried over outside the meetings. Sometimes a group of us would go dancing at the GAA Firehouse on Saturday night, aglow in fraternal hugging and lip-smacking. Once I was taken on a tour near the piers of the famed "trucks," a kind of free, outdoor gay bathhouse, but our penchant for political chit-chat in the midst of slurping and groaning drew sharply reprimanding looks. And for the fourth Gay Pride day in late June 1973, our gay scholars contingent gathered in force in Washington Square Park to enjoy the festivities.

That particular day, however, had its downside. Bette Midler, just rising to stardom after having made her early reputation singing in gay bathhouses, put in a deft, if brief, appearance. But for some reason the bill was ineptly filled out with a torch singer full of incongruous pseudo-sobs for her man, and an electric guitarist who complained bitterly about being unable to get his album of homosexual love songs distributed. "You can guess why!" he shouted at the crowd. "Because they're talent-less," some wag yelled back.

One episode that day highlighted serious rifts in the move-ment. When Silvia Rivera, a well-known street queen, de-manded access to the microphone to "plead the transvestite cause," the master of ceremonies barred her way, insisting that "we are here today for entertainment not politics." But Silvia was not to be denied. Elbowing her way to the mike, she let the audience have it between the eyes: "How many of you white, middle-class motherfuckers have been in jail? Been raped? Had your noses broken? *I* have, honey. And so have plenty of your sisters. And they're still in jail, and still being raped. And what are *you* doing about it?—*nothing!*"

"Politics" having intruded, the emcee allowed a representative from Radicallesbians to respond to Silvia. Though the RL spokeswoman's short hair, butch drag, and tough manners struck me as imitative of male stereotypes, she saw nothing ironic about lambasting Silvia, and all transvestites, for aping female stereotypes—for "perpetuating outmoded notions of femininity." In retaliation, the editor of DRAG magazine, re-splendent in a floor-length green gown and a platinum wig, angrily threw her tiara into the crowd. "Farewell, my sometime friends," she sobbed, and stomped offstage in her size twelve pumps, the glitter on her gown sparkling in the afternoon sunlight.

My own sympathy was with the transvestites. As I wrote in my diary that night, "I thought the point of gay lib was 'vive la différence.' Vive *our* difference, RL (and much of the crowd) seemed to be saying today. And 'our', moreover, is defined by numbers and power—the same majoritarian tyranny the move-ment protests in the society at large. Thus prejudice and oppres-sion, the targets of protest, get reproduced in the ranks of the protesters. And the oppressor rests comfortable in the knowl-edge that the oppressed will take over the function of denounc-ing each other."

Like so many belated converts to a cause, I sometimes sounded like the truest believer, zealotry replacing nuance. When the *New York Times* asked me to review Al Carmines' popular stage piece *The Faggot*, I persuaded the editor to let me include Jonathan Katz's militant agitprop play *Coming Out!* in the discussion, and then proceeded to praise it far above *The Faggot*. I ardently hailed the Katz work for demanding an end to oppression and providing a context for struggle, and fervently denounced the Carmines play for confirming the stereotypic image of gays as frivolous and trivial. I was pointing to real attributes in both works, but also indulging a Manichean need to release my own spirit from any suggestion of taint.

Judging from the deluge of mail, I was not alone in that need. Defenders of Carmines angrily denounced me for confusing "the solemnity of gay rhetoric with gay pride," calling it a "disservice" to the movement and a philistine rejection of an artist's right to his own vision. Carmines himself picked up that theme and reprimanded me (with considerable graciousness, given what I'd done to him) for asking a "subjective theater piece" to be a "political position paper." He exempted himself as "an artist" from such humdrum considerations.

But Carmines' detractors joined me in protesting his "naive" view that a theatrical work about gay life staged in 1973 could avoid having a political dimension and political consequences. And I myself, continuing to sound like one of King Arthur's knights, wrote a rebuttal denouncing Carmines for his "grandiose" insistence that as an artist he was "above the fray." First of all, I declared, striking a few good sparks from my plunging Excalibur, Carmines' claim that *The Faggot* "is art is only slightly less bizarre than the pretense that it is not politics." I scorned his apparent belief that " 'politics' is something confined to legislators and agitators." Such credulity, I insisted, "was dangerous. The vacuous, plastic creatures he has put on the stage reinforce negative social attitudes about gay life. These, in turn, reinforce oppression and discrimination. If Carmines can't see this, he's alarmingly innocent. To mislabel that innocence 'Art' is to compound ingenuousness with affectation."

Whew! Such furious militance brought to bear against so comparatively slight a target was more than a little like stretching a butterfly on the rack. Years later, I was able to make a somewhat sheepish apology to Carmines for having overstated the case, an apology he accepted in good spirit. But back in 1973, zesty with the unfamiliar juices of affirmation, I was prepared to take on all comers at full tilt.

Indeed, the new gay politics was unleashing plenty of emotional and psychic heat, and GAU generated its full share of libidinal energy. Bonding was intense, lifelong friendships sworn and sometimes maintained, sexual couplings and uncouplings frequent. In my own case, forming new friendships felt far more urgent than having sex, and only once did I actually go to bed with a member of the group. But that once was hardly run-of-the-mill; it put me further in touch with some of the pain I'd been carrying around, with the buried need for love and the long-harbored sense that I was unworthy of it.

"José" was in his early twenties, one of the youngest in our group and the only Hispanic. Increasingly drawn to each other at the meetings, we finally arranged to spend some time alone—and when we did became immediately physical. It started out in a standard enough way: our bodies felt good together, and excitement was quick. But then, with the help of some grass, what José called our "trip vibes" kicked in and we made passionate love to each other's bodies. As I groaned in pleasurable disbelief (how could he enjoy stroking and licking my scrawny, unattractive legs?), José whispered reassurances ("It's because I love you that deep inside") soothing, alarming sounds in my ear.

Abruptly, Cousin Louie was in my head. Cousin Louie who had never been "quite right"—my father's retarded nephew, always grinning, always gentle, his gait awkward, listing like a ship in trouble as he clumsily tried to navigate across a room. "Cousin Louie had loved me, loved me when I was what?—three? five?" I wrote in my diary that night, "Cousin Louie, unseen in 30, 35 years, but still alive in my head. I started to cry. Louie loved me. Louie had loved me. Where was Louie? Where was the love? My arms stiffened up; the fingers on my hands curled in, like a spastic's, like Louie's. I tried to stroke José's hair, but my fingers stayed locked. I couldn't get the gentleness in my head into my hands. My touch was jerky, awkward—like Louie's must have been when he tried to pat my head. Oh the pain, Louie! The pain of never being able to stroke easily, calmly, gently, of never being able to command the gestures that would express the feelings, that would win other people's recognition that the feelings did exist, that you were no idiot—only the hands that couldn't comply with the heart.

Louie, Louie—thanks for the love. I cried and cried last night.
José—thanks for bringing that buried love back, for not stopping when I cried, for knowing I needed the tears and not
reassurances that might abort them. . . . Under careful supervision, they let you touch me, Louie. The beautiful, blond God/
baby put nervously, momentarily within your reach. I touched
you back last night."

Soon after the evening with José, and as if released by it, I
became seriously involved with someone who was not himself
a member of GAU but was friendly with several people in it.
Stanley was a filmmaker, deeply sweet and affectionate, a
scrawny, manic mix of absolute mush and magnate imperialism,
undersized and over thirty—a promising departure in every way
from my pattern of infatuation with borderline young hoods.
We took to each other immediately and intensely. But it was
hardly all gain. Because I had long since separated sex and
intimacy, the attempt at recombination brought plenty of irri-
table anxiety—and seismic quarrels—in train.

A brief attempt to live together heightened the irritability.
My chief tactic for dealing with a closeness I both wanted and
feared was to accuse Stanley of being too "adoring." As I wrote
in my diary, "He follows me around the apartment, chattering
maniacally at my heels or gazing mistily at me as I speak adultly
about our separateness. I say he disappears in the puppy. I say
I want a person, not an appendage, say it crisply, coldly, cutting
his personage down to where I insist I don't want it to be. The
pedestal and its base will ruin us, I say, say it brilliantly, elevating
myself through superior perception to Olympian heights I claim
to dislike. Being Just, I try to speak of terror, too, of my eternal
equation of love with suffocation. How did I become Danny?"

We soon decided that we were moving much too quickly, that
the relationship had taken on all the outer shape of a commitment before our affection had had a chance to solidify. But
when Stanley returned to his own apartment, I felt no less
unhappy—torn between the competing fears of loneliness and
entrapment, the wish for closeness and the need for solitude.
In the privacy of my diary I tried to persuade myself that I
wasn't really in love, other than with the idea of it ("Isn't it
wonderful, Marty's involved with someone! Ah, the wonders

wrought by Liberation!"), tried to persuade myself that "a deeper liberation would be one that surrendered the one-to-one model of intimacy as *the* definition and signpost of 'maturity.'" I told myself further that "I have no envy of Stanley's being. I'm therefore detached, unpossessive. This, some would argue, allows for the possibility of genuine love. I tend to believe it ordains mere friendship."

Yet beneath the defensiveness, I knew that my own calcifications were getting in the way of a committed intimacy that in fact I had long wanted but had been reluctant to pursue out of a settled conviction that intimacy could never last and that its withdrawal would leave me shattered. After one tearful day, I wrote this in my diary: "Crying at my distancing postures, at my age printed in the postures; crying that new rhetoric and old desire aren't enough together to mark a passage."

Yet despite the deep resistance and the fierce recriminations, Stanley and I hung together, the swift alternations in mood, the gnashing provocations not quite enough to overbalance the sweetness of the times when we did connect, when, our anxieties temporarily at bay, we were able to see clearly the full extent of our attachment to each other. Sensibly, we stopped talking about a life partnership and started building, day by day, the history that might in the future convert that hope into a reality.

Stanley could be impishly impatient with the self-important scholars of GAU who were out to change the world, and with the sometimes windy meetings that kept us apart. But as an activist himself, he supported my involvement, even as it increasingly branched out beyond GAU. And in fact working in GAU seemed to be amplifying my energy, creating enough for a variety of involvements.

Though I was putting in long hours on GAU's fall conference, I found myself far more willing than previously to participate as well in assorted other gay causes and events. And they seemed, in the summer and fall of 1973, to proliferate. A group of activist gay lawyers started to put together what became the Lambda Legal Defense and Education Fund, an organization designed to work for gay rights along the lines of the NAACP's Legal Defense Fund; when they asked me to serve on the group's advisory board, I immediately accepted, all my earlier hesitations about playing an activist role gone. I also accepted invitations to speak on "the new homosexuality" at a variety of campuses, to an overflow crowd at the stodgily prestigious Andiron Club in New York, and to the academic freedom committee of the ACLU (the national board, unlike the New York branch, had previously been reluctant to protest discrimination based on sexual orientation).[26]

My experience at Swarthmore was emblematic. The gay liberation group on campus consisted of twenty women and two men, one of whom told me, "I wish I'd been *in* the closet at some point so I could have had the fun of coming out"—though the "fun" of being out at purportedly avant-garde Swarthmore had included having rolls thrown at him in the dining hall and receiving a death threat in the mail. The lesbians on campus deeply impressed me. "Like lesbians everywhere," I wrote in my diary, "they seem so much more closely bound and adultly assertive than gay men. Perhaps to be doubly removed (woman, lesbian) from the culture's power center is to be, characterologically, doubly blessed."

During my public talk at the college, I had a brief scare. A burly-looking guy at the back of the hall yelled out, "Homosexuality is decadence. The proof is Nazi Germany." As my lesbian friends in the front row nodded encouragement, I held my ground. "You don't know your history," I yelled back, "Hitler and Himmler despised and murdered homosexuals. Nazi Germany is proof that homophobia, not homosexuality, is the best index of a society gone mad." As my friends noisily applauded, the man noisily stormed out of the hall.

I had a different sort of run-in with "The David Susskind" television show. Thinking they might do a program on homosexuality, Susskind's people had me up for a once-over. But when, during the interview, I suggested that the gay experience had some important light to cast on gender and sexuality in general, they flared with indignation. It was the standard liberal scenario: *we* might accept *you*, but it will be on *our* terms; there can be no suggestion that *you* might inform or change *us*. I decided the show would be yet another Susskind Public Service broadcast—trash the victims in the guise of exploring their plight—and declined to participate. I had no confidence, I told them, that the subject would be treated with respect, and I didn't want to be used as this week's titillation. My outspokenness was as much a surprise to me as to them. It was as if all those years only a paper-thin wall had separated me from my own indignation at being bullied and patronized—and it was now punched through with ease.

# 21

---

# ORGANIZING

O|NE DAY LATE IN May 1973 I got a call from a man who identified himself as Howard Brown, Mayor Lindsay's former commissioner of health. He said he had been "inspired" by my example in coming out and asked if he could talk with me about his own pending decision to do the same. We met a few days later, hit it off instantly, and talked away the afternoon. A charming raconteur, he regaled me with tales of the Lindsay administration. He told me how the mayor—"a good guy" in Howard's view—had thoroughly checked out the (false) rumor that Howard was having an affair with the head of the search committee that had recommended him as health commissioner. He told me how badly he had felt at his inauguration when he and his lover of many years drove to the ceremony in the same car but then, on arrival at City Hall, had to get out on different sides, the lover to disappear into the anonymous crowd, Howard to be greeted by his sister, who stood in on the receiving line as his "closest family member."

Howard also confided that he had had a heart attack several years earlier and doubted if he would live more than another ten years (in fact he died in a mere year and half, at age fifty). He said he wanted to spend his remaining time "trying to reach mid-America" and thought the best way to do so was to stress that homosexuals were, except for their sexual orientation, "jes folks." When I protested that characterization, arguing that our special history had created a special—and valuable—perspective that had to be affirmed, Howard listened carefully, smiled impishly, and said, "Well of course we're different—why, heavens, honey, I roam around the apartment every night in high heels!—and of course we have a unique perspective, but we shouldn't stress all that just now; maybe later, after we've won acceptance, we can go on to make our special contribution."

I solemnly protested that as "false assimilationism," as kowtowing to the culture's sex-negative, gender-stereotyped values, as reinforcing the American zeal for homogenization, its entrenched suspicion of human diversity. Those values, I argued, were desperately in need of renovation—thus the importance of maintaining the integrity of a gay subculture uniquely positioned to challenge them. But Howard would have none of it, playfully denouncing me as "starry-eyed" and "impractical."

That was not all we disagreed about. Howard also believed that an exclusively homosexual lifestyle *was* pathological. Indeed, he considered himself "diseased." And he didn't think that mattered one way or another for the gay movement. "It's possible and necessary to argue for civil rights," he insisted, "even for those who in some way—be it psychologically, spiritually, or physically—do not measure up." Howard had internalized the negative psychoanalytic model that had ruled the roost when we were both young even more fully than I had. Having now moved toward the liberationist model, I would argue repeatedly with him about the destructive inadequacy of the psychoanalytic view. But he remained immovable.

Despite these serious differences, Howard and I quickly became good friends. There was much about him that I admired: his sharp intelligence; the lovely way his eyes would twinkle with bashful self-deprecation even as his voice boomed with affirmation when he talked about wanting to devote the rest of his life to "this *last* cause," his own; above all, his essential sweetness—his quickness to hold himself to account while overpraising everyone else. Everybody's best press agent, Howard's introductions at parties became legendary: I'd like you to meet John Smith, *the* finest young doctor in the city, or *the* most brilliant lawyer, or *the* best cook, or the possessor of *the* most beautiful cleft chin—Howard always managed to find *some* trait about which he could sing superlatives. In my reading of his character, this extravagant praise was simultaneously an index to Howard's generosity of spirit *and* to the degree self-hatred, engendered by homophobia, had turned him into a devout people-pleaser, eager to praise *you* so that you would not hate *him*.

After Howard publicly came out—in a milestone story on the front page of the *New York Times*—he became a whirlwind of activity on behalf of the gay movement. He was forever filling his spare bedroom with a visiting gay high school teacher from Akron, flying to speak to a fledgling gay group in Fort Worth, appealing for funds to help an incipient gay publication get off the ground. And in his own home he entertained his new circle of gay activists constantly and lavishly.

One evening he invited Stanley and me to a dinner party that he grandiosely billed as a "summit meeting," an effort to get the leaders of gay organizations talking to each other in order to avoid duplications of effort. It turned instead into a routine social affair, and a rather sluggish one at that. Though Howard valiantly tried to keep us task-oriented, everybody else seemed to be having an off-night. One of Mattachine's leaders drank too much and kept barging into the conversation with punchy irrelevancies. One of Lambda's leaders, suffering from flu, remained morbidly silent, absorbed in internal lamentation. And Stanley and I, in one of our positive phases, couldn't keep our hands off each other or our minds on any topic other than eternal love.

The following week, whether in compensation or retaliation, Stanley and I decided to take Howard to the Gilded Grape, a transvestite/transsexual hangout whose volatile, dramatic crosscurrents appealed to us. Howard was entranced with the place. At the end of the evening, thrilled at having seen the new brand of drag queen machisma in full cry, he fervently announced that he had resolved a matter that had long troubled him: he *would* appear in drag at the upcoming transvestite STAR ball (to which he had been invited as guest of honor). Not to "would be elitist."

At one point Howard and I combined forces to co-sponsor a benefit at the The Ballroom cabaret for a new gay magazine called *Out*. Neither of us had much faith in *Out*—in fact it lasted for only two issues—but we nonetheless felt we should pitch in with a fund-raiser (I also gave the magazine a one-act play of mine for its first issue). Smack on the cover of that first issue, the editor placed a cartoon of Norman Mailer, coyly dressed in a windblown skirt and blouse, designed to illustrate Andrea Dworkin's lead article, "Why Doesn't Norman Mailer Become the Woman He Is?"

Then in its second issue, *Out* published a letter from the writer Dotson Rader protesting the cover and insisting that we all leave Norman in peace "because he was having trouble with his writing." At which point Mailer, whom I knew slightly, sent me a sharp note. Rader had assured him, Mailer wrote me, that he had never sent *Out* such a letter and Mailer demanded to know why *Out* was "attacking" him. I called the editor of *Out*, who told me that Rader had sent his letter privately to Arthur Bell, the *Village Voice* columnist; Bell had then turned it over to the magazine.

With that information, I wrote Mailer that in my view "the publication of private correspondence can't be justified legally or ethically," but neither could Rader "be justified in claiming never to have written such words. That is all I know of the matter and all I hope to know." I added, since Mailer had assumed that I was the editor of *Out*, that I had no connection with its daily operations and had simply lent my name and some of my writing to it "because I believe in the necessity of its existence, and hope for its future potential. Perhaps you will understand those feelings from your early connection with the [*Village*] *Voice*."

In his reply, Mailer said he was "going to try to get to the bottom-bottom of all this" and told me to send him a copy of the cover that had originated the trouble. The peremptory tone irritated me. "I'm not going to run any errands," I wrote back. "Having taken myself out of the center of a mess you gratuitously put me in, I'll let you go the rest of the way to the bottom-bottom on your own. I have confidence in your resources."

Mailer responded indignantly that *he* was the injured party. Having confirmed that *Out* had published Rader's letter without permission, why had I done nothing to indicate my displeasure to the editor? And why did I not seem to realize that his previous letter to me had constituted an apology for having "jumped in" without knowing the facts? "This is getting silly" I wrote back, "perhaps none of us wants to go to work. . . . (1) I *did* remonstrate with *Out* for publishing Dotson's letter. If I failed to tell you, it was a disservice to myself. Of course I've had no report from you of any remonstrance to Dotson. (2) If . . . your second letter to me . . . constitutes your notion of an apology, you may yet get to be President." This time Mailer really did apologize and on a more or less cordial note, we agreed to let the matter rest.

Literary testiness on the gay issue was not confined to heterosexual writers. When I attempted to raise funds among well-off gays in the arts for another, far more substantial publication, *Gay Sunshine*, I ran mostly into indifference but also into some huffy disdain. *Gay Sunshine*'s devotion to lengthy articles on literary subjects had limited its circulation even within the gay world, and my plan was to put together a sustaining fund for the journal by getting fifteen or so individuals each to pledge fifty dollars a month.

I wrote only to people I knew personally, and I enclosed two sample issues of *Gay Sunshine*. Most of them never responded. Of the four who did, two said they would think about it (but never sent money), one pledged the desired fifty dollars (but never sent money), and the fourth, the playwright/director Arthur Laurents, perhaps speaking for the silent others, wrote me a blistering note, scorning *Gay Sunshine* as "provincial," deploring "the tendency in the gay movement to be turned on by verbal exhibitionism," and concluding, "I don't think freedom is enough compensation for no sense of humor, no depth, no style, no illumination, etc."

Howard, too, was having trouble raising money among well-established gays. Sometimes when I saw him for a late night drink, his kewpie-doll face would pucker with disappointment as, near tears, he would tell me how he had gone to see Dr. So-And-So that afternoon, a wealthy, closeted physician for whom he had earlier done favors in his capacity as health commissioner; Howard had asked the doctor for an anonymous contribution and been turned down cold with some version or other of "I'm-all-right-Jack." This particularly grieved Howard because at just this time a crucial campaign was being mounted within the American Psychiatric Association to drop homosexuality from the category of "disease" (a campaign won late in 1973), and funds were badly needed to carry on the struggle. Howard could never get over the insularity and indifference of closeted gay eminences, whether in the arts or medicine, and no amount of reminding ourselves that we, too, had once (and recently) been locked away in fearful silence, could quite dull our sense of indignation.

But Howard, despite all his ritual mannerisms of self-abasement, was a fighter. In the fall of 1973, he combined forces with Bruce Voeller and Ron Gold, who had disgustedly resigned from what they called the "do-nothing" Gay Activists Alliance to form Gay Action, Inc. (soon changed to the National Gay Task Force). In October Howard asked me to serve on NGTF's board of directors and, flattered to be included in the company of such pioneering activists as Barbara Gittings and Franklin Kameny, I readily agreed. On October 16 we held a sparsely attended press conference to announce the official launching of the new organization, with Howard speaking succinctly and eloquently of the need to mobilize national resources on behalf of the gay struggle for civil rights.

Though pleased to lend my name and energy to NGTF—and its board of directors did turn out to be very much a working board—I had serious doubts about the new organization from the beginning. The same night of the press conference, I set down my conflicted feelings in my diary:

NGTF clearly wants to pattern itself on the ACLU or NAACP—which means it can make a valuable contribution, but in the liberal, reformist mode: "let us in" rather than "let us show you new possibilities." Structurally, too, I can sympathize with wanting to do away with the marathon GAA membership discussions on whether to buy one or two typewriters, but decisions from the top down may carry limitations as severe (if different from) those of participatory democracy—especially since it's not clear in whose name we're speaking, the nature of the constituency, its ability (once existent) to implement decisions, to countermand the board. All hands assure me that a constituency (à la CORE or NOW) will develop and will have power. We'll see.

As the Task Force was being launched in October, the Gay Academic Union was completing months of work on its two-day November conference, "The Universities and the Gay Experience." We had put in long hours without any confidence that the conference would in fact come off. How many gay academics, we wondered, would actually show up? How many would prove willing to attend an event in which their own sexuality might somehow get publicized, with resulting repercussions for their jobs and reputations? Would the few women who had struggled along in GAU all these months be able to draw enough other women to the conference to form a sizable contingent—and to give GAU the legitimacy it sought as an organization for gay men *and* lesbians?

As we prepared for the conference, the volatility of our meetings sometimes made us doubt whether we could hold together as an organization, let alone carry off a successful event. Not only did the role of women in GAU continue to agitate our working sessions, but the issue of bisexuality soon proved divisive as well. I myself had been increasingly drawn to the bisexual model touted in the counterculture as a standard against which all who aspired to *bona fide* membership in the Sexual Revolution should measure themselves, not pausing to worry over the contradiction with my previous view that sexual orientation was imprinted and immutable.

I was well aware, however, that bisexuality was not the equivalent of, and could with some people be a fortification against, gender nonconformity. To have sex with both genders in the same way—to be *always* dominant, *never* yielding—worked against the realization that we contain many, sometimes contradictory selves. Indeed, my skeptical side wanted to relegate bisexuals to some distant category of indecision, wanted to see their lifestyle not as a function of free-spirited polymorphous perversity but rather as a paralysis of will, an impaled inability to break away from the security of a traditional marriage and take on the still onerous image of being homosexual.

It was precisely that argument that raged within GAU. Most of our group regarded bisexuality with suspicion. It was a cop-out, they argued, a failure of nerve. It rendered being gay provisional, made it seem a varying impulse rather than a steady state. But that attitude struck me as simplistic, too, and I went with the minority side of the debate, with the view that a bisexual capacity was probably intrinsic to human nature (before socialization bred it out of most of us). Still, I cautioned that such an assumption—seemingly on the side of human liberation—could become the latest "scientific" dictum used to intimidate and control "deviants"—in this case exclusive homosexuals *and* heterosexuals. Having been made to feel guilty for most of my life about my homosexuality, I was trying not to yield too readily to the new cultural imperative that threatened to instill guilt instead for *exclusive* homosexuality.

Back and forth we went in the debate. At one point I suggested that those who claimed that bisexuality was a function of "lower consciousness," the preserve of cowards and poseurs, might themselves be trying to avoid coming to grips with their own erotic impulses toward members of the opposite gender. For that I was characterized as some sort of latter-day Horatio Alger, forever fixated on Self-Improvement, forever unwilling to accept himself *as is*. The nerve having been hit (wasn't the refusal to "settle" for who I already was precisely what a decade of psychotherapy had done to me?), I defensively answered that *they* were fixated on self-congratulation—though calling it self-affirmation.

Protracted and sometimes heated though our arguments were, the standoff was essentially friendly and the give-and-take invigorating. We were, after all, getting to some basic issues long ignored, both within ourselves and within the larger society, and exploring them meant, inevitably, a certain amount of turmoil and disagreement. The fact was, turmoil and all, we were developing trust, forming bonds, and, mostly in high spirits, moving toward the climactic conference.

By October, with a hundred last-minute chores to be done, we put aside high philosophy and grappled with the immediate issues of registration forms and coffee cake. Though we still had no idea how many people would show up, acceptances to speak arrived from Edgar Z. Friedenberg, Wilson Carey McWilliams, Barbara Gittings, and Richard Howard, and their likely drawing power seemed to guarantee at least a minimal turnout.

Barbara Gittings and I were chosen as the keynote speakers. In the weeks preceding the conference, I put in long hours preparing my remarks, going through several drafts (declaiming each one to Stanley's tired ear), determined to "get it right," to speak my mind as fully and cogently as possible.

On the morning of November 23, the members of GAU gathered early and nervously at the City University of New York's John Jay College, the site of the conference. The vast lobby looked ominously empty, and as we set up the registration tables and took our assigned places behind them, we anxiously wondered whether we hadn't overreached ourselves.

But then they started to come, even before the official 9:00 A.M. opening time for registration, and in a steady, happily noisy stream that continued for hours, overwhelming the registration tables, throwing the organizers into a tizzy of delight. In the end, 320 people actually registered, and it was clear that another hundred or so, preferring not to sign their names to anything, simply milled anonymously about, surreptitiously sitting in on an occasional workshop or panel. Equally gratifying, more than seventy women showed up—far more than we had dared hope. Throughout the two-day conference, a separate women's caucus met at regular intervals, and at the end a majority (35–22), satisfied that GAU was at least not blatantly sexist, formally voted to affiliate.

The two days of panels and workshops, moreover, were hugely successful. The variety of experiences and insights that the speakers offered vividly attested to the range of gay life*styles*, even as they seemed miraculously to blend into a coherent whole. And the response from the audience was throughout warm, excited, generous. Nonetheless, when it came time for my keynote address, I mounted the podium with my heart in my mouth. Stanley blew me a kiss from the back of the auditorium, and that helped get my mouth to open. I began by telling the overflow crowd that "a seemingly absurd phrase" had been haunting me ever since I began preparing my remarks: "Honored Rabbi, dear parents, relatives, and friends . . ." The phrase was the opening of my bar mitzvah speech, delivered at age thirteen to the congregation of Sinai Temple.

That speech had marked my official rite of passage to manhood, and the phrase had haunted me, I said, because "today, too, is a rite of passage. Not for me alone, but for us together; not into manhood or womanhood as those states have been traditionally defined; not sanctified by supernatural doctrine;

not blueprinted by centuries of ritualized behavior; not greeted by kinship rejoicing and social acceptance; not marked by the extension of fellowship into the established adult community"— but nonetheless a rite of passage, that historic point in time when gay women and men decided to organize themselves around their skills, using them to fight homophobia, to protest the notion that same-gender love and lust affront the laws of nature, to place ourselves "in the forefront of the newest and to my mind most far-reaching revolution: the recharacterization of human sexuality."

I expressed the hope that the conference would mark the beginning of "the long march through those particular academic disciplines and institutions with which we find ourselves affiliated." But marching, I warned, "is notoriously hard work. And institutions are notoriously resistant." Neither dedication nor competence guaranteed success. In the short run, they probably guaranteed heightened resistance. "Because we challenge the exclusive heterosexual lifestyle by which the majority in this country all at once defines biologic truth, social necessity, and personal essence, our work will be difficult and frustrating. Because we are asserting our own worth and our special perspective, the work can be joyful."

But, I further warned, self-worth was not a function of self-congratulation: "If we mean seriously to challenge sexual stereotypes, we cannot assume any automatic truths. If we wish to inaugurate a profound debate on sexuality, we cannot set the topics or terms, nor announce in advance the nature of the conclusions. Nor can we afford to dismiss out of hand information or arguments that might discomfit our own theoretical models—we cannot, that is, if 'liberation' is to be more than a slogan and 'revolution' more than a posture."

As a case in point, I argued that we should welcome not shun current research investigating whether homosexuality had a hormonal or genetic component, even though we recognized that the scientific world's continuing concern with the "causes" of homosexuality was propelled by the assumption that homosexuality was an "error" to be corrected. As scholars, I said, we must never support the suppression or avoidance of evidence— "not under the most severe ideological pressure nor in the name of the most sublime political advantage." Our function was to welcome research and then to insist that it not be misused for repressive purposes. If, for example, future studies did prove that homosexuality had a genetic component, we would need insistently to remind the scientific world that that discovery merely provided insight into how certain sexual patterns got formed, *not* whether a particular pattern was "good" or "bad"— the latter was a moral judgment reflecting cultural not scientific imperatives.

I then turned in my speech to a consideration of the risks and gains of "coming out." I spoke of the risk of losing jobs or never being hired; the risk of laying ourselves open to categorization as that "thing"—a homosexual; the risk of our public avowal being treated as a vaguely unclean bit of exhibitionism. In my own case, I reported, the risks had proved minimal because of my secure, tenured position. I stood "in awe," I said, "of the courage of those students and untenured faculty who are coming out in increasing numbers; indeed, the untenured among us—those with the most to lose, as the world measures loss—have been setting the pace for their more privileged and protected colleagues."

Though the risks were heavy, I went on, they were perhaps inescapable by-products of becoming political, "of openly uniting with others—no less frightened, complex, and private—to end the common oppression." And the personal gains of doing so were profound: the quieting of self-doubt, the comfort of becoming part of a community. That emerging community would be shaped, I cautioned, as much by process as by ideology—as much by how co-workers treated each other as by how they fronted on the world.

The internal feuding and divisions that already characterized the gay movement were, I submitted, to some extent unavoidable: the diversity of lifestyles among gay people required divergent expression. Besides, we were in the ambivalent position of being products of the same set of cultural values that we were organizing to protest against—"values that confuse maleness with machismo, femaleness with docility, bisexuality with indecision, and sexuality with orgasm."

But if the gay movement was destined to be marked by controversy, perhaps it need not, I argued, be marked by mutual recrimination and contempt. And I used the close of my speech

to make a plea that we "at least try to proceed as friends reinforcing each other's confidence, instead of as adversaries as-
sailing each other's deviations. The former builds community,
the latter perpetuates powerlessness. The one does the work of
the revolution, the other the work of the oppressor."

My hope for GAU in particular, and the gay movement in
general, I concluded, "is that we can serve as a genuine alternative to the sexist models that dominate our culture; that we
will refuse to talk of human beings—gay or straight—as single
impulses, fixed essences, judgable objects; that we will offer, in
opposition to the current vision of homogenized humanity, our
celebration of human diversity.

"The goal is utopian, and must partly fail. But only utopian
goals, I believe, will allow us partly to succeed."

Just how utopian was amply demonstrated in the immediate
aftermath of the conference. Six of us, three men and three
women, had been elected at the conference as GAU's steering
committee. At our first meeting a month later, one of the men
didn't show up at all and the second arrived stoned, launched
into a lyric account of how much he was turning on a woman
friend in bed—"she's letting herself go enough to moan and
make noises"—and suggested that we prepare *now* for the even-
tual split of GAU into male/female factions. It was as if our
enemies had sent in an *agent provocateur*. The women were furious at what had amounted to a caricature sexist monologue,
but decided, "for now," to try to get done the organizational
work for which we had been empowered. How long they would
remain committed to GAU, however, remained to be seen.

In the weeks and months following the conference, moreover,
as committees and rhetoric proliferated apace, the danger
loomed that GAU would simply turn into one more liberal academic talkfest. Gay academics, it became apparent, were academics first and gays second—that is, they loved to talk and
argue; were cautious by inclination and training; distrusted class
analysis, confrontational politics, and interracial cooperation;
and were wedded to mainstream notions—petition and pressure
the government for legislative action—of how to achieve social
change.

Indeed by 1974 the gay movement in general was heading

into the same set of interlocking dilemmas that have characterized protest movements throughout our history. How to
prevent a radical impulse from degenerating into reformist tinkering? How to mobilize a constituency for substantive change
when most of the members of that constituency prefer to focus
energies on winning certain limited concessions, like civil rights
legislation, and show little interest in joining with other dis-
possessed groups to press for systemic social restructuring? How
to appeal to a country on behalf of an oppressed minority when
the country's instincts are deeply conservative, when, in the
aftermath of the black struggle and the Vietnam war, it was sick
to death of moral demands, when it smugly assumed its prej-
udices and values were somehow divinely ordained?

Knowing that my own expectations were always too high, I
tried to resist feeling discouraged. But that was hard to do in
the face of continuing hostility both within and without the
movement. It hurt when *Gay Sunshine* printed a dismissive article
on the conference, claiming that the large attendance was simply
due to the academic penchant for networking ("They were looking for contacts . . . their gayness a gimmick to push their
careers"). And it was sobering when the head of the American
Association of Teachers of French (and publisher of the *French
Review*), in declining to print a notice of GAU activities, sent us
this bit of invective: "Please do not expect any cooperation from
our organization for the publicizing of your philosophy of life.
Self-restraint is one of the necessary qualities of all mature
adults, and pampering, publicizing, and advocating a weakness
such as yours would be a pathetic indication of the decline of
our society."

Stanley and I decided that it was time for a vacation. We used
the occasion of a scheduled string of lectures about Black Mountain that I was due to give at several North Carolina colleges in
February 1974 to rent a car and take a leisurely twelve-hundred-
mile drive down the Eastern Seaboard. Our epiphany came at
St. Andrews Presbyterian College, in Laurinburg, North Carolina, the heart of the Bible Belt.

The entire school had been assigned *Black Mountain*, so my
reputation, in every sense, preceded our arrival. Since they al-

ready knew from the book that I was gay, I nervously conferred with Stanley about whether I had the political obligation to press ahead in my formal speech to the college with a liberationist rap. Sharing my inflamed Northern fantasy about being burned alive by grimacing rednecks, and rattled by the prospect of being an unwilling victim of Marty's penchant for martyrdom, Stanley hastened to assure me that we had fully discharged our political duty just by showing up in the flesh in enemy territory. I speedily and gratefully agreed, and that night confined myself in my speech to the topic of "Non-Traditional Education."

But I hadn't counted on the peculiar wiles of the Southern undergraduate. Following the speech, Stanley and I were carted off as guests of honor to an enormous beer blast in one of the dormitories. The party was already in progress when we arrived, the huge dining area emptied of chairs and tables, and several hundred undergraduates were alternating frenzied dancing with multiple trips to the gigantic beer kegs that lined the side walls. "My God," I whispered to Stanley, "it's an *auto-da-fé!*" "I need some grass," he hoarsely responded.

As if overheard, one of the undergraduates instantly produced two joints. They proved so strong that for the next three hours I felt certain I was swaying on the deck of an ocean liner. Spacy and emboldened, I executed a courtly bow in front of Stanley and invited him to dance. He visibly blanched, hissed in my ear that I should *kindly* remember where we were, and then, when I persisted, refused to go out on the dance floor until the music got frenetic enough to allow only for a non-touching frug.

But some little gremlin put a quick end to that. As we were gyrating away, a safe three feet from each other, the music abruptly shifted to a foxtrot. We both shrugged "what the hell" in unison—as if our fate had been foreordained—wrapped our arms around each other, closed our eyes (more in prayer than ecstasy), and waited for it all to come down. A hush quickly fell over the room, and within seconds, all the other couples had stopped dancing and had formed a huge, nearly silent circle around us. "I guess this is good for their heads," Stanley's strangulated voice whispered in my ear. At just that moment, a husky young man tapped Stanley on the shoulder—and asked if he could cut in. As the crowd burst into applause and the music shifted back to a frenetic beat, he and I, soon surrounded by other couples, frugged away in delirium.

Shortly after that, an undergraduate named Randy, a rugged, mustachioed specimen of gorgeous Southern manhood, politely introduced himself. "Sir," he began, "ah am a heterosexual male, but ah want to thank you for showing people down here that you should be whoever you are." Simultaneously stunned by his beauty and his graciousness, I thanked him for thanking me. As the evening progressed, I found Randy increasingly at my side, and increasingly stoned. At one point, his hand was very decidedly on my ass.

Then, as it grew late, Randy asked if he could "have a word" with me, and the next thing I knew I was following him up the winding five flights of stairs to his dormitory room. When we reached the door, he grandly flung it open—and there, lying naked between black satin sheets, was Randy's girlfriend. "Howdy," she said, with utter nonchalance, and went back to staring at the television set positioned above the bed. Clearly a threesome had been arranged in my honor—possibly to inaugurate my, or possibly Randy's, conversion. When I recovered, I politely declined to remove my clothes and join them in bed. (So much for my theoretical defense of bisexuality!).

As I headed back down the stairs, Randy was hot at my heels. It was time, I decided, to give him a taste of his own shock tactics. "Don't play so many games," I said, putting my arm firmly around his waist and kissing him hard on the lips. He went instantly limp, looked swooningly doe-eyed—the macho man turned to proverbial putty, the ideal fantasy incarnated. I decided not to press my advantage. Leaving Randy stupefied on the stairs, I rejoined Stanley for one final foxtrot.

As we drove back to New York, Stanley and I replayed the events at St. Andrews over and over, chuckling with disbelief at the unpredictable turn of events, at our impassioned reception. Always the moralist, I decided the whole experience proved that the sixties were alive and well, that countercultural values had not waned but, rather, had become retrenched and localized. And those values now seemed everywhere among the young—in Laurinberg, North Carolina no less than in Manhattan. How could we not feel optimistic? Stanley and I asked each other. How could we not go on believing in a new day that seemed so palpably about to dawn.

# NOTES

1. See Kenneth Lewes, *The Psychoanalytic Theory of Male Homosexuality* (Simon and Schuster, 1988), for a full discussion of the contrast between Freud's views on homosexuality and the simplistic, polemical dogma that supplanted them. On the negative gay image in film, see Vito Russo, *The Celluloid Closet* (Harper & Row, 1981; reissued 1987).

2. Kubie's response, and those of Knight and Baitsell that follow, are from Wardell B. Pomeroy, *Dr. Kinsey and the Institute for Sex Research* (Harper & Row, 1972), pp. 296–97, 280, 287. For more on the reception of Kinsey's work, see Janice M. Irvine, *Disorders of Desire: Sex and Gender in Modern American Sexology* (Temple University Press, 1990), esp. pp. 64–66.

3. Some of the material in this section, as well as the "Harvard" section that follows, has been taken and partly reworked from my essay "Gay in the Fifties," as published in my collected essays *About Time: Exploring the Gay Past* (Gay Presses of New York, 1986).

4. Two books have been of special value in this discussion of the shifting psychoanalytic views of homosexuality: Ronald Bayer, *Homosexuality and American Psychiatry* (Princeton Univer-

sity Press, 1987 edition); and Kenneth Lewes, *The Psychoanalytic Theory of Male Homosexuality* (Simon and Schuster, 1988). See also, Richard A. Isay, *Being Homosexual: Gay Men and Their Development* (Farrar, Straus & Giroux, 1989). The Hooker quote is from Bayer, *Psychiatry*, 51.

5. For this and many other historical references, I am heavily indebted to John D'Emilio's pathbreaking *Sexual Politics, Sexual Communities: The Making of a Homosexual Minority in the United States, 1940–1970* (University of Chicago Press, 1983).

6. The Senate document is printed in Duberman, *About Time*, 148–56.

7. Bayer, *Psychiatry*, 49–53.

8. Duberman, *About Time*, 195–97.

9. Lewes, *Theory*, 111–14.

10. For the early years of Mattachine, see Stuart Timmons, *The Trouble with Harry Hay* (Alyson, 1990).

11. D'Emilio, *Politics*, 81.

12. Bayer, *Psychiatry*, 30–33; Lewes, *Theory*, 206–12.

13. *The New York Times* article is reprinted in Duberman, *About Time*, 203–09.

14. Bayer, *Psychiatry*, 39 (Menninger); D'Emilio, *Politics*, 144 (Academy).

15. For more on Kameny (and Gittings), see D'Emilio, *Politics*, especially 152–7, 169–71.

16. For a detailed account of the pre-Stonewall homophile movement in New York City, see Toby Marotta, *The Politics of Homosexuality* (Houghton-Mifflin Co., 1981), chs. 1–3.

17. *Time*, Jan. 21, 1966, as quoted in D'Emilio, *Politics*, 138.

18. On the depiction of gays in film, see Russo, *Celluloid, passim*.

19. D'Emilio, *Politics*, 206–07.

20. D'Emilio, *Politics*, 199–200, 211–19.

21. D'Emilio, *Politics*, 216.

22. Bayer, *Psychiatry*, 102–03. See also Gary Alinder, "Gay Liberation Meets the Shrinks," in *Out of the Closets*, Karla Jay and Allen Young, eds. (Douglas, 1972).

23. These observations derive from a series of interviews for my forthcoming book on the Stonewall generation.

24. The O'Leary/Vida letter *was* printed in *Lesbian Activist*, March 1973.

25. Both my article and the correspondence surrounding it are reprinted in Duberman, *About Time*, 272–96.

26. See Marotta, *Politics*, for more on the anti-discrimination activities of the NYCLU.